LOTUS 72

© Haynes Publishing 2012

Ian Wagstaff has asserted his right to be identified
as the author of this work.

First published in September 2012

All rights reserved. No part of this publication may be
reproduced or stored in a retrieval system or transmitted,
in any form or by any means, electronic, mechanical,
photocopying, recording or otherwise, without prior
permission in writing from Haynes Publishing.

A catalogue record for this book is available
from the British Library

ISBN 978 0 85733 127 4

Library of Congress control no. 2012936196

Published by Haynes Publishing,
Sparkford, Yeovil, Somerset BA22 7JJ, UK
Tel: 01963 442030 Fax: 01963 440001
Int. tel: +44 1963 442030 Int. fax: +44 1963 440001
E-mail: sales@haynes.co.uk
Website: www.haynes.co.uk

Haynes North America Inc.
861 Lawrence Drive, Newbury Park,
California 91320, USA

Printed in the USA by Odcombe Press LP,
1299 Bridgestone Parkway, La Vergne, TN 37086

COVER CUTAWAY: *Tony Matthews*

LOTUS 72

1970 onwards (all marks)

Owners' Workshop Manual

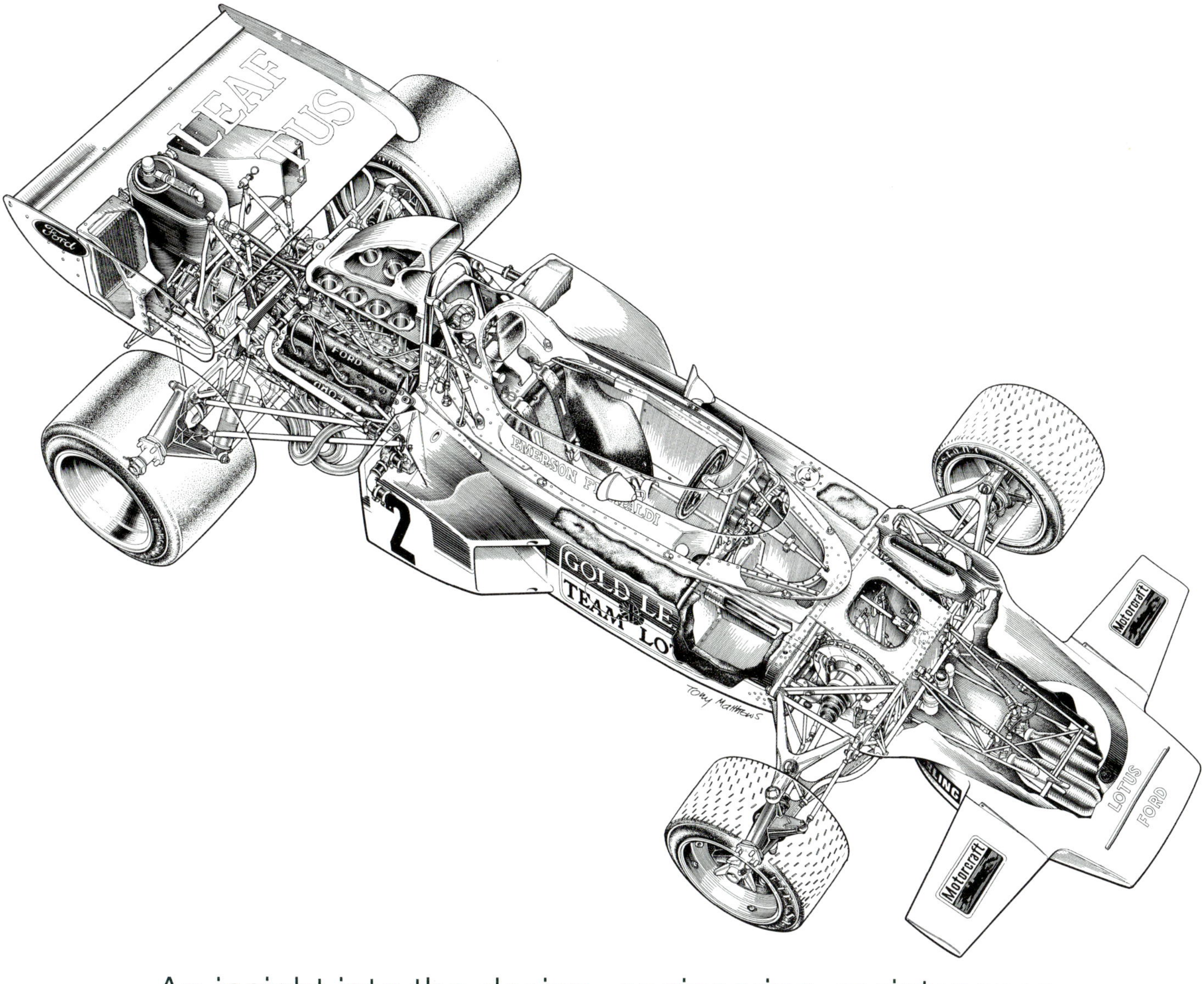

An insight into the design, engineering, maintenance and operation of Lotus's legendary Formula 1 car

Ian Wagstaff

Contents

6	Introduction
Acknowledgements	6

8	The Lotus 72 story
The early years in Formula One	10
Enter the Cosworth DFV engine	12
Launch of the Lotus 72 and its first championship	14
The time of Fittipaldi	17
Decline and fall	20
Subsequent Lotus Formula One history	22
Lotus 72 factory drivers	24
The designers	30

38	Anatomy of the Lotus 72
Specifications	41
Aerodynamics	43
Chassis	56
Cockpit	59
Suspension	63
Brakes	69
Wheels and tyres	71
The Cosworth DFV engine	74
Hewland gearbox	82
Electrics	85

86	The driver's view
Emerson Fittipaldi	88
John Miles	90
Reine Wisell	92
Tony Trimmer	93
Brian Henton	94
Historic racing	95

98	The mechanic's view
Eddie Dennis	101
Derek Mower	104
Ian Dawson	106
Typical between-race checks	108
Pre-race/demonstration preparations	115
Servicing the Cosworth DFV	118

120	Restoration & historic racing
Buying and maintaining a Lotus 72	122
Insurance	126
Racing opportunities	127
Restoration projects	130
Classic Team Lotus	139

142	Individual chassis histories
Chassis histories	144
The private entries	150

154	Epilogue

155	Appendices
Lotus 72D specification (1973)	155
Lotus 72 World Championship Grand Prix race history	155
Lotus 72 non-World Championship race history	157
Extracts from FIA Year Book of Automobile Sport, 1972	159
Useful contacts	161

162	Index

Introduction

Over 40 years after its launch, the Lotus 72 still stands out as one of the best-known Grand Prix cars of all time. Exactly how you remember it may depend upon your age. There are grown men, including some very senior names in motorsport engineering, who, when I mentioned the fact that Haynes would be including it amongst the first of its racing car 'workshop' manuals, waxed lyrical about their Corgi toy versions, or how many 1/12th scale Tamiya plastic models they'd made of the car. One said that it was the shape of the Lotus 72 that schoolboys drew on the covers of their exercise books.

There are many reasons why Colin Chapman and Maurice Phillippe's Lotus 72 should be remembered: it was a bringing together of a series of innovations such as torsion bar suspension and inboard front brakes that, together as a package, took two drivers' and three Constructors' World Championships back to Hethel. For me, it was the distinctive wedge shape that, at the time, seemed so very dissimilar from every other car on the Formula One grid. All the others appeared to trace their ancestry back to the Cooper-Climaxes, but this one appeared to be from a futuristic era. It's difficult to explain now just *how* different it looked.

My first sighting came at Silverstone during the 1970 International Trophy – not the Lotus 72's finest hour. The now infamous anti-squat and anti-dive features were still installed. Later in the year I stood on the outside of Clearways at Brands Hatch as Rindt imperiously swept past an out-of-fuel Brabham to win the British Grand Prix. The Lotus 72 had definitely arrived.

My most abiding memory, though, is of looking down from the press box in the tower that once stood on the outside of Silverstone's Woodcote corner. Fittipaldi and Hailwood were in a frenetic battle for the 1972 International Trophy. The fearless Hailwood's arms flailed as he sought to hustle his Surtees TS9B through what was then one of motor racing's most daunting bends. By contrast, Fittipaldi's arms appeared rock steady. I doubt there will be any demand for a manual on the Surtees TS9B.

Acknowledgements

A book such as this would be unthinkable without the support of Colin Chapman's son Clive and Classic Team Lotus. This operation painstakingly keeps fresh and alive the Lotus legend, and I'm very grateful to Clive and his staff, including team manager Chris Dinnage, for their assistance and being given access to 72E/5 and to the archive of Lotus 72 drawings.

I must also thank those who were involved with the Lotus 72 during its era as a current Grand Prix car and were able to share their thoughts with me. These include drivers Emerson Fittipaldi, John Miles, Reine Wisell, Brian Henton and Tony Trimmer, and mechanics Eddie Dennis, Derek Mower, Ian Dawson, Tony Cleverley and Stan Collier, as well as designers Martin Waide and Nigel Bennett. My thanks, too, to John Manchester and Andrew Noakes for their assistance with the Cosworth DFV engine, and William Hewland with regard to the Hewland FG400 gearbox.

A Lotus 72 was raced in 2011, although as I write this there's unlikely to be one in actual competition this year. The cars are, though, often demonstrated, and from the industry that restores and maintains these historic artefacts I must thank CGA Race Engineering (Colin and Alastair Bennett), R&J Simpson Engineering (Bob Simpson and Gary Anderson), Simon Hadfield Motorsports (Simon Hadfield), Hoole Racing (Sid Hoole and Peter Lawrence) and Hall and Hall (Rick Hall).

To these must be added Rebecca Hale, Stuart and Oliver McCrudden and David Addison from those who continue to organise races for 1970s Formula Ones, and Sean Walker, David McLaughlin and Bill Pohlad who've been lucky enough to actually drive 72s, as well as Adrian Hardy of Ellis Clowes who advised me on how to insure them. For assistance with many of the photographs, my thanks to Dave Hill, archive librarian at Ford Photographic, and Nicola Hartley of Sutton Images.

Such is the nature of Lotus that there are myriad books that mention the type 72. A number of these have been consulted and, in particular, I must acknowledge the works of Doug Nye and that definitive book on the car, Michael Oliver's *Lotus 72: Formula One Icon*.

Finally, I must thank one of motorsport's top engineers, Andy Brown, who has guided me through many of the aspects of this project. Despite a career that's seen time at March and with the Leyton House Formula One team, being assistant technical director on the Galmer that won the Indianapolis 500 in 1992, a senior figure at Champ Car team PacWest, chief engineer for Panther during the Sam Hornish IRL championship-winning years and latterly lead race engineer with Target Chip Ganassi Racing, Andy was like the proverbial schoolboy when I suggested that we visit Hethel. The Lotus 72 is like that; it brings out an enthusiasm in people that few other individual racing cars have ever achieved.

Ian Wagstaff   June 2012

'The 72 was a fantastic car to drive. It was the best racing car that I drove during my long racing career.'

Emerson Fittipaldi
World Champion, 1972 and 1974

(Sutton Images)

Chapter One

The Lotus 72 story

Team Lotus was an integral part of the Grand Prix scene for over a quarter of a century. For six of those seasons the type 72 was its frontline car. Its story encompassed one of the most exciting eras of Formula One racing and some of its greatest drivers, including two World Champions, and designers. In many ways, the Lotus 72 defined its era.

Over the period 1958–94, Team Lotus rose to become one of the truly charismatic manufacturers in Grand Prix racing. During that time its cars won 73 Grands Prix and took seven constructors' championships plus six drivers' titles. It produced many famous cars during this time but perhaps none more so than the Lotus 72 that contributed 20 of those GP wins as well as three constructors' and two drivers' championships. Its distinctive wedge shape made it stand out from the grid right at the start of its long career and, particularly in its later black and gold John Player Special livery, it became the car that defined a Grand Prix racer for a whole generation of fans.

The experts also appreciated its position in history. In 2003 *Motor Sport* magazine asked a panel of experts, including a goodly number of engineers, to list the greatest Formula One cars to have raced since the World Championship was instigated in 1950. The Lotus 72 was placed second, beaten only by the Ferrari F2002. Considering the Italian car had been current the previous season and was therefore to the forefront of memory while the type 72 dated back three decades, this spoke volumes for Colin Chapman and Maurice Phillippe's design.

The early years in Formula One

Under its magnetic founder Colin Chapman, Lotus progressed through a series of sporting trials cars and then sports cars to its first single-seater, the Lotus 12. This appeared in Formula Two guise at the 1956 London Motor Show. A 1.9-litre version of the Coventry-Climax FPF engine and then a 2.2-litre unit enabled Team Lotus to use the Type 12 to enter its first Formula One races in 1958. The little, front-engined, spaceframe car was replaced by the advanced but unreliable Type 16. However, the days of front-engined Formula One cars were now over and it was only with the rear-engined Type 18, introduced in 1960, that Lotus was able to produce a Grand Prix winner. The car was suitable for Formula Junior, Formula Two and, with a 2.5-litre Climax FPF engine, Formula One. It led its debut Grand Prix and then took Team Lotus's first ever Formula One victory, a non-World Championship affair at Goodwood. The manufacturer's first Grand Prix win came shortly after when Stirling Moss drove private entrant Rob Walker's version to first place in

BELOW: Examples of every single Lotus Formula One car were on the grid for the Classic Team Lotus Festival at Snetterton in 2010. From right to left on the front row are Types 12, 16, 18 and 21. *(Author)*

LEFT: **The Lotus 25 makes its debut at Zandvoort driven by Jim Clark. Its monocoque construction was Grand Prix racing's equivalent of the** *Dreadnought* **battleship, making all its opponents obsolete overnight.** *(Sutton Images)*

Monte Carlo. Lotus was now a major contender for overall honours, with Moss winning a second World Championship round at Watkins Glen late in the year. Moss and Innes Ireland also won a number of non-championship races that season. Lotus had arrived as a Grand Prix car constructor.

In 1961 the British constructors – most of whom, like Lotus, were still using the four-cylinder Climax engine – were caught napping by the introduction of an initially unpopular 1.5-litre formula. In its favour, Lotus had the fact that the world's number one driver, Moss, was competing with one of its cars. His undoubted brilliance meant that a Lotus 18 again won the Monaco Grand Prix, to which he added the German Grand Prix. At the Nürburgring his car was fitted with streamlined bodywork, a joint project between Lotus and privateer team UDT-Laystall. This made it appear similar to the Type 21 that had been introduced in 1961 but which was only used by the factory team that season. It was with one of the latter that Ireland scored the factory's initial Grand Prix win, the United States Grand Prix at Watkins Glen. The car was patently underpowered and this victory only came in the absence of the all-conquering Ferraris, who had already wrapped up the championship at the penultimate round.

The first Lotus to make use of the Coventry-Climax FWMV V8 engine – which, along with the BRM P56 V8, would herald a period of British dominance – was the Type 24. The car was introduced at the start of the 1962 season and proved a winner at early non-championship races in the hands of Jim Clark. A number of private teams, including UDT-Laystall (which bought four), acquired the spaceframe 24s, thinking them to be 'state of the art', and weren't best pleased when Team Lotus appeared at the first Grand Prix of the season with the revolutionary 25. Like the 72, this was to become one of the truly great designs of Grand Prix racing. The car was described by designer Chapman as having 'a twin-tube ladder frame, stressed-skin riveted structure'. It was Formula One's first modern semi-monocoque and, as such, the forerunner of every GP car built over the past 40 years.

The Type 25 was also Team Lotus's first World Championship winner. The incomparable Clark narrowly missed the title in 1962 despite coming first in three Grands Prix. The following season he dominated the championship, winning seven out of ten rounds. The Lotus 33, the 25's immediate successor, looked very similar but had a stiffer monocoque plus a lengthened wheelbase to accommodate the latest flat-crank Climax FWMV engine. In 1965 Clark again conquered the championship, this time with six race victories. In the 25/33 concept Team Lotus can perhaps be said to have produced the first of its icons.

A 3-litre formula was introduced for 1966, and initially Team Lotus struggled, using a two-litre version of the 33 and the 43, which was built for the highly complicated and unsuccessful 3-litre BRM H16 engine. Clark managed to win the 1966 US Grand Prix with the latter but it was never going to be the answer. Even BRM itself abandoned the H16 configuration for a V12. Help, though, was at hand in the shape of vehicle manufacturer Ford and the engine that was to power Team Lotus cars to five constructors' championships, three of them won by the 72.

Enter the Cosworth DFV engine

The 3-litre Cosworth DFV has claim to be the greatest Grand Prix engine of all time; it was certainly the most successful, with 158 wins over the period 1967 to 1983. It also could be said to be Colin Chapman's baby as much as that of Cosworth's Keith Duckworth. The latter had joined Lotus in 1957 as a gearbox engineer, and it was there that he first worked alongside Mike Costin, who was to be his partner at Cosworth. Their company was formed later the following year and soon became a successful builder of Formula Junior Ford 105E-based engines. Formulas Two and Three followed.

Meanwhile, there was dissatisfaction with the 1.5-litre Formula One. It was simply too small for what was supposed to be motor racing's ultimate category. A well-driven, Group 7, big American V8-powered sports racer could beat the lap times of an F1. There was talk of a replacement 2-litre formula, which would, at least, allow the use of stretched versions of existing engines. Then, at a meeting between interested parties and the FIA's sporting commission, the CSI, in Paris, Chapman made the case for a 3-litre rule. The FIA accepted this. That put Coventry-Climax – Formula One's most successful engine manufacturer over the 1959–65 period – out of the picture. Chapman, having called for a 3-litre formula, would have to look for a new engine supplier.

The first season of the 3-litre formula saw a hotchpotch of answers, and for many it was a stopgap and often unsatisfactory season. The simple, Oldsmobile-based V8 Repco 620 used by Brabham was the answer in both 1966 and 1967. Ferrari looked an early favourite with its V12 design, but its 1966 season rather fell apart. Also using a V12 Italian power unit was Cooper, but its heavy Maserati engine was based on the 2.5-litre unit from an even earlier formula. Gurney also plumped for a V12, this being a new engine from Weslake, but initially had to fit a 2.7-litre version of the Coventry-Climax also used for the 2.5-litre formula of 1954–60. Others, too, took the 2.7-litre route, while some, like Lotus, were even more undersized when they temporarily settled on 2-litre Coventry-Climax and BRM engines from the 1.5-litre years. McLaren, in its first Formula One season, built a full 3-litre car with a Ford V8 IndyCar engine and then an unreliable Serenissima V8. BRM took the most complicated route with its H16, and it was that, as mentioned, that Team Lotus used for the final part of the 1966 season.

The H16 was, though, only a temporary solution for Team Lotus, enabling Chapman to pursue the engine he really wanted – a purpose-built design from Keith Duckworth. Ford engines had been the basis for much of Duckworth's work and so it's perhaps not surprising that the car maker's public affairs director Walter Hayes, who was also responsible for competition affairs, should already have been thinking about a Formula One engine even before Chapman approached him. Despite the fact that Duckworth had

BELOW: Cosworth co-founder Keith Duckworth tests what was arguably his greatest creation, the 3-litre DFV. *(Ford)*

ABOVE: Another highly significant Lotus to make a Zandvoort debut, the Type 49. This time the result was victory first time out, not only for the car but also for the Cosworth DFV engine that was later to power the Type 72. *(Ford)*

never designed a complete engine before, Ford agreed to back him to the tune of £100,000. (That sum also included the design of the Ford Cortina-based FVA Formula Two engine.)

The initially 400bhp, 90° V8 DFV ('Double Four Valve') was designed to be a stressed part of the first chassis in which it was installed, the Lotus 49. Thus, while many other manufacturers were to use it in the seasons to come, it was originally an integral part of a Lotus and would be a fitting power unit for the Lotus 72 that was to come.

Until the 72 arrived, the Lotus 49 was probably the most outstanding car of the 3-litre formula's early years. It was a straightforward monocoque car with the engine mounted on the rear bulkhead and looks that hearkened back to the 25 and 33. The car and engine won first time out at the 1967 Dutch Grand Prix with Jim Clark at the wheel, and was used by Hill to take the 1968 World Championship following the Scot's tragic death at a Hockenheim Formula Two race early in the season. It took Lotus from an age when cars looked simple, with little regard to aerodynamics, to one where the wing had become 'king'. Despite the lack of an engine cover it initially appeared to have clean lines, which were first destroyed by an upswept engine cowl and then by a series of rear aerofoils that ranged from those high up on struts to much lower affairs mounted directly to the wheel uprights. The Type 49 also took Formula One from a time when all Grand Prix cars had to be painted in the national colours of their entrants (in the case of Team Lotus, a British livery of green) into the modern era of sponsorship, when it appeared early in 1968 in the red, white and gold colour scheme of Gold Leaf cigarettes. By 1970 the car was well past its first flush of youth but was still used as an alternative when the 72's teething troubles proved too much.

13

THE LOTUS 72 STORY

ABOVE: The failure of the four-wheel-drive Type 63 was to lead to the Type 72. *(Ford)*

BELOW: The first Lotus 'wedge' was the attractive Type 56 gas turbine Indianapolis car, seen here at Vel's Parnelli Jones Racing Collection in Torrance, California. *(Author)*

Launch of the Lotus 72 and its first championship

Lotus was, however, heading up a blind alley. Experience of four-wheel-drive for the Indianapolis 500 persuaded Chapman that this might be the way to handle the 3-litre power that was now available. The result, the Lotus 63 that appeared in 1969, was a failure and underlined the need for a more conventional car, albeit one that bristled with new features, to replace the 63. Again, Team Lotus's experience in the Indianapolis 500 was brought into play. For 1968 Team Lotus had built four Pratt & Whitney gas-turbine-engined cars. Arguably they were the most attractive cars ever to be seen at the Speedway on account of their wedge shape. (An experimental Formula One version, the 56B, was raced alongside the 72 at occasional races in 1971.) The shape was repeated in the short-lived de Dion axle Lotus 57/58 F1/F2 project; in the Formula Ford 61 (although purely for aesthetic reasons) and, to a certain extent, the 63 and the Formula 5000 Lotus 70. However, arguably its most dramatic iteration was to be the 72, which stood out from the crowd at the start of the 1970 Formula One season. The rest of the grid still, in some ways, visibly hearkened back to the Cooper-Climaxes that heralded the rear-engine era. The technical details of the 72 will be described in the forthcoming pages. Suffice to say that in 1970 it just appeared so different to the rest. The drivers for Team Lotus that season would be the mercurial Austrian Jochen Rindt – who had at long last won his first Grand Prix the previous year and was generally regarded as the fastest driver of the immediate post-Clark era – and the cerebral Englishman John Miles.

Colin Chapman and designer Maurice Phillippe, who would carry out the detail work,

spent a long time discussing what the car would be like, the Type 56 Indianapolis car playing a large part in their thinking. The result was specifically designed to work with Firestone's latest, light construction tyres. A low unsprung weight, an all-up weight that was near the limit, and smooth pitch-free characteristics enabled it to make better use of the softer tyre compounds than the rest of the grid. Relocation of components meant better weight distribution, with the radiators split and moved to the sides of the cockpit. Torsion bar suspension and inboard front brakes with double universally jointed driveshafts, let alone its radical wedge shape, made it stand out from the rest of the Formula One grid. But there was nothing specifically new in any one of these features. Indeed, there is an argument that the Lotus 72 was a fairly orthodox racing car for its period. After all, torsion bars were fitted to such as the 1939 Mercedes-Benz W163, while side radiators were already to be found back in 1914, when they appeared on the Hughes-Rayfield Special that was entered for the Indianapolis 500. What *was* special was the way in which Chapman and Phillippe put them all together and made them work as a package. A total of 83 component manufacturers supplied product for the new car.

Radical anti-dive and anti-squat features meant that the handling was found to be suspect during its first two races, the 1970 Spanish Grand Prix and the BRDC International Trophy at Silverstone, and revisions were made. In the heat of Spain another problem arose. The insulating material used to prevent the transfer of heat from the brakes to the universal joint wasn't up to the job, and during practice the bolts holding the left brake disc snapped on Jochen Rindt's car. The material was replaced by a steel spacer and ventilated discs replaced the original solid ones.

Rindt and Miles had to revert to their Team Lotus 49s for the Monaco Grand Prix, and the Austrian won a dramatic last-minute victory, his second win at a World Championship event. A four-week gap between Grands Prix enabled Lotus to remove both the anti-dive and ant-squat geometry from Rindt's car and the anti-squat from Miles's. Concern over the size of the suspension bolts led to Rindt again driving a Type 49 in Belgium. Paying driver Alex Soler-Roig tried to qualify what was Rindt's normal 72 but did insufficient laps, leaving Miles as the only Type 72 driver that day. However, success was just around the corner: Rindt then won four consecutive Grands Prix with his revised 72 and arrived at Monza with the championship almost in his grasp. At Zandvoort for the Dutch Grand Prix he led for all but the first two laps, but his victory was soured by the death of his friend Piers Courage, who was driving a De Tomaso for entrant Frank Williams. Rindt was now just one point adrift of Jackie Stewart in the World Championship stakes and was contemplating retirement if he took the title. By this stage Chapman was confident that he had the best car on the grid and that, if no problems occurred during the races, the championship was there for the taking.

At the physically demanding Clermont-Ferrand circuit in the Auvergne, Rindt had adopted a wait and see policy, having been hit in the face by a stone during practice and

BELOW: Rindt testing at Snetterton prior to the 1970 Spanish Grand Prix. Problems were already becoming apparent. *(Ford)*

15

THE LOTUS 72 STORY

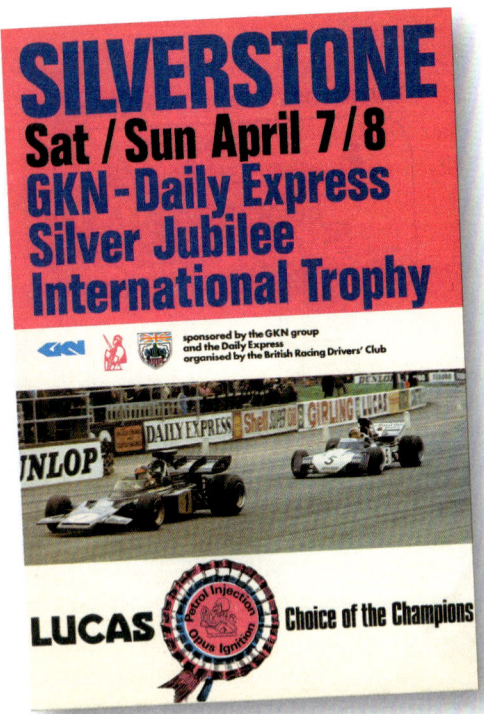

ABOVE: The 1973 Silverstone International Trophy programme celebrated the previous year's Fittipaldi versus Hailwood battle. *(Author)*

ABOVE RIGHT: Fittipaldi leads Henri Pescarolo's Politoys at the 1971 British Grand Prix. *(Ford)*

only qualifying in sixth place. Once up to second he began to put the pressure on Jean-Pierre Beltoise, taking the lead when one of the Frenchman's tyres began to lose air. For the first time in his career Rindt now led the World Championship. 'It is now quite clear that the Lotus 72 is a sensation car,' he told his biographer Heinz Prüller.

Next up was the British Grand Prix at Brands Hatch, an undulating and bumpy surface that Rindt felt was ideally suited to the Type 72. Ferrari's Jacky Ickx led initially before retiring with a broken differential bearing. Rindt now led on the slippery track, closely pursued by Australian Jack Brabham in one of his own cars. With 12 laps to go the Austrian had a moment at Clearways and Brabham slipped through. Unlike at Monaco, Rindt didn't harry Brabham; the state of his tyres just wouldn't allow him to. However, for a second time that year he overtook Jack on the last lap, sweeping past at Clearways as the latter ran out of fuel. Victory was almost taken away when the scrutineers declared the highest point of the rear wing to be more than permitted, and it took over two hours before they decided that the wing was legal by a matter of just one millimetre.

Concerns over the safety of the Nürburgring took the German Grand Prix to Hockenheim that year. Here Rindt battled frenetically with the Ferraris of Ickx and 'Clay' Regazzoni and the March of Chris Amon. Eventually it was all down to Ickx and Rindt, with the latter grabbing the lead for the final time on the penultimate lap. The next Grand Prix was Rindt's national event at Zeltweg. It was pointed out to Chapman by some of the other teams that the Lotus 72 was half an inch too wide. That meant ten hours' work for the mechanics to slim down the radiator intake with power saws and files. In the race, the Austrian was fighting his way back from sixth place when his DFV failed.

Going into the Italian Grand Prix, Rindt looked an almost certain champion – victory would give him the title, providing Brabham didn't finish higher than fifth, and there would still be three rounds remaining. During practice Rindt ran without wings, finding the car almost 800rpm faster on the straights. Denny Hulme was to say that when Rindt went past him he felt as if his McLaren was painted on the road. John Miles was also sent out without wings but quickly returned to the pits, as he felt the car to be undrivable in this guise. Brazilian driver Emerson Fittipaldi, who had joined Team Lotus at the British Grand Prix – where he had made an impressive debut at the wheel of a Type 49 – had been entered in a 72 for the first time but crashed towards the end of the Friday practice.

On the Saturday morning Rindt was entering the Parabolica when his car was seen to weave slightly and then turn sharp left into the crash

16
LOTUS 72 MANUAL

barriers, resulting in a fatal accident. It would be seven years before an Italian court would conclude that front brake-shaft failure had caused Rindt to lose control but that improperly installed safety barriers had been the cause of his death. The team remined unsure. Fear of fire meant that although Rindt's other safety belts were fixed, his crotch straps were not. There was little, therefore, to prevent him being pulled down into the cockpit, and as a result the lap belts had cut his throat. Ironically, in an age when flames were an all too common occurrence, the car didn't catch fire.

The car was impounded, although its newly installed development engine (number 901) was removed and would be used in Emerson Fittipaldi's car the next time the factory Lotus 72s reappeared. Miles' car and the blue 72 that privateer Rob Walker was now entering for Graham Hill were withdrawn. Chief mechanic Eddie Dennis recalled that the team rapidly headed for the border, being stopped once 'presumably to see if we had Jochen's car on board.'

Team Lotus absented itself from the next championship event, the Canadian Grand Prix, leaving the Rob Walker car as the sole 72 there, while John Miles understandably walked away from Grand Prix racing. Because of the uncertainty over what had caused Rindt's accident, solid brake shafts were fitted to Hill's car at St-Jovite. These would be used in all the Type 72's subsequent seasons.

At this point it was still possible for Jacky Ickx to take the championship if he won all three remaining Grands Prix. The Belgian ticked off the first of these with a victory. However, at Watkins Glen Team Lotus's youthful new pairing of Emerson Fittipaldi and Reine Wisell finished first and third, securing a posthumous championship for Rindt. It was a race won more by the misfortunes of others and, therefore, hardly one of Fittipaldi's greatest, but it was one of the most meaningful.

The time of Fittipaldi

Having won the championship, albeit in sad circumstances, Team Lotus now entered a season in which, for the first time since 1960, it was not to win a single Grand Prix. The drivers' inexperience and the fact that Fittipaldi was seriously injured in a mid-season road accident didn't help as a number of minor changes were made and new low-profile Firestone tyres fitted. The turbine-engined, four-wheel-drive Type 56B also acted as a distraction that year.

By the end of the season the car, though, seemed to be coming right, and the following year Fittipaldi took five Grand Prix victories to become the youngest World Champion at the time, although his new teammate Dave Walker failed to score a single point. Four non-championship victories also fell to the Brazilian, who had helped to develop it into the quickest

BELOW: In 1972 Dave Walker achieved an unenviable record of becoming the first driver not to score a point during the season that his teammate won the World Championship. This is the Australian in Argentina. *(Ford)*

car in the Formula One field. This was the year that the Lotus 72 first appeared in what was to become the iconic black and gold livery of John Player Special. The change of brand presented the sponsor with the opportunity to give the car a name akin to the contenders for the Indianapolis 500, which were invariably called the something or other Special. It worked hard to persuade the public to refer to it as a JPS, but history decided that it was still a Lotus 72. As *Motor Sport* magazine's hard-line Grand Prix reporter Denis Jenkinson said, 'It's a Lotus-Cosworth, not a JPS-Ford.'

In the main it was easier to tell the origins of a car by its name in the 1970s than it ever would be by the 21st Century. Mike Kettlewell, writing in the 1972 edition of the *Autocourse* annual, was perhaps prescient when he wrote: 'One cannot condone the adoption of this Indianapolis-type practice in Formula 1 … the thought of, in years to come, John Player Specials battling with Yardley Black Labels, Brooke Bond Tea Bags, Rothmans King Sizes, Mum for Men Specials, etc, when they might all be from the same chassis manufacturer is frightening … One naturally accepts the fact that commercialism is all-important in Formula 1, but it cannot be allowed to get too out of hand.' One wonders what Kettlewell would have thought of the World Championship being eventually won by an energy drinks supplier. However, it was less than a decade since BRP team owner Ken Gregory had first persuaded a sponsor to fund a Grand Prix team and far less since the Lotus 49 had become the first Formula One car to appear completely in a sponsor's livery. Kettlewell did reckon that the new JPS image had improved the morale of Team Lotus.

Champion became the spark plug supplier in 1972, taking over from Ford's own brand Autolite, while Texaco replaced Shell as the fuel and lubricant sponsor. Another change was that Maurice Phillippe had left, to be replaced as chief designer by Martin Waide, a long-standing employee of Lotus.

The early season, non-championship races augured well for the rest of the year, with Fittipaldi winning the Race of Champions at Brands Hatch and the International Trophy at Silverstone. Then came the first European World Championship race of the season, the Spanish Grand Prix. It had been two months since the previous round, South Africa, in which the Brazilian had opened his account with a second place. A poor start followed by his fire extinguisher going off during the second lap was perhaps not the way to get going, but Fittipaldi quickly outwitted his rivals into first place and his second World Championship victory. A couple of races later and the Grand Prix teams were at Nivelles for the first time for the Belgian Grand Prix. Fittipaldi took pole but was again beaten off the line. By lap nine he was in the lead and pulling away into the distance. He now led the championship outright. He also took another non-championship victory. He was to score four of these that year with the Type 72, as he also won the rather bizarre Rothmans 50,000 Formule Libre race at Brands Hatch later in the year.

For scoring purposes, the championship was divided into two halves. Fittipaldi now put the championship out of reach for his competitors by winning three of the next four rounds, starting with the British Grand Prix at Brands Hatch. Again he was beaten off the line but won after a frantic battle with Jacky Ickx (Ferrari) and Jackie Stewart (Tyrrell). Two races later it was again a story of pole, beaten away from the start, and a closely fought battle for

BELOW: One of the great sights of motorsport in the 1970s, a Lotus 72 powering through Silverstone's Woodcote corner. In this case it's Emerson Fittipaldi's, in practice for the 1972 International Trophy. *(Author)*

victory. With three races to go Fittipaldi had a 25-point lead in the championship and there were only nine points available for a win.

The championship would be secured at Monza, but not before 72/7, Fittipaldi's intended car, was damaged when its transporter blew a tyre near Milan and it was flung out into a garden. The spare car, 72/5, was quickly prepared and a new Series 12 DFV installed. A mechanically troubled practice meant that Fittipaldi was back on the third row of the grid, added to which a leaking fuel tank had to be replaced 35 minutes before the start. However, this time the Brazilian made a lightning start, taking the lead on the demise of the two Ferraris. Aged just 25 he had become the youngest-ever winner of the world title, and the 72's place in history was secured.

The following year the incredibly rapid Ronnie Peterson joined Fittipaldi, meaning that Lotus had two top-line drivers for the first time since 1969. Australian Ralph Bellamy had now taken over as Formula One designer, and Goodyear – whose tyres were less suited to the weight balance of the 72 – had replaced Firestone as the tyre supplier. There were more Grand Prix victories, including Lotus's 50th when Emerson took the Spanish race. Peterson broke his Grand Prix duck and then won some more. This, though, was the year of Jackie Stewart's final World Championship, and the Lotus pair finished behind him in second and third. Reward, though, came in the shape of the Constructors' Championship, indicating that it was, perhaps, not a bad idea to employ two such talented drivers.

The season had begun well, with wins for the new champion in the opening two rounds, Argentina and Brazil, and at the fourth, Spain, but that was that for the Brazilian. Buenos Aires, a five-way battle, was to be remembered by Fittipaldi as his best race in a type 72. At Interlagos he was never headed, an emotional victory as São Paolo was his home town. The Montjuich Park round was the first at which all cars had to have deformable structures around the fuel tanks. Peterson led but lost his gears, leaving Fittipaldi to win with an almost flat rear tyre.

The team took four Type 72s to Zolder for the Belgian Grand Prix for Fittipaldi and Peterson, the first time this many 72s had been to a race meeting. However, Fittipaldi could only manage third place, Jackie Stewart won and the balance of power shifted to the Scot, who by halfway through the season had established a lead in the championship that he was not to lose. Changes in tyre technology, problems with the gearbox and braking performance combined against the 72, but now Peterson was coming into his own. His long-awaited first Grand Prix victory came at Paul Ricard.

At Zandvoort, Fittipaldi had a massive practice accident following wheel failure. From a period when he had scored 41 points in six races he was now in one where he would score only a single point in a similar number of rounds. However, Peterson returned to the victory circle in Austria, repeating the result in Italy. The Swede was now proving quicker than the Brazilian, who needed to win in Monza if

LEFT TOP: Emerson Fittipaldi suffered from metering unit failure at the Race of Champions in 1973. *(Author)*

LEFT MIDDLE: Ronnie Peterson retired with gearbox failure at the non-championship Brands Hatch race. *(Author)*

LEFT BOTTOM: Fittipaldi accelerates away from Druids corner during the above event. *(Author)*

ABOVE: Colin Chapman in JPS livery. *(Ford)*

19

THE LOTUS 72 STORY

ABOVE: Peterson (leading) and Fittipaldi formed the front row of the grid at the Osterreichring in 1973. The Swede went on to win. *(Ford)*

Decline and fall

Fittipaldi now left to join McLaren and win another World Championship. Jacky Ickx, the team's main rival towards the end of 1970, replaced him, but could only take one, non-championship victory with the ageing 72. This should have been the last appearance of a factory entered 72. Peterson, by contrast, won another three Grands Prix with the car. However, it should not have been like this…

Ralph Bellamy wanted to design what he saw as a '100lb lighter Lotus 72'. During the course of its development the weight of the 72 had crept ever upwards. The result was a new car for 1974, the 76 (or John Player Special Mark 1), which had problems with its fuel, oil, cooling and braking systems and was still the same weight as the 72. Ronnie Peterson became so exasperated with the Type 76 that he pleaded for the 72 to be brought out again. The 72 continued to play its part, and not just as a substitute. At the 1974 German Grand Prix the mechanics built a special for the Swede to race after he'd crashed chassis number 72/8 in practice. One of the new cars, 76/2 (also known as JPS/10*), had been taken along as a spare. Its tub, along with radiators and front suspension, was mated to the 72's engine,

he was to have any chance of retaining his title. He came second to Peterson that day, annoyed that no team orders had come into play. You can forgive Lotus. Fittipaldi was now known to be leaving them at the end of season, and to take the championship he would have had to win all three remaining rounds, with Stewart failing to score a single point. As it was, another second place, at Mosport, helped Fittipaldi to salvage second place in the drivers' championship. This, and a win at the final race of the season, Watkins Glen, enabled Team Lotus to retain the constructors' championship.

* It was considered that the type 72s were also John Player Specials, and thus the first Type 76 was designated JPS/9. It followed on from the first eight chassis numbers, even though four of these never appeared in JPS livery. The last 72, 72/9, appeared after the launch of the Type 76.

RIGHT: Ronnie Peterson wins a Grand Prix at last. His mount, 72/6, had been built halfway through the 1971 season and been updated to 72E specification with deformable structures around the tub for 1973. A well outboard cantilevered rear wing was also a feature of the car by the time it took the Swede to victory at Paul Ricard. *(Ford)*

20
LOTUS 72 MANUAL

TOP: At the Nürburgring in 1974 Peterson raced a hybrid consisting of the rear end of a 72 grafted on to the tub and front suspension of a 76. *(Ford)*

ABOVE: Jacky Ickx was in 72E/5 for the 1974 German Grand Prix, finishing fifth, one place behind Peterson in the hybrid 72/76. *(Ford)*

ABOVE: Peterson demanded that he drive a 72 and not a 76 in the 1974 Monaco Grand Prix. He was vindicated when he took the car to a hard-fought victory. *(Ford)*

gearbox and rear suspension set, not an easy task. A 72-type nose cone was also fitted. The 'special' finished fourth, which led to both Lotus 76s having 72-type rear ends for the Austrian Grand Prix.

Peterson's first win of the year had been earlier in the season at Monaco, where Chapman and team manager Peter Warr had relented to Peterson's demands and both of the Team Lotus drivers had 72s instead of 76s – Ickx's, it was said, had been brought out of Chapman's personal museum. Team Lotus, it seemed, was in a state of disarray. However, despite a spin and the fact that he hit Carlos Reutemann's Brabham as he returned to the track, Peterson fought his way to victory. The next win, a hard-fought typical Peterson drive, would come in Dijon, France. Goodyear, though, was not including Lotus in its development work. There would be just one more win for the 72, a thrilling 0.8-second victory at Monza ahead of former Lotus driver Fittipaldi.

With the failure of the 76, Team Lotus had no option but to roll out the 72 again for 1975, but it was now well past its sell-by date and the season was a disaster. It didn't help that John Player significantly reduced its funding, having first told Chapman that it intended to withdraw altogether. A record number of 72s started the South African Grand Prix, but that was because a couple were locally based cars (three 72s were to find their way into

ABOVE: **Emerson Fittipaldi may have won the World Championship for McLaren in 1974, but in Italy it was Ronnie Peterson who won with his ageing Lotus 72.** (Ford)

South African privateer hands). Ickx finished second following a truncated Spanish Grand Prix; it was the best result of the season for Lotus. The Belgian left before the British Grand Prix, to be replaced by no fewer than three less experienced British pilots, novices Jim Crawford and Brian Henton and Team Surtees driver John Watson. At the US Grand Prix Peterson finished fifth and Henton 12th as the Lotus 72 disappeared into history, scoring two last points even after six seasons.

Subsequent Lotus Formula One history

Lotus was now in trouble. Following the disaster of the 76 and the prolonged use of the 72 it had fallen behind in terms of Formula One development. Thus the slim 77 was seen as an interim car, although Mario Andretti did win the particularly wet 1976 Japanese Grand Prix with one. However, its successor, the 78, introduced the concept of a 'wing car' under which an area of low pressure was generated, increasing the loading on the tyres. Regular visits to the winner's circle returned, with four victories for Andretti and one for Gunnar Nilsson during 1977. Tragically, Ronnie Peterson, who had returned to Lotus after an absence of a couple of seasons, was killed, like Rindt at Monza, at the wheel of a 78 the following year.

The 79 that followed capitalised on the experience gained with the 78 and went further towards being a true a true 'ground effects'

ABOVE: **An example of Chapman innovation that was ultimately deemed to be in breach of Formula One regulations, the twin-chassis Type 88.** (Nick Collins)

RIGHT: **Suspecting that the 88 might not meet with official approval, Lotus also produced the unsuccessful Type 87 for 1981. Elio de Angelis sits on the grid for that year's British Grand Prix. The Italian would be Team Lotus's first Grand Prix winner since the days of Andretti, but at the wheel of the later Type 91.** (Author)

vehicle. In 1978 it took the company to its last drivers' and constructors' championships. Champion Andretti took a further six Grand Prix victories for Lotus that year while Peterson won twice. The 79 was, perhaps, the last of the truly great Lotus Grand Prix designs, but it had its deficiencies, which showed up once the opposition began to understand ground effects. A second-generation ground effects car, the 80, was a failure, while the simpler 81 also failed to win a race.

At the beginning of the 1980s Chapman began work on a twin-chassis concept in which an aluminium honeycomb monocoque with conventional suspension formed a primary chassis, while a secondary chassis, made in moulded carbon-composite, was supported by its own framework and carried the bodywork, sidepods, wings and radiators. The 86 was only seen as a test bed, but the more sophisticated 88, the first composite F1 car to run, actually got as far as the racetracks before being banned. The conventional but largely uncompetitive 87 was run at the same time and was followed by an improved version, the 91, which lacked sufficient speed to be truly competitive (although, with Elio de Angelis, it did win Team Lotus its first Grand Prix since 1978), and a further development, the 92, which was the last Lotus to use a Cosworth engine derived from the DFV (the DFY).

The turbocharged Renault-engined era began with the test bed 93T and then the 94T, which incorporated the old 91 chassis. The latter wasn't particularly competitive but it did return Lotus to nearer the front. However, Chapman had suffered a fatal heart attack just after the first 93T was completed. Arguably Team Lotus was never the same without Chapman's relentless drive. De Angelis and Ayrton Senna, who replaced a long-serving but, as far as Lotus was concerned, winless Nigel Mansell for 1985, would ensure that there were more Grand Prix victories.

At the end of 1986 John Player and Sons withdrew its backing and the last link with the 72 was severed. Honda replaced Renault as the engine supplier, and computer-controlled 'active' suspension was featured on the 99T. From 1988 Team Lotus' fortunes deteriorated. With Honda's withdrawal and the end of the turbo era, Lotus used Judd engines on a customer basis. More powerful but heavier and longer Lamborghini V12 engines powered the Type 102 in 1990. It was back to Judd for 1991 and then, in 1992, the Ford name returned with HB V8s powering the Lotus 107s. There was little continuity in engine use during those final years and eventually Mugen Honda power units were fitted before, in 1994, Team Lotus applied for an administration order to protect it from its creditors.

In 2010 Malaysian entrepreneur Tony Fernandes secured the right to use the Lotus name for his new Grand Prix team. Group Lotus has since terminated that agreement, and following an acrimonious 2011 season in which there seemed to be two Lotus teams, the only cars to carry the Lotus name in 2012 were those of the former Renault F1, in which Group Lotus had bought a share. However, these recent projects should be seen as being Lotus in name only and not true Team Lotus cars.

ABOVE: Lotus's next great success after the 72, the Type 79 took Mario Andretti to the 1978 World Championship. It was to be Lotus's last world title. *(Ford)*

BELOW: The familiar JPS livery disappeared for 1987 to be replaced by that of another cigarette manufacturer, Camel. Honda engines also replaced Renault for the Type 99T. With this, Ayrton Senna scored Lotus's final two Grand Prix victories. *(Author)*

23

THE LOTUS 72 STORY

LOTUS 72 FACTORY DRIVERS

RIGHT: It took two hours to decide that Rindt's wing was legal following his victory in the 1970 British Grand Prix. *(Ford)*

A total of 12 drivers started races with the Lotus 72 for Lotus, with a 13th, Spaniard Alex Soler-Roig, failing to qualify for the 1970 Belgian Grands Prix. Former Lotus factory driver Graham Hill also drove a Rob Walker-entered 72 in Grand Prix while a further five drivers competed in South African Formula One races.

Jochen Rindt

World Champion 1970 with Lotus 72. Four Grand Prix wins with Lotus 72.

Austrian Jochen Rindt was known for his outright speed, making his mark in a Formula Two Brabham-Cosworth, winning as an almost unknown at Crystal Palace during Whitsun 1964. This led to a one-off drive in Rob Walker's Brabham-BRM in the Austrian Grand Prix later in the year and a contract with Cooper for the following three seasons' Grands Prix. At the same time he joined Roy Winkelmann's F2 team. He rapidly became one of the leading contenders in the junior category, which in those days featured plenty of Grand Prix drivers, and also won the 1965 Le Mans 24-hours with

RIGHT: Another victory for Rindt at the 1970 British Grand Prix. The wing controversy has yet to rear its head and Chapman is cheerful, although Eddie Dennis appears thoughtful. *(Ford)*

RIGHT: Jochen Rindt took the lead of the 1970 British Grand Prix on lap 5, losing it to Jack Brabham on lap 69 only to regain it on the final tour.

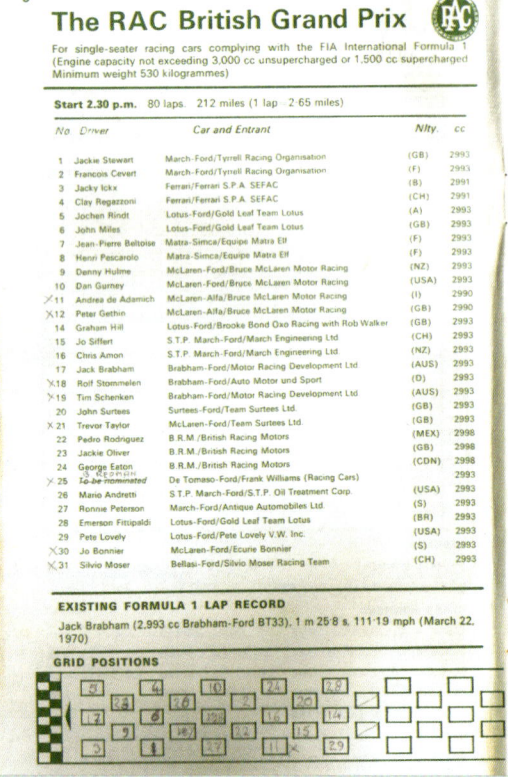
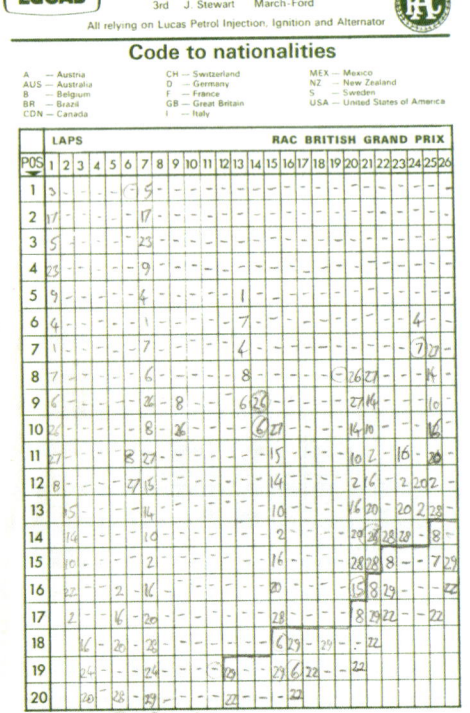

Masten Gregory in a North American Racing Team-entered Ferrari 275 LM.

Firmly established as an experienced driver by the end of 1967 and with his Cooper contract now at an end, Rindt was able to transfer to a more competitive team after three frustrating years. Mechanical trouble, however, ruined his year with Brabham, and for 1969 he reluctantly left to join Lotus on the proviso that he would have equal number one status with Graham Hill. He now proved himself to be a potential Grand Prix victor, particularly at Silverstone where he famously diced with Jackie Stewart before an aerofoil came adrift. Finally, at the end of the year he scored the first of his six Grand Prix victories by winning the US GP. By now he was arguably the world's fastest Grand Prix driver but was handicapped by the age of the Lotus 49.

The start of the 1970 season must have been frustrating, with the new 72 obviously needing development. However, an old 49C was pressed into action for the Monaco Grand Prix, and in what was probably the finest drive of his career he pressed Jack Brabham so hard that the Australian slid into the barricades, leaving Rindt to win. Reunited with the 72 at the Dutch Grand Prix, Rindt proceeded to win four consecutive races and to take a commanding lead in the World Championship. Tragically, he was killed in practice for the Italian Grand Prix when his Lotus 72 swerved into a crash barrier. At this point Jacky Ickx could have still won the championship, but this became impossible once new Lotus team leader Emerson Fittipaldi had driven his 72 to victory in the US Grand Prix.

ABOVE: **It was wet at Monaco in 1972, very wet, but Fittipaldi managed to snatch third place in the closing stages.** *(Ford)*

Emerson Fittipaldi

World Champion 1972 with Lotus 72. Nine Grand Prix wins with Lotus 72 (also World Champion 1974 with McLaren).

Brazilian Emerson Fittipaldi moved rapidly through Formula Ford and Formula Three, having arrived in Britain in 1969. The following season he competed in a works-supported Formula Two Lotus and was given the opportunity to drive a factory Lotus 49 in that year's British Grand Prix. Starting as number three driver for Gold Leaf Team Lotus, he rose to team leader following the death of Rindt, using a

LEFT: **Emerson Fittipaldi took nine Grand Prix wins with the Lotus 72.** *(Ford)*

ABOVE: Fittipaldi wins the 1970 United States Grand Prix. It was only his fourth appearance at this level.
(Sutton Images)

Lotus 72 to win what was only his fourth Grand Prix, the 1970 US. In one and a half seasons he had progressed from FF contender to Grand Prix winner.

Problems with the 72 meant a lean 1971, but five wins the following season saw him take his first World Championship, at the time the youngest person to do so. He won the first two Grands Prix of the following year but his season fell away with only one more victory. A change of team to McLaren for 1974 saw him take back the title. Again he started the next year well but he couldn't retain the championship.

Having won 14 Grands Prix he now made a shock move to his brother Wilson's team. Following five dismal seasons with Fittipaldis he quit driving in Formula One at the end of 1980, and moved into management of the team until it folded at the end of 1982.

Fittipaldi revived his career in North America, initially in sports car racing before moving on to IndyCars. After driving for a couple of small teams he joined Patrick Racing. In 1989 he won both the CART championship and his first

ABOVE AND RIGHT: Jean-Pierre Beltoise (BRM number five), Emerson Fittipaldi (Lotus number one) and Mike Hailwood (Surtees number five) battled it out for the lead of the 1972 International Trophy at Silverstone.

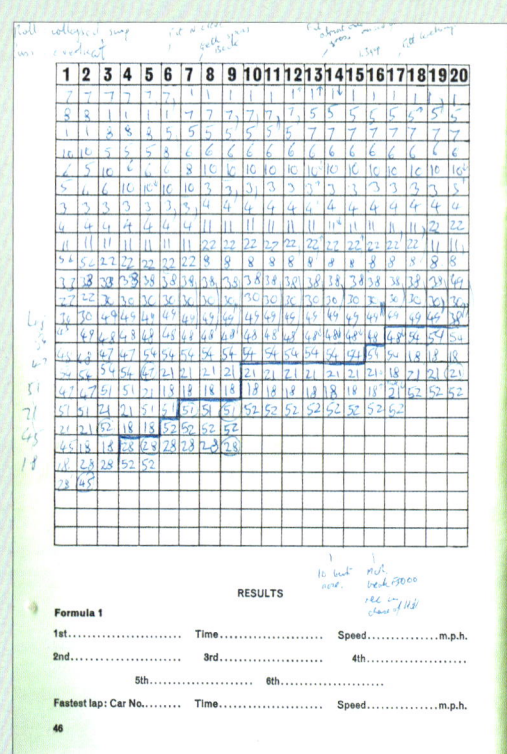
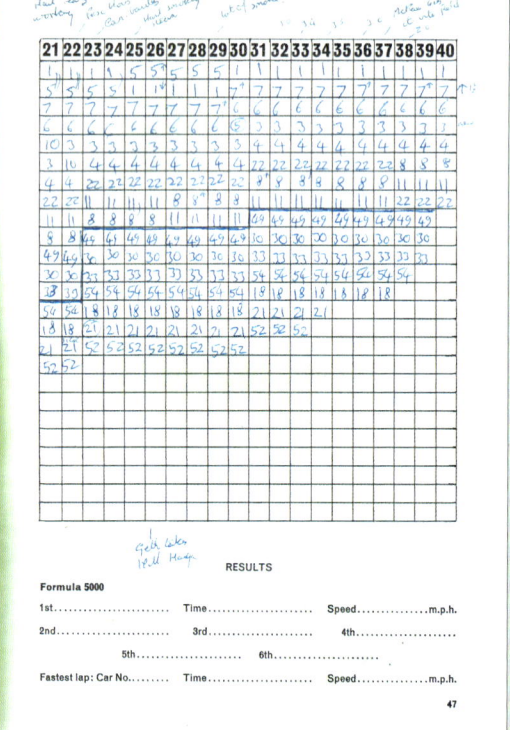

Indianapolis 500 in dramatic fashion after a last-minute dice with Al Unser Jr. Fittipaldi was then driving a Penske for Pat Patrick and the following year he joined Penske's own team, with whom he remained for the final six seasons of his career, winning a total of 22 CART races for the two teams. He won his second Indy 500 in 1993, taking the lead from another former World Champion and Team Lotus driver Nigel Mansell.

Ronnie Peterson

Seven Grand Prix wins with Lotus 72.
When Ronnie Peterson joined Team Lotus in 1973 he and Fittipaldi gave it an 'all-star' line-up for the first time since the Rindt/Hill pairing of 1969. The spectacular Swede had first come to notice in a Formula Three Tecno, winning the 1969 Monaco F3 race. He underlined his undoubted ability during three seasons driving Marches, first with Colin Crabbe's privately entered 701 and then with a factory 711 and 721, finishing second in the 1971 World Championship (with four second places) as well as winning the European Formula Two Championship the same year. However, he still had to win a Grand Prix before he joined Team Lotus. He was to be with the team for the rest of the 72 'era', winning seven of his ten eventual Grand Prix victories with the car.

During 1973 Peterson claimed nine pole positions with the Lotus 72, regularly out-qualifying Fittipaldi. The failure of the 76 and the then age of the 72, meant that Team Lotus couldn't give him a car worthy of his talents for his third year with the team and, after three seasons, he returned to March, with which he won the 1976 Italian Grand Prix, his third F1 victory at Monza.

After another season away from Team Lotus, this time with the Tyrrell six-wheeler, he returned to act as 'number two' to Mario Andretti, driving Lotus 78s and 79s and scoring a further two wins before he died tragically following injuries received after the start of the Italian Grand Prix. Having scored four second places that year – all behind Andretti – to add to his victories, he was again placed second in the championship. It has been said that he was the fastest driver of his time.

Peterson and Fittipaldi were easily the most prolific users of the Lotus 72, with 40 and 38 Grand Prix starts respectively. The Swede was also the only driver, apart from World Champions Rindt and Fittipaldi, to win GPs with the car.

ABOVE: **Arguably the fastest driver of his era, Ronnie Peterson, like Fittipaldi, scored his early Grand Prix victories at the wheel of Lotus 72s.** *(Ford)*

BELOW: **A committed Ronnie Peterson at the French Grand Prix in 1974.** *(Ford)*

ABOVE: Ickx in the pack with a Type 76 in 1974. The McLaren M23 (no. 6) behind apes the wedge shape of the older Type 72. (Ford)

RIGHT: While waiting for the 56B turbine car to be finished during practice for the 1971 Dutch Grand Prix, Dave Walker took out the Type 72 intended for Dave Charlton. He crashed the car and the South African became a non-starter. (Ford)

Other Team Lotus factory drivers who raced the 72

Much of the initial testing of the Lotus 72 was carried out by John Miles, himself a talented engineer. The Englishman had been promoted into the Formula One team initially to develop the 4WD Lotus 63, which he raced in 1969. Following an accident, Graham Hill left the Lotus team and Miles became number two to Rindt for 1970. As such he raced a 49 twice and a 72 on seven occasions, his best result being fifth in South Africa with the former. Following Rindt's accident Miles had had enough and left the team.

His place was taken by Swede Reine Wisell, who came third in his first Grand Prix, the 1970 US – a result that was to prove his best in a 22 GP career. He continued to drive the Lotus 72 in 1971, leaving to join BRM for the following season and then returning to JPTL to race a 72D in the two North American Grands Prix. His subsequent two seasons were spent driving Marches. Spaniard Alex Soler-Roig also drove a 72 in 1970, failing to complete enough practice laps to qualify for the Belgian Grand Prix.

The following year Formula Three champion Tony Trimmer had a one-off drive in a factory 72 at the Brands Hatch Race of Champions. The Englishman, who had carried out testing duties with the 72, was also entered for the British Grand Prix that year as a reward, but this was withdrawn, officially because of a shortage of engines. Trimmer's F3 title successor, Australian Dave Walker, also drove the car at the Hockenheim Rindt Memorial Race prior to becoming number two to Fittipaldi in 1972. While Fittipaldi proceeded to win the World Championship, Walker, who had also driven the 56B turbine car in 1971, failed to score a single point and left the team at the end of the year. Prior to dominating Formula One racing in South Africa with Scuderia Scribante's 72, Dave Charlton had a one-off drive in a factory version at the 1971 British Grand Prix.

The Fittipaldi and Peterson all-star line

72 TRIVIA

1969, **1970** and **1971** Monaco Formula Three support race winners Peterson, Trimmer and Walker all later drove Lotus 72s.

BELOW RIGHT: 1975 was a disaster. Jacky Ickx could only manage eighth at Monaco, and left the team mid-season. *(Ford)*

RIGHT: Ronnie Peterson drove a Tecno in Formula Three during 1969, the year that he won the Monaco Formula Three race. *(Author)*

up of 1973 lasted just one year. In 1974 Peterson was joined by another former Grand Prix winner, Belgian Jacky Ickx, who stayed with the team for much of the 72's remaining life. However, theses were now troubled times at Team Lotus and the Belgian was unable to add to his eight GP victories, although he did take the 1974 Brands Hatch Race of Champions in the rain. Today he's probably better known as a six-times Le Mans 24-hours winner.

Halfway through the 1975 season Ickx left the team, which then used three relatively inexperienced British drivers to fill the gap. Formula Atlantic champion Jim Crawford was given two races in the car, as was Brian Henton. John Watson, who had been driving for Team Surtees, was also put in a 72 for the German Grand Prix, as he already had experience of the Nürburgring. By this time the 72 was hardly the machine for a young driver to prove himself. Crawford resurrected his career in North America, where he became known for his raw speed and intense bravery at Indianapolis. Henton returned to Formula Two to win the 1980 European title. Further Grands Prix did follow with private entries and then with Toleman, Arrows and Tyrrell, but with no success. By contrast, Watson went on to fame in Formula One, winning five Grands Prix with Penske and McLaren, challenging for the world title in 1982 before finishing third.

LEFT: Jim Crawford participated in just two races with the Lotus 72. His Grand Prix career then stalled, although he won the 1982 British Formula One championship before moving to the USA. He finished sixth at Indianapolis in 1986 despite still suffering from injuries received there the previous year. *(Ford)*

THE LOTUS 72 STORY

The designers

The 'fathers' of the Lotus 72 could be said to be Lotus founder Colin Chapman, who was responsible for the basic concept, and designer Maurice Phillippe, who carried out the detailing. Once the Lotus 63 4WD had proved to be the wrong way to head, the pair spent many hours discussing what they should do next. Chapman drew up a specification to take advantage of Firestone's new light-construction tyres. Phillippe, who had taken over the design of the Lotus IndyCars from Len Terry, had already been responsible for the turbine-powered Type 56 and its radical wedge appearance. The embryonic 72 was already taking shape.

Phillippe left Lotus towards the end of the second year of the Type 72. Development work on the car was subsequently continued first by Martin Waide and then by Ralph Bellamy. Lotus team manager Peter Warr was to write that by the time Phillippe resigned, the Type 72 was so far ahead of the field that his successors, Waide and Bellamy, had mainly to concern themselves with just updates.

Colin Chapman

Qualified structural engineer Colin Chapman had begun his design career with an Austin 7-based sporting trials special in 1948, progressing through a series of sports racing cars. Major racing success for his Lotus marque came with the 750 Formula Mark 3. Lotus Engineering commenced trading in 1952, the year the Mark 6 sports car went into production. At the time Chapman was still working for British Aluminium, and it was not until 1955 that he was able to devote himself full-time to Lotus. His designs were no longer confined to motorsport and in the second half of the 1950s the evergreen Lotus 7 and the pretty little Elite coupé went into production. Such had become Chapman's reputation that he was invited to redesign the chassis of the Vanwall Grand Prix car a full two years before the first Lotus Formula One car, and he was also called upon to improve the BRM's suspension. His understanding of tubular chassis dynamics, suspension design and aerodynamics were considered to be ahead of his time.

Chapman was also an accomplished racing driver in his own right, winning the marque's first race, a five-lap scratch encounter at Silverstone in 1950. The following year he was extremely successful in 750 Formula races, winning a string of events. He more than proved his worth in the sports racing cars that followed, competing at Le Mans in 1955 and 1956, and in the latter year was offered a drive by Vanwall in the French Grand Prix. He failed to start following a practice crash.

Chapman's first single-seater design, if one excludes outside work, was the Type 12, a multi-tubular spaceframe front-engined car used in both Formula Two and Formula One. First raced in 1957, this was powered by various sizes of the Coventry Climax FPF engine. It was followed by the wider and stiffer Type 16. By now, though, front-engined cars were fast becoming dinosaurs. Chapman's Type 18, the first of his rear-engined designs, was, as related above, the car that took Team Lotus into the winner's circle as a Formula One operation. In addition Chapman designed a series of great sports racers during this period, the 11, 15 and 23 – Stirling Moss was to describe the Type 15 as his favourite car.

BELOW: **Chapman and Rindt discuss the prototype at an early Hethel test.** *(Ford)*

ABOVE: Chapman and his driver line-up at the 1970 United States Grand Prix. Fittipaldi (seen here in the car) will go on to win and secure a posthumous World Championship for Rindt. *(Ford)*

If Chapman hadn't been hailed as a genius by 1962, he certainly was when the slim, monocoque Lotus 25 descended from its transporter in Holland. By this time Chapman was starting to build a design team with such men as Len Terry, who helped develop the 25 into the 33 and designed the Indianapolis 500-winning Lotus 38.

Although there were times when his concentration was elsewhere, such as on Lotus road cars or the Moonraker boat concern, he continued to lead his team from the front, inspiring but demanding the utmost from its members. He remained innovative, as illustrated by the unique twin-chassis design of the Types 86 and 88 with their use of composites. Motor racing was robbed of one of its giants when he suffered a fatal heart attack in 1982.

According to Nigel Bennett, Chapman was 'an inspirational character to work with. His strength was having inspirational ideas and getting people to work on them. Only a small percentage of them were good, but he was not constrained by anything.'

Maurice Phillippe

In 1965 Len Terry left Lotus, suggesting that Maurice Phillippe – an aerospace designer and then development engineer on the Ford Anglia engine – should join the company. Like Chapman, Phillippe had been a member of the 750 Motor Club and had built and raced his own cars, including the MPS 750 Formula car and the Delta Formula Junior. He also raced an ex-Keith Duckworth Lotus Seven. Aircraft industry influences were strong in the early days

LEFT: Detail design on the Lotus 72 was carried out by Maurice Phillippe. *(Ford)*

31

THE LOTUS 72 STORY

of Lotus (Chapman saw National Service with the RAF) and Phillippe, a very private person, had worked at De Havilland.

Phillippe could be said to have been thrown in at the proverbial deep end, drawing the BRM H16-powered Type 43 and then becoming joint chassis designer with Chapman of the championship-winning Type 49, the first of the Cosworth DFV-powered Lotuses. 'In its early stages the 49 had quite a few problems and it was a testing time for Maurice,' recalled Martin Waide, who was to succeed him. 'I think he sorely tried Chapman's patience.'

The detail work on the Type 56 Indianapolis gas turbine car – what could be described as the first of the 'wedges' – was the work of Phillippe, leading to his co-operation with Chapman on the like-shaped 72. However, prior to the 72 he produced the attractive but ultimately doomed Type 63 four-wheel-drive Grand Prix car.

Waide remembered how Phillippe worked: 'He was the fastest draughtsman and most intuitive creator of welded parts I've ever seen.

ABOVE: Phillippe left Team Lotus to design Indy and Formula One cars for Vel's Parnelli Racing Team. *(Derek Mower collection)*

BELOW: 'We finally got there.' The VPJ4 was perhaps the design that should have replaced the Lotus 72. *(Author)*

He worked so fast that the area around his drawing board would be black with graphite. It came at a price. He didn't stop long enough to do analysis, calculations for strength, stiffness, fatigue life. Basically, his works were artistic renderings. I'm being a little cruel here. This is why parts failed although the cars looked lovely. He would fill ring-bound sketch books in the evening and then come into the office and use the one that he liked for the design the next day. He worked extremely hard. His work was his life.'

Phillippe was to leave Team Lotus in the autumn of 1971 to join the Vel's Parnelli Racing Team, initially to design an IndyCar and then the sophisticated VPJ4 Formula One that could be said to have been a derivative of the Type 72. According to Lotus team manager Peter Warr it was 'a car that fitted exactly the brief that Colin Chapman had given his designers for 1974.'

Waide was to recall looking at the VPJ4 with Dave Baldwin, another former Team Lotus designer who went to the Vel's Parnelli team. 'We finally got there,' Baldwin observed.

Phillippe later became chief designer for Tyrrell, but that team never returned to its World Championship-winning ways of 1969, 1971 and 1973, and victories were infrequent. He eventually set up his own consultancy, being responsible, along with fellow ex-Lotus and Vel's Parnelli man John Baldwin, for the March 89CE Indy car with its lamentably slow Alfa Romeo engine. He died the same year in tragic circumstances.

Martin Waide

Martin Waide was apprenticed at Alvis in Coventry. He took part in Formula 1172 races with an early Cooper and noticed that Lotus was advertising for a design draughtsman. He still reckons that because he was the last to be interviewed, he got the job. He moved to Cheshunt, where Lotus was then based, and into the drawing office of Lotus Components, the arm of the company responsible for customer racing cars. Mike Warner, who ran Lotus Components, described Waide as 'diminutive and very, very clever' during the time that he worked for him.

At Lotus Components he started to draw

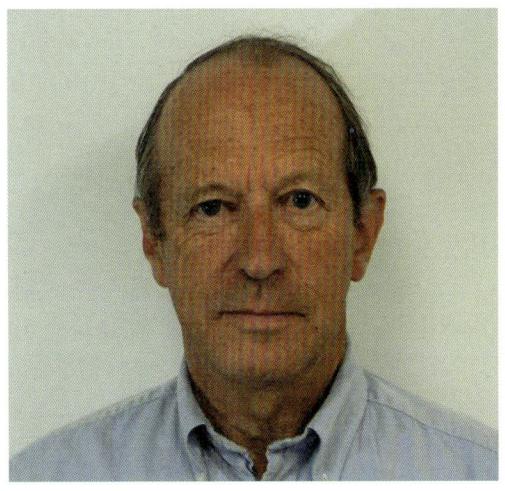

LEFT: Martin Waide was one of the many Team Lotus 'old boys' who attended the Classic Team Lotus festival at Snetterton in 2010. *(Martin Waide collection)*

the Type 26R, the racing version of the Elan, under the watchful eye of Len Terry. He carried out all the mechanical design of the Type 30 sports racer and also the Europa. The Group 7 Type 30 was intended to be Lotus's contender in the large-engined sports car races that were popular in the mid-1960s. Unfortunately the Ford V8-engined car was no match for the McLaren-Oldsmobiles and Lola-Chevrolets. Waide also worked on the de Dion Formula Two Type 58 that was abandoned, the Europa-like BOAC 500 class-winning Type 62 Group 6 prototype, and the Type 70 Formula 5000/A.

Waide took over the development design of the Type 72 from Phillippe for the 1972 season. He rebuilt the car to meet the new safety regulations and to accommodate the Goodyear tyres. It was also suggested that he then spend the rest of the season strengthening it to withstand Ronnie Peterson's press-on style of driving.

After more than a decade with Lotus, Waide moved to the USA and a post with S&W Engineered Products on spring and shock absorber development. In the 1980s he turned his attention to the aircraft industry and, in particular, unmanned military planes. The practical output of some of his efforts can been seen in the General Atomics Predator and Boeing's unmanned helicopter, the A160T Hummingbird. A need to return to engineering basics then led to his work on the TigerCat 3V2, a Harley Davidson-powered three-wheeled car that's considered a motorcycle in most states of the USA and is intended to go into production in 2012–13.

ABOVE: **Ralph Bellamy designed the Type 76 for the 1974 season. The intention was that it should prove 100lb lighter than its predecessor, but it turned out to be the same weight.** *(Ford)*

Ralph Bellamy

Ralph Bellamy was appointed chief Formula One designer late in 1972. Australian Bellamy, who was regarded as an ideas man, had first worked in Formula One with Brabham and then McLaren, being responsible for the M19 with its rising rate suspension. He briefly rejoined Brabham before becoming part of the Lotus team. Bellamy's first complete car at Team Lotus was the Formula Two Type 74 that borrowed some of the features of the 72, such as torsion bar suspension and inboard front brakes. As far as the 72 was concerned, Bellamy believed that the car was already efficient and he tended to confine development work to the aerodynamics.

For 1974 Chapman famously specified a Formula One car that was to be 100lb lighter than the Type 72 but have suspension and geometries identical in principle to the older car. The result was Bellamy's 76, which was unreliable, suffered from unsatisfactory handling and, despite intentions, didn't save any weight. This car was quickly abandoned, but Bellamy was one of those who worked on Lotus' next World Championship-winning car, the innovative Type 78. Peter Warr was to write that Bellamy's input into the ground effects cars was important, while Nigel Bennett reckoned that ground effects was actually discovered by Bellamy and Peter Wright by accident in a wind tunnel, after pannier pods on a model fell off when the tape holding them became hot and sagged – the nearer the pods got to the ground, the more the downforce increased.

Following this, the easygoing Bellamy left to work for a number of racing car manufacturers including Fittipaldi, Ensign, March, Ralt and Lola, designing a variety of Formula One, Formula Two, Formula 3000 and Indy cars, before returning to his native land in the 1990s. He has continued his involvement in the sport there, working on V8 Supercars and Super Touring.

Designer's view: Martin Waide on the Lotus 72

'I was given a Formula One baptism at the 1971 South African Grand Prix. I was invited as an observer but I think the idea was to find out whether the rest of the team could put up with me! Within weeks of returning I was appointed chief designer. Peter Warr's comment was, "Better the devil you know than the one you don't." I'd already designed another early "wedge" car, the Formula 5000/A Type 70. This car made its debut at Phoenix in the USA with Mario Andretti driving, supported by myself and just one mechanic. Andretti convincingly put the car on pole, and I think it was that design and that performance that made Chapman think "Maybe Martin can help with the Formula One team."

'Appointed chief designer in September 1971, I needed support in the design office but was surprised to find a dearth of applicants in response to a full-page advertisement in *Autosport*. I was surprised to find how unattractive Team Lotus was as a design centre in 1971. Ralph Bellamy eventually "turned up", although he appeared to have had no job title.

'I thought, "We'd better get on with this. The 72 is going to be Emerson's car for the season so we'd better make it competitive and safe." It still had Timken bearing hubs of an

identical design to the disastrous Lotus 64 Indy car. There's one thing that you never do with a Timken taper roller bearing on a hub, and that's you never make the inner member the rotating part. Maurice got it backwards. The 72 had the same design, although, unlike the 64, it hadn't failed yet, but I knew that this was imminent. I therefore redesigned the entire rotating system of the hubs. I went back to a conventional, safe design, with new uprights and hubs and at the same time changed the diameter of the front because the car was heavily weight-biased to the rear. I put on a lighter front wheel nut with smaller thread, which led the way to much smaller threads later on.

'The MelMag disc wheel seemed to be exactly what I was looking for. This was a very light, hot pressed magnesium wheel. In the event of an accident it was also unlikely to fracture. The 72s were thus equipped with these, and they became the standard for four or five races; but manufacturing problems caused too many failures. The left-hand front wheel failed in practice and Emerson was lucky to get away with only a broken ankle. The possibility of being sued by the driver because of the failure

ABOVE: The final official race appearance of Ralph Bellamy's Type 76 was at the 1974 Italian Grand Prix, although one was an unauthorised starter at Watkins Glen. There would be no choice but the ageing 72 for the following season. *(Ford)*

LEFT: Ralph Bellamy in discussion with Ronnie Peterson at the 1973 Argentine Grand Prix. *(Sutton Images)*

35

THE LOTUS 72 STORY

of its product caused MelMag's manufacturer to cease supply, even though I'd have liked to have continued with them. Team Lotus went back to cast magnesium wheels. I felt bad about Fittipaldi's ankle. I'd broken mine once and knew what it was like.

'The regulations had now changed, in that a deformable structure was mandatory. With an existing car this was quite a challenge. The only practical way to convert existing chassis was to put a layer of structural foam between the metal chassis and the lightweight glass fibre. Chapman queried whether this would be legal, but the cars passed scrutineering. We were much helped by the fact that the radiator ducts were outside the main tub.

'For 1972 I introduced the anvil-shaped airbox and, initially, very deep side plates for the rear wing. I knew, talking to aerodynamicists, that ultimately we'd have ground effects. Over the winter we'd built a wing with very large end plates. There are photographs that show this at a rollout with large Texaco decals on the end plates. The wing was tested at Snetterton and proved to result in excellent stability. I now wonder why it wasn't used by the team, which went back to a large, two-piece wing.

'We were doing well. Emerson was fantastic; his car-set skills were good and he was aided by the fact that the car was extremely benign. There were several reasons for this – it had rising rate suspension, it was universally adaptable to different circuits, and the torsion bars were in the fuel tanks at the front. It was fit and forget. All we did was change the ride heights, damper settings and aerodynamics.

'I remember we put a small Formula Two wing on for Belgium. That was when I had the courage to put the wing on the oil tank.

BELOW: Dave Walker, seen here in the wet at Monte Carlo, was one of the Team Lotus drivers during Martin Waide's time as chief designer. *(Ford)*

The elliptical oil tank was structural and formed the cantilever wing mounting. The airflow over the engine bay and under the wing was much improved.

'In May 1973 I left the company, as I felt I could not longer see my way forward. I had no designer and no staff and I think Chapman had his eyes on other things, although he was motivated again when things began to get interesting with ground effects. I don't regret not being there after 1973. The race results eventually plummeted. I feel that the design team had an absolute loss of direction in the middle 1970s, with a debasement of what had been achieved. They wandered around for four years before they got their act together with the Type 78.

'I'm still puzzled by what happened to 72/4 [the privateer car raced by Graham Hill], which, after 1970 initially languished in a corner of Rob Walker's workshop covered in a tarpaulin. Walker was now allied with John Surtees, but nobody looked at the 72. I believe this to have been because the "not invented here" feeling was so strong. The championship-winning design was, fortunately for Lotus, ignored, and not understood. That was exactly what we wanted; the Surtees TS9 was hardly up to Lotus 72 standards.

'De Havilland and the aircraft industry had an influence on Lotus. Its technology was slightly refined WW2 aluminium aircraft structural techniques. Construction methods, riveting, flanging, panel forming, were such as were used in metal aeroplanes. Some of our fabricators had come from the aviation industry and we even used aircraft terms. The designers had line of sight to each other's drawing boards and a common data pool. You couldn't beat that for efficiency.'

NIGEL BENNETT

In the summer of 1975 Team Lotus team manager Peter Warr was involved in a serious road accident, and former Firestone race tyre engineer Nigel Bennett – who was to become one of the great Indy car designers – stood in for him.

'It was a real struggle. In its last year the car wasn't competitive. There was a battle to make it work. I can remember races where rubber bushes were going in and coming out on the rear suspension. It was designed with a rearward weight distribution. At Firestone we provided tyres which suited that, but when Firestone pulled out in 1974 and was replaced by Goodyear, Goodyear wasn't about to make special tyres for Lotus. Ferrari and McLaren had far more conventional cars, with outboard front brakes which put far more heat into the front tyres, and the 72 would just not get the front tyres up to temperature. That was the main problem. It would be the same with the Types 76 and 77. Only with the 78 and its outboard front brakes would this be solved.'

During the time that Bennett was with Firestone, Lotus, along with Ferrari, was probably its leading contracted customer. 'We gave them almost everything they wanted. Now all the manufacturers balance their cars to make the most use of the available tyres. But back then Firestone developed front tyres that were specific to Lotus.

'Chapman believed the unsprung front weight was particularly important. Other manufacturers, seeing the success of the 72, thought about fitting inboard front brakes. Testing with other teams, Firestone came to the conclusion that unsprung front weight wasn't that all important.' Bennett told Chapman about this, which resulted in his telling Len Terry to redesign the Type 77 with outboard front brakes, thus transforming it.

On Warr's return Bennett stayed on at Team Lotus as a test and race engineer before moving to Ensign, where he was reunited with Bellamy, and thence to Lola and a career that revolved around IndyCar racing. Moving from Lola to Penske he became one of the most successful IndyCar designers, his cars winning 53 races and five championship titles. He was, recalled, Penske's Nick Goozee, 'the last of the gentleman designers'.

ABOVE: Nigel Bennett went on to become one of the great Indy car designers, working for Penske in Dorset, to where he eventually retired. *(Author)*

'The Lotus 72 was a hard car to work on. It was a battle, a lot of work with a mass of changes.'

Ian Dawson
Team Lotus mechanic 1975

Chapter Two

Anatomy of the Lotus 72

With features such as torsion bars and inboard brakes, the Lotus 72 was a unique racing car. However, its use of the Cosworth DFV engine made it representative of the 'English kit cars' that dominated the 3-litre Formula One, while is innovative wedge shape was one that others were to copy. During its long life, it underwent a host of changes to remain competitive.

(Author)

BELOW: There was nothing new about side radiators. They were featured even as far back as 1914 on the Hughes-Rayfield Special. This failed to qualify for the Indianapolis 500 when its English-born driver Hughie Hughes destroyed its crankcase while showing off the day before qualifying. *(Indianapolis Motor Speedway)*

As the Lotus 72 competed over six seasons – an inordinately long time for any factory car to be part of the Grand Prix grid – it understandably underwent myriad changes. The car that ended the 1975 season was very different from that with which Rindt and Miles first competed. The removal of anti-squat and anti-dive meant that it was much changed even between its debut and the string of victories that gave the Austrian the World Championship in its first year. Mandatory deformable structures introduced later in the car's life were a significant change, while in its final season alone the 72 was repeatedly altered in an attempt to remain remotely competitive.

There were some remarkable ups and downs in its career as its specification changed.

The failure of the Type 76 meant that the 72 had to remain in service when it was past its sell-by date, and it was an almost impossible task for Team Lotus to make it anything other than a shadow of its World Championship self, whatever was done to it. However, it's a measure of the fact that Colin Chapman may have been a year or two ahead of the rest with his basic design that the 72 remained as competitive for as long as it did.

In total, nine Lotus 72 chassis numbers were issued – 72/1 to 72/9 – although two were a complete rebuild of another. They broadly ran in original, B, C, D, E and F specifications. The surviving cars exist in a variety of specs.

Just how much could be and ultimately was altered can be seen at the car's final British Grand Prix appearance. Three cars were entered with contrasting approaches to the problems that now beset the ageing design. The newest of the cars, 72/9, was – as near as possible within the regulations – converted back to 1973 specification. The narrow front track was again used, as were soft spring rates, while the cables that had lately actuated the torsion bars had been replaced by the original steel links. The battery was again located at the rear. By contrast the other two cars now had coil spring rear suspension, while all three had stronger CV joints on the front brake shafts that were taken from the rear suspension.

ABOVE: Rindt testing the Lotus 72 in original specification at Snetterton prior to its race debut in Spain. *(Ford)*

RIGHT: Removal of the anti-squat and anti-dive features created the 72C, seen here at Brands Hatch. *(Ford)*

40
LOTUS 72 MANUAL

Specifications

The basic tenets of the Lotus 72's design were a very low unsprung weight and low drag. At launch the car was near to the minimum weight limit of 530kg thanks to the use of lightweight alloys and magnesium. Weight distribution was 35/65% front and rear. The initial wheelbase was 8ft 4in (2.54m) and the track 4ft 9in (1.45m), although these figures would change.

Lotus 72
The original specification with anti-squat and anti-dive and Hewland DG300 gearbox. 72/2 ran in this specification for just two races, 72/3 for three.

Lotus 72B
The anti-squat geometry was removed from the rear suspension but the anti-squat left in place at the front. The Hewland DG300 gearbox was also retained. 72/1 ran in this specification from the 1970 Belgian Grand Prix until the end of the season, when the monocoque was taken to pieces and much of the car carried over to create 72/4.

Lotus 72C
A total redesign that involved removing most of the anti-squat and anti-dive from the suspension. The monocoque was strengthened while the lighter and smaller Hewland FG400 gearbox replaced the DG300. Both 72/2 and 72/4 were still in this configuration at the end of their active racing careers. 72/3, 72/4 and 72/5 were all built to this specification, while 72/2 was converted to it for the 1970 Dutch Grand Prix.

ABOVE: The removal of the majority of anti-squat from 72/1 caused it to be redesignated as the only 72B. Its second race as such was the 1970 Dutch Grand Prix, where John Miles dropped back to seventh after a spin. *(Sutton Images)*

Lotus 72D

This specification, which first appeared at the 1971 Monaco Grand Prix and was used for two seasons, featured twin parallel links at the rear. 72/3 and 72/5 were converted to it during the 1971 season, while 72/6, 72/7 and 72/8 were all built as 72Ds.

Lotus 72E

The 72E specification was introduced to meet the 1973 mandatory regulations for deformable structures around the tub. 72/5, 72/6, 72/7 and 72/8 were all converted to this in 1973. 72/3, which was now in private hands, was converted a year later. 72/9 was built as a 72E and remained so for the rest of its career, as did 72/3, 72/6 and 72/7.

Lotus 72F

72E/5 and 72/8, both still factory entries, were converted to 72F, the final specification, during the summer of 1975. An oil tank was placed between the rear bulkhead and the engine, thus creating a 5in (127mm) longer wheelbase.

ABOVE: Fittipaldi at the 1971 US Grand Prix. Clearly evident are the separate radiator pods that identify a pre-deformable structure 72, and the first of the tall airboxes. Also obvious on this 72D is the rear outward-mounted damper, the original inboard location having proved to be too hot. *(Ford)*

LEFT: Peterson leads Fittipaldi at Monza in 1973, driving 72/6 and 72/7 respectively, both in 72E specification. *(Ford)*

BELOW: Swansong. Brian Henton in 72F/5 at the 1975 United States Grand Prix. *(Ford)*

Aerodynamics

The aerodynamic form of the Lotus 72 was designed to generate the maximum possible download under new wing regulations. As far as Formula One racing was concerned, wings had first appeared two years previously at the Belgian Grand Prix, although they had earlier been seen elsewhere, notably on the Chaparral Can-Am sports-racing cars. Lotus had already experimented with a small, strut-mounted aerofoil on a Type 49T during practice for a 1968 Tasman Series race in New Zealand. Jim Clark had suggested this device to his mechanics, but with Colin Chapman back in the UK and unaware of it the decision was taken not to race with it. Interestingly, March founder Robin Herd recalls that he experimented with a wing on the McLaren M2A back in 1966. Fresh from the Royal Aircraft Establishment, the young

ABOVE: This small strut-mounted aerofoil appeared on a Type 49T during practice for a Tasman Series race in New Zealand – the first time a rear aerofoil was used on a Lotus 49.
(Roger Leworthy)

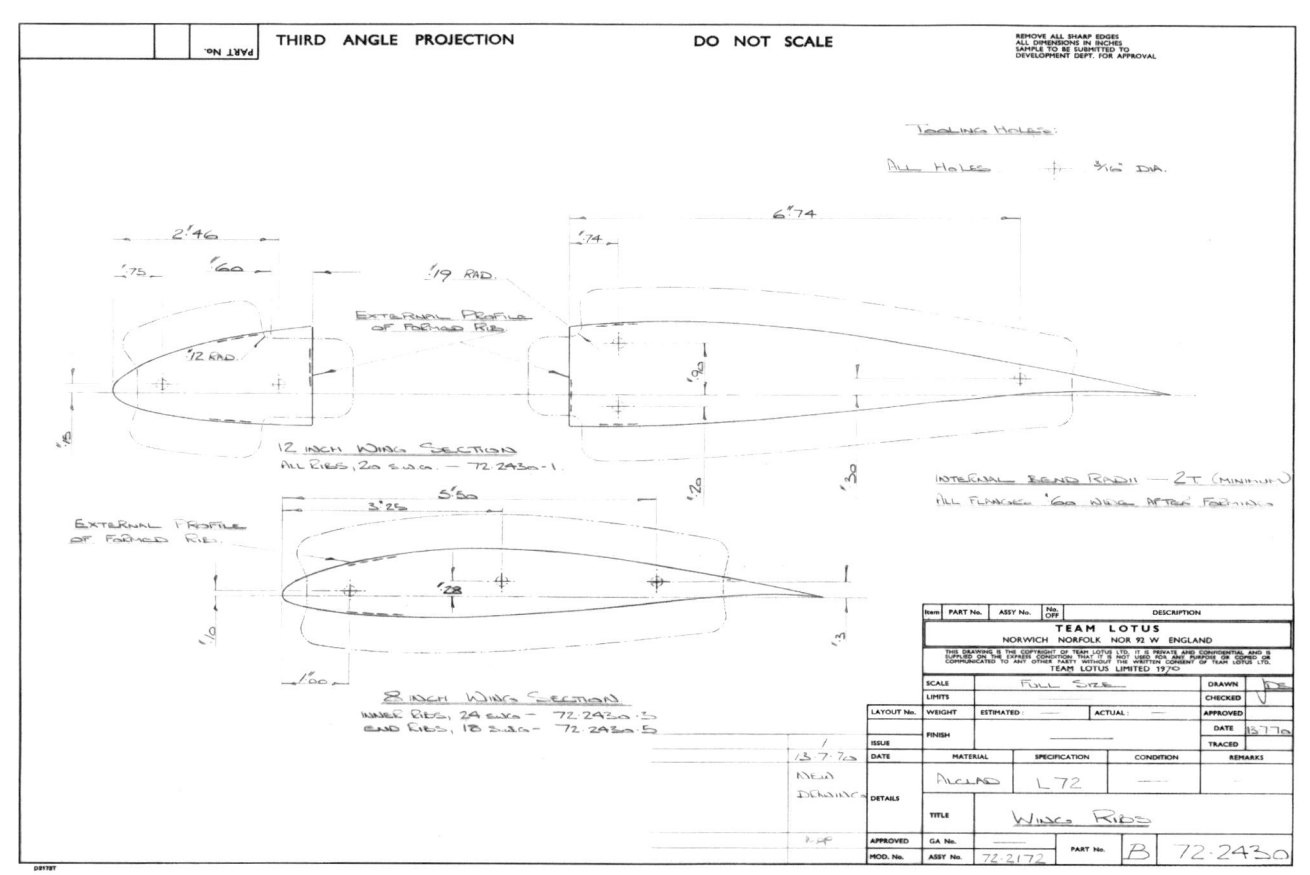

(Classic Team Lotus)

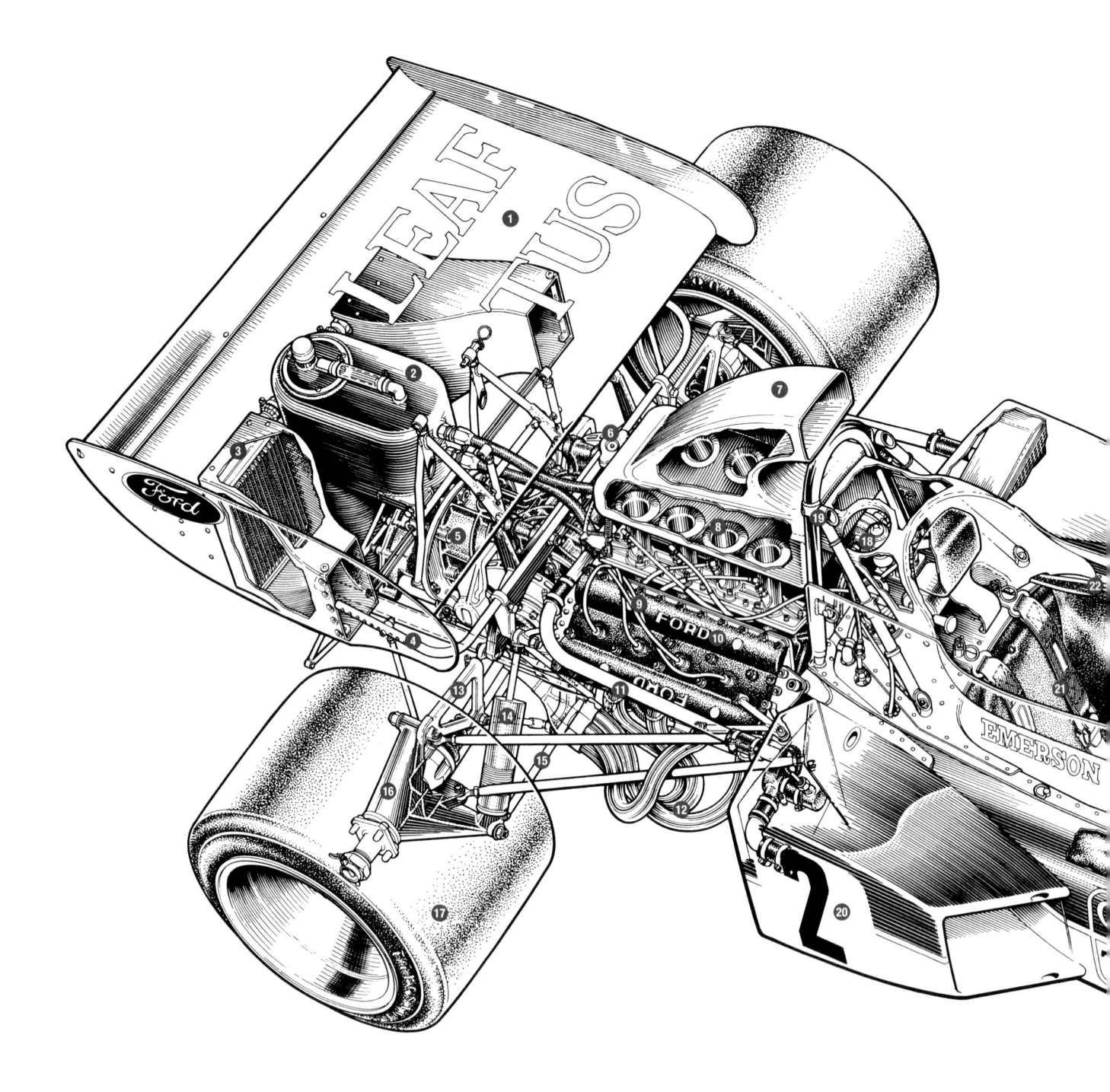

This cutaway lays bare the Lotus-Cosworth 72D in its 1972 guise, as driven by Emerson Fittipaldi.
(Tony Matthews)

1 One-piece rear wing
2 In-line oil tank
3 Oil cooler
4 Rear anti-roll bar
5 Hewland FG400 gearbox
6 Water cap
7 Single-scoop airbox
8 Inlet trumpets
9 Spark plug leads
10 Cosworth DFV engine
11 Water pipe
12 Mild steel exhaust system
13 Rear camber adjusters
14 Rear damper
15 Twin parallel links
16 Rear upright
17 Low profile Firestone tyre
18 Fuel pump
19 Roll hoop
20 Side radiator pod
21 Six-point harness
22 Wiring harness
23 Walpres wing mirror
24 Monocoque chassis
25 Perspex cockpit moulding
26 Smiths cockpit instruments
27 Steering column
28 Fuel filler cap
29 FPT rubber fuel bag
30 Front anti-roll bar
31 Cooling vent
32 Square-section tubular-steel footbox, carrying brake, accelerator and clutch pedals
33 Inboard front brakes
34 Front wishbone
35 Front upright
36 Front wheel hub
37 Brake master cylinders
38 Adjustable nose plane
39 Nosecone
40 Fire extinguisher
41 Fine vertical blade

45

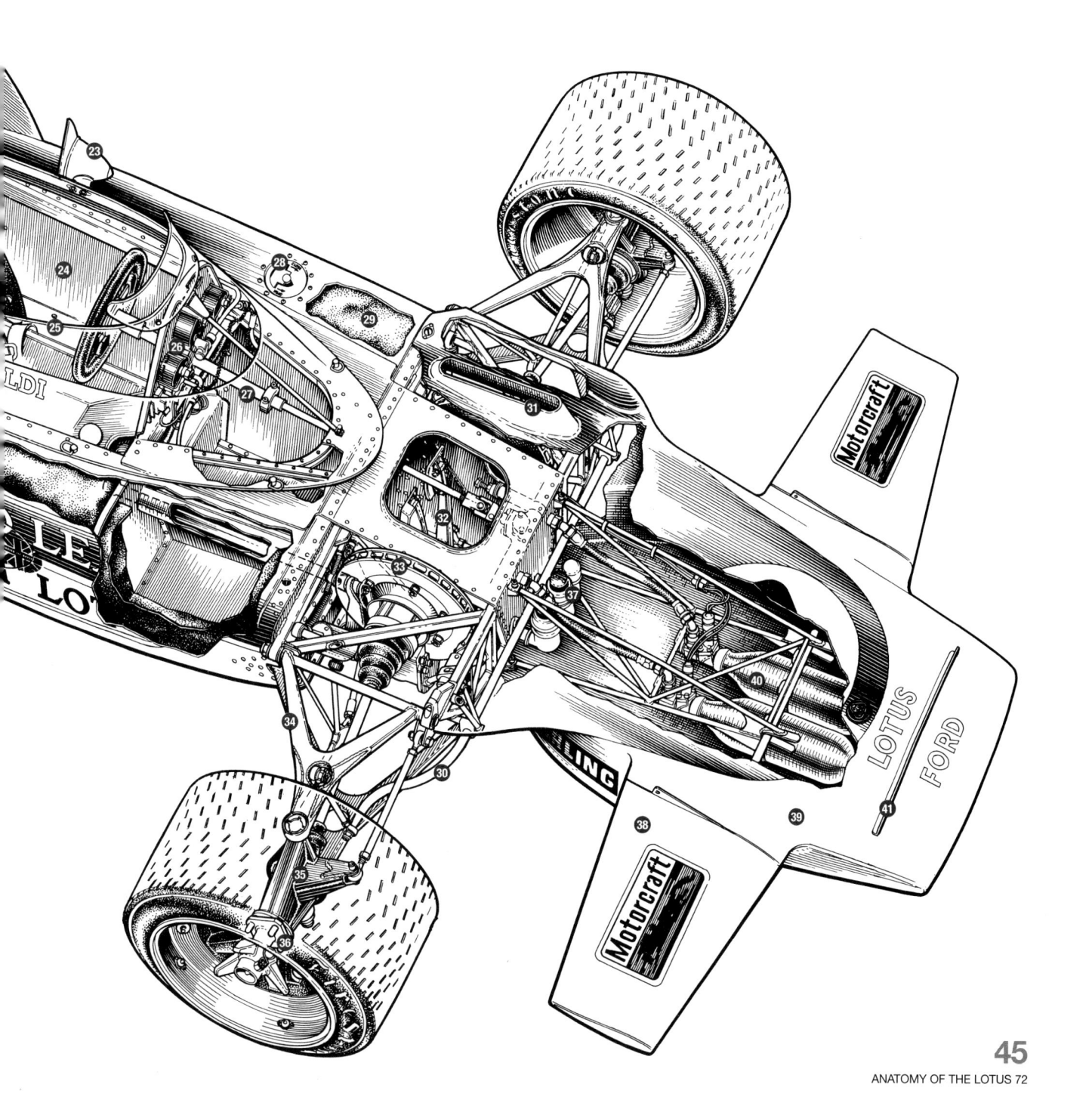

ANATOMY OF THE LOTUS 72

THIRD ANGLE PROJECTION — DO NOT SCALE

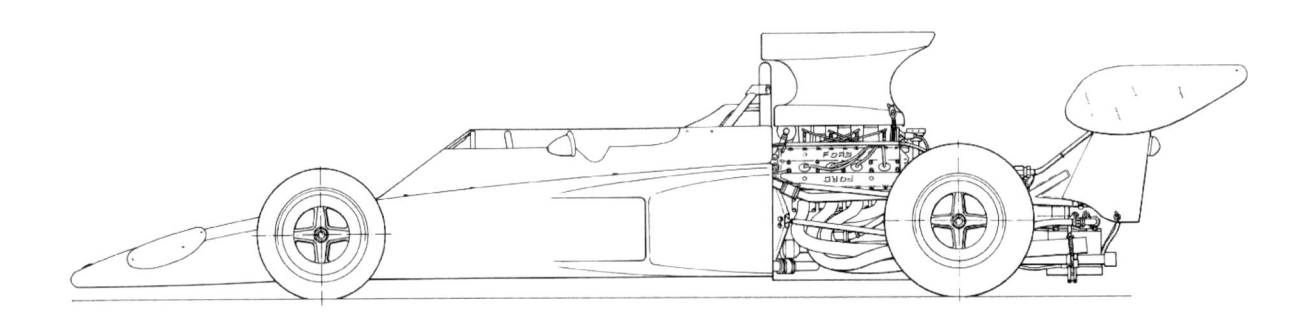

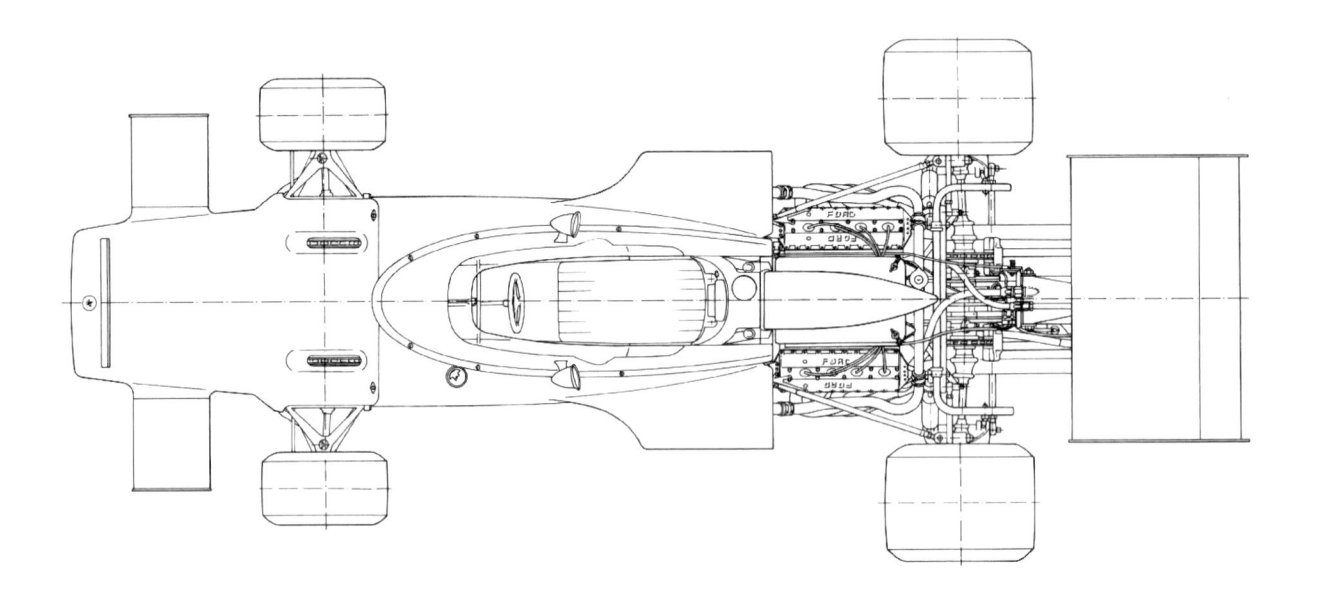

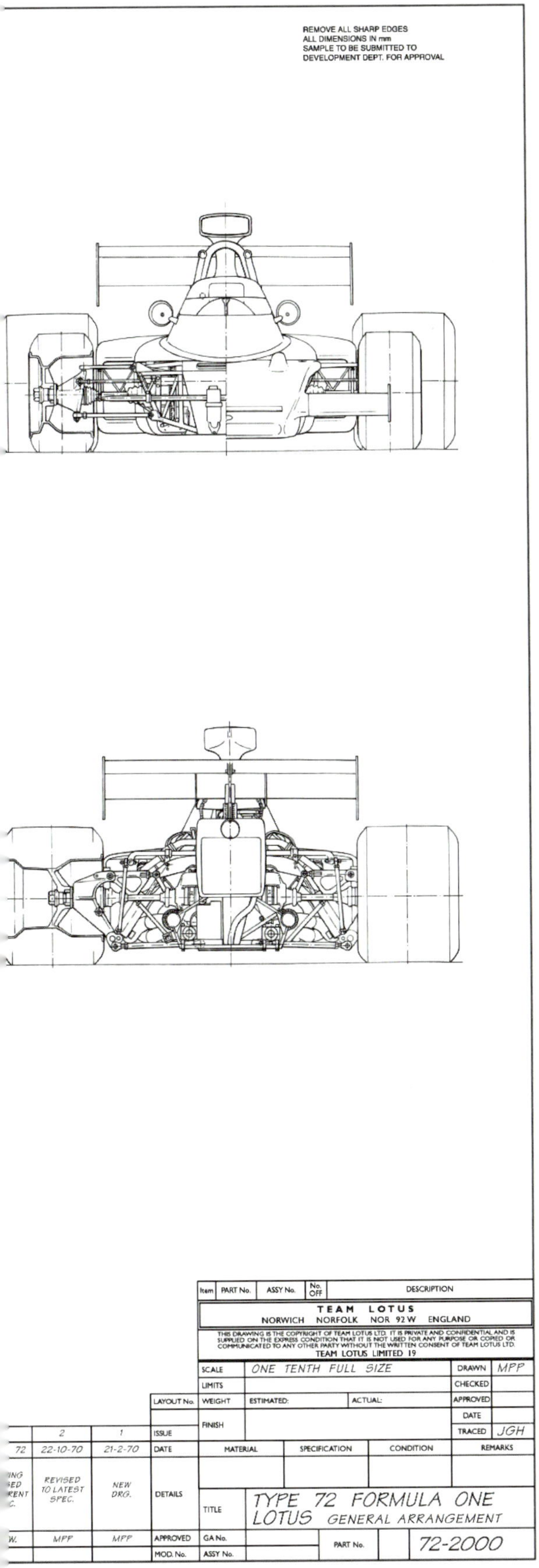

Herd tried one out during testing and found that the car was two seconds a lap faster. It's perhaps a reflection of the times that the wing idea was then shelved – probably, but bizarrely, for no better reason than that the team was too busy on other matters.

During 1968 and 1969 the strutted wings grew higher, wider and more fragile. That they couldn't continue as they were was made all too clear when both Graham Hill and Jochen Rindt crashed their Lotus 49s in the 1969 Spanish Grand Prix. The result was a mandated return to sanity and much lower, more strongly fixed wings typified by those on the Lotus 72 and its early 1970s rivals.

The wedge-shaped profile of the Type 72 was dramatically different to anything else then found in Formula One. However, it dated back two years before its launch to the particularly smooth appearance of the Lotus 56, the gas turbine, four-wheel-drive car that led the 1968 Indianapolis 500 until nine laps before the end. A spare turbine chassis, known as the 56B, was used in F1, but this wasn't raced until 1971, by which time the shape of the 72 had become familiar. Other 'wedges' that preceded the 72 were the 57/58 F1/F2 prototype; the spaceframe Lotus 61 production Formula Ford that first appeared in 1969, and the short-lived Type 63 four-wheel-drive Formula One car of

(Classic Team Lotus)

BELOW: Legendary shape preserved in wind tunnel model at Hethel. *(Author)*

ABOVE: Wings on the Lotus 49 and its competitors grew higher and higher. This is Jackie Oliver at Monza in 1968. The following year they would also sprout high-level wings at the front. *(Ford)*

the same season. The Type 70 Formula 5000/A car that, like the 72, appeared in 1970 can also be said to have been wedge-shaped. The 56 had already proved that this profile was effective in reducing positive lift.

To enable this shape to be created the radiators were located either side of the car, towards the rear of the cockpit rather than in the then traditional position of the nose. John Miles, who did the vast amount of the early testing of the 72, recalled: 'Some of the inspiration for the shape came from Indy, and if you're going to make that shape you've got to stick the radiators somewhere else. Anyway, Chapman is quoted as wanting a more rearward weight distribution than previously.'

The aerodynamic effect of the wedge shape was initially enhanced by a three-tier tail aerofoil and broad, adjustable nose planes. The former was mounted over a three-gallon saddle oil tank that was wrapped over the gearbox. The idea behind the three-tier concept was that it enabled the wing assembly overall to run at a greater combined incidence than would have been possible with a one-piece wing that would have stalled. The wings were removed in practice for the 1970 Italian Grand Prix.

Early in 1971 a one-piece rear wing was fitted. A cylindrical in-line oil tank replaced the earlier version to clean up the airflow below this. Two oil coolers were mounted either side of the tank. A third generation single-piece design appeared the following season which also saw a number of alternative wing, wing mount and oil tank revisions. An aerodynamically shaped conical oil tank was

LEFT: Limited testing at Snetterton before the car's first race revealed that the engine was running hot due to insufficient air getting through the ducts in the sidepods. As a result the pods were pointed further out into the airstream and the resulting gap filled in with a strip of fibreglass. *(Ford)*

ABOVE: The original saddle oil tank position was similar to that of the Type 49B/C. Mounted over it at this stage was a three-tier aerofoil. *(Ford)*

RIGHT: Broad adjustable nose planes enhanced the wedge shape as seen here on an early version, 72/3. *(Simon Hadfield Motorsports)*

ABOVE: To create a wedge shape, Chapman located the radiators either side of the 72. *(Author)*

LEFT: Chapman instructed that both front and rear wings were removed during practice for the 1970 Italian Grand Prix. *(Sutton Images)*

49
LOTUS 72 MANUAL

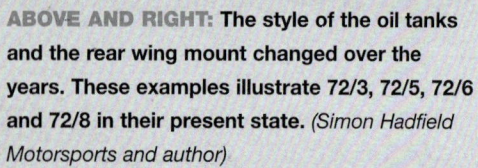

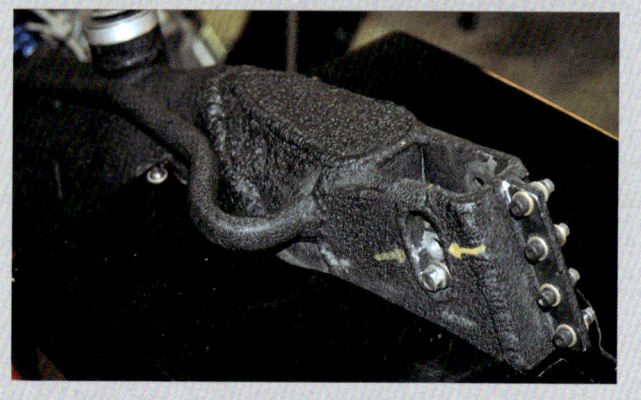

ABOVE AND RIGHT: The style of the oil tanks and the rear wing mount changed over the years. These examples illustrate 72/3, 72/5, 72/6 and 72/8 in their present state. *(Simon Hadfield Motorsports and author)*

fitted in 1972. A longer, lower tank which acted as a wing mounting was fitted to one of the cars for the 1973 German Grand Prix, thus removing the need for a temporary spaceframe that had been used to mount the wing 10in (254mm) further back. In 1975 a new oil tank was located between the tub and the engine, replacing that over the gearbox and throwing more weight forward.

One trend-setting feature of the Lotus 72 was the concept of the engine airbox that was first fitted to the car for the 1970 British Grand Prix. This forced air into the engine's injection trumpets, initially from ducts sited on either side of the rollover bar. At the same event the

TOP LEFT: 72/6's oil filler cap. *(Author)*

ABOVE: Side-mounted oil radiators on 72E/5. *(Author)*

BELOW: The first appearance on a Type 72 of the single airbox already pioneered by other teams was at Silverstone in 1971. *(Ford)*

RIGHT: The distinctive anvil-shaped airbox was drawn by Martin Waide for 1972.
(Author)

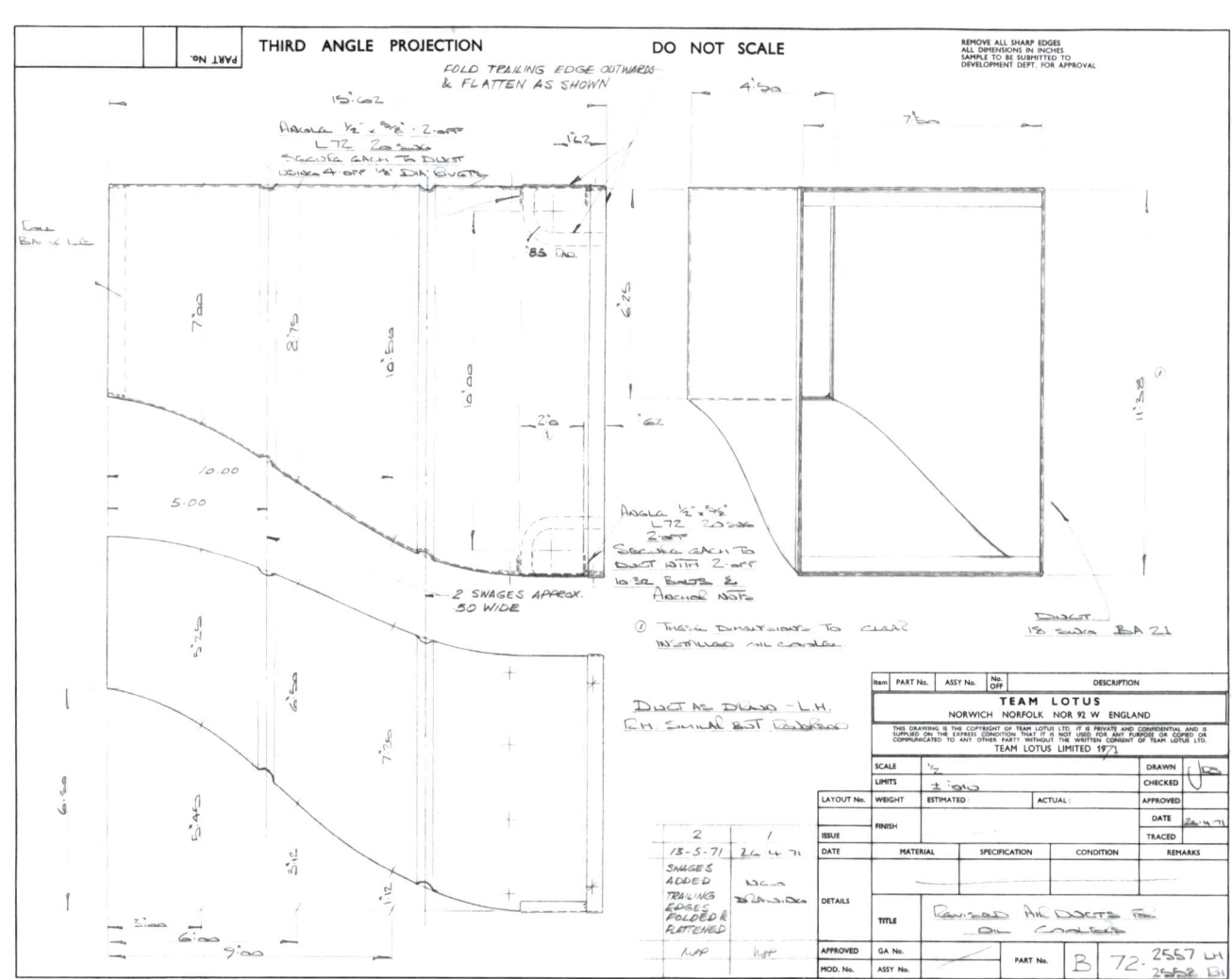

(Classic Team Lotus)

following year, this lop-eared style was replaced by a tall, single-scoop version, with a series of distinctive anvil-shaped alternatives appearing in 1972–73. At a sponsors' launch early in 1972, where an anvil-shaped airbox was seen for the first time, the Lotus 72 also appeared with deep side plates to the rear wing. These were used in practice for a non-championship event but never in an actual race.

Far-overhung wing mounts that extended rearwards were fitted for 1973, before rules changes the following year limited the amount of rear wing overhang allowed; these stated that the trailing edge of the rear wing was to be no more than one metre behind the centre line of the rear wheels. This meant that Lotus had to remove the lower and longer oil tank and wing mounting and return to a more conventional position. The oil tank could no longer be located behind the gearbox and was thus returned to a position above it. The handling balance suffered as a result of these changes. Work around the engine and engine cover had already interfered with the airflow to the rear wing, a problem that was exacerbated by bringing the wing forward.

The distinctive chisel nose remained in place throughout the 72's six active years. A fine vertical blade placed transversely across the nose reduced the positive lift by slowing down the flow of air over the front part of the body. As it curved gently towards the front, the underside of the nose in 1970 didn't prevent lift. Subsequently, parallel front wings with much greater camber were developed, to which winglets were fitted along the trailing edge. In the summer of 1972 drawings were made of a full-width nose, but it was never used. However, by 1973 the aerodynamics of the Type 72 were more refined than at its launch.

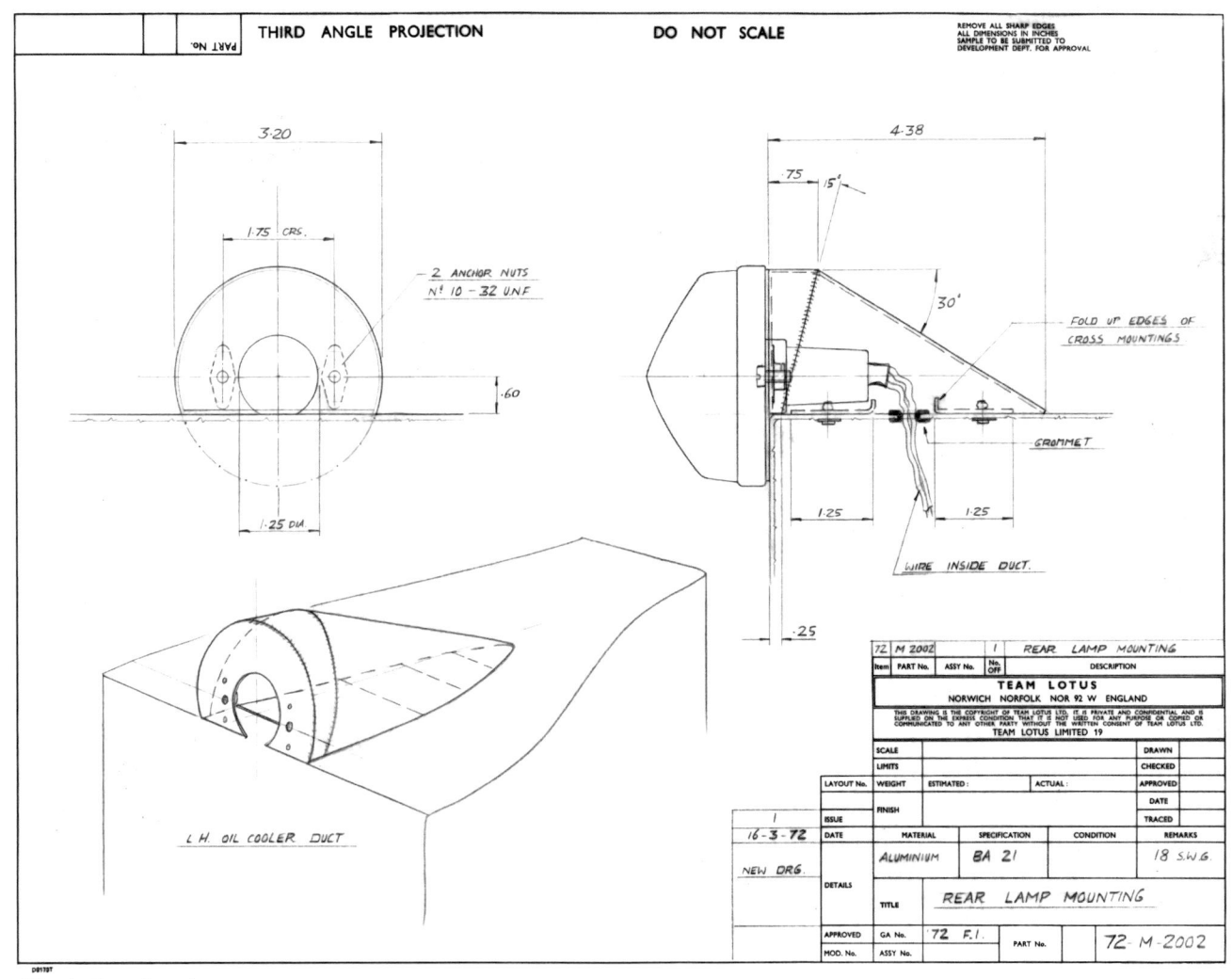

(Classic Team Lotus)

RIGHT AND BELOW: 72E/5 retains the same wing as it would have used in 1975. *(Author)*

BELOW: Top of 72/6's wing. The JPS victory decals became a feature of the Lotus 72's livery. *(Author)*

BELOW RIGHT: Underside of the wing now fitted to 72/6. *(Author)*

RIGHT: A vertical blade was fixed transversely on the nose to reduce lift. *(Author)*

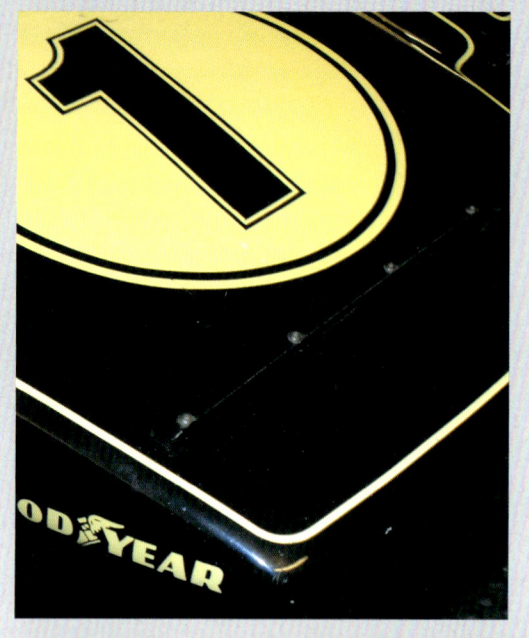

ABOVE: The chisel-shaped nose remained in place throughout the 72's life, despite a full-width nose being considered in mid-1972. *(Author)*

54
LOTUS 72 MANUAL

THE BUNGEE WING

In 1972 Team Lotus ran what has been described as the 'bungee wing' on the Type 72. The regulations stated that the rear wing had to be firmly fixed. Colin Chapman pointed out to Martin Waide that a scrutineer testing the wing would probably be able to exert no more than one-eighth of the downforce that would be applied down the straights at, for example, Monza. He then ordered Waide to fit a rubber bush into the wing. 'He didn't tell me how to do it. He just said "Do it," and walked away with a twinkle in his eye.'

Moveable aerodynamic devices, it should be noted, had been banned in Formula One since the middle of 1969.

Waide selected a large, 2½in rubber and steel cylindrical bush that just fitted in the wing section, on top of the rear oil tank. As a result the wing de-pitched at speed, although, as Eddie Dennis recalled, 'If you sat on it you couldn't move it.'

Down the high-speed straights the wing would reduce its angle of incidence. In the corners it would revert to its normal position, providing needed downforce.

For the British Grand Prix the wing grew additional supports in the form of struts (which were, in fact, telescopic) from the trailing edge to the gearbox, to allay other teams' suspicions. For months nobody twigged what was happening. Then McLaren's Denny Hulme pointed out that as he followed Emerson Fittipaldi down the straights, so his helmet would suddenly come into view. The rubber bush was quietly shelved. 'It was a bit tongue in cheek,' said Dennis.

ABOVE: It was at the Austrian Grand Prix that Denny Hulme (seen here in third) **noticed that all was not what it seemed.** (Sutton Images)

RIGHT: The tub tapers forward as can be seen during the rebuild of 72/6. *(R&J Simpson Engineering)*

RIGHT: The original monocoque chassis was made from 18-gauge NS4 magnesium alloy and 20-gauge L72 aluminium sheet. This is Team Lotus's 72/5 chassis, damaged at the 1973 Dutch Grand Prix and left unrestored. *(Classic Team Lotus)*

ABOVE: This shot of the prototype during testing at Hethel clearly illustrates the front of the car at the start of the 1970 season. Included are the solid inboard disc brakes, the steep forward raking of the front wishbones, and the original location of the fire extinguisher and the battery. *(Ford)*

Chassis

The chassis is of monocoque construction, in this case more of a 'bathtub' than in the Lotus 49, which had become the norm after being introduced by Chapman in 1963 with the 1.5-litre Lotus-Climax 25. It is formed over steel internal bulkheads. The inner panels were initially made from 20-gauge L72 Alclad aluminium sheet, the outer ones from softer, more malleable 18-gauge NS4 magnesium alloy that followed the compound curves where the tub waisted in towards the hip-mounted radiator ducts. Problems with cooling in Spain for the car's first race meant that the radiator draft-includer ducts were enlarged by outrigging them on the spacers between the pod and hull. However, at the 1970 Austrian Grand Prix it was noted that this took the car beyond the mandated 110cm maximum width, and the pods were drawn back in. The conditions in Austria were much cooler than in Spain. Not only was cooling there adequate but the engine now pulled an extra 200rpm on the straight.

The tub tapers forward in side view to create the distinctive wedge shape. The inner panels slope sharply forward towards the floor to make room for the FPT rubber fuel bags that feed a collector tank behind the sloping seat back panel, with the fuel tank mounted on the top. Projecting from the front of the tub is the $5/8$in square-section, tubular steel frame front subframe. This carries the pedals, master cylinders, front suspension and a thin

FAR LEFT: A thin tubular frame projects forward of the footbox. *(Author)*

LEFT: The battery and fire extinguisher were originally located in the front tubular frame. On 72/6 they're now sited under the driver's legs. This particular car uses a Yuasa battery and a Lifeline Zero 360 extinguisher. *(Author)*

FAR LEFT: Alloy plates from the cam covers are bolted to ear-like brackets on the upper corners of the tub. *(Author)*

LEFT: There's nothing revolutionary about the structure from the section behind the cockpit to the roll bar. With the DFV acting as a stressed member, the Type 72 is here no different to any other 'English kit car' of the period. *(Author)*

tubular forward frame to support body mounts and, originally, the battery and Graviner fire extinguisher, as well as providing the locating points for the nosecone. The battery and fire extinguisher have now been located under a small panel beneath the driver's legs in some of the cars. At one point the battery was also located under the oil tank. In addition the footbox provides the mounting points for the front brake discs and calipers.

From the back of the car up to the roll bar, the Type 72 is like any standard Formula One car of its period, the so-called 'English kit car'. As with the Lotus 49, a Cosworth DFV engine is utilised as a stressed member, bolted against the monocoque rear bulkhead. At the top of the engine, alloy plates from the cam covers are bolted to ear-like brackets on the upper corners of the tub. The DFV is held at the bottom by two large bolts.

Originally a C-shaped subframe was attached to the rear of the engine. The single upper wishbone mountings and rear anti-roll bar were located on to this. An A-shaped lower wishbone was located on to the back of the engine and a sandwich plate fitted to the transaxle. Later a simple fabricated beam was mounted to the lugs on the gearbox side plates. This carried the inboard pickup for the single

LEFT: The footbox structure carries the three pedals. *(Author)*

57

ANATOMY OF THE LOTUS 72

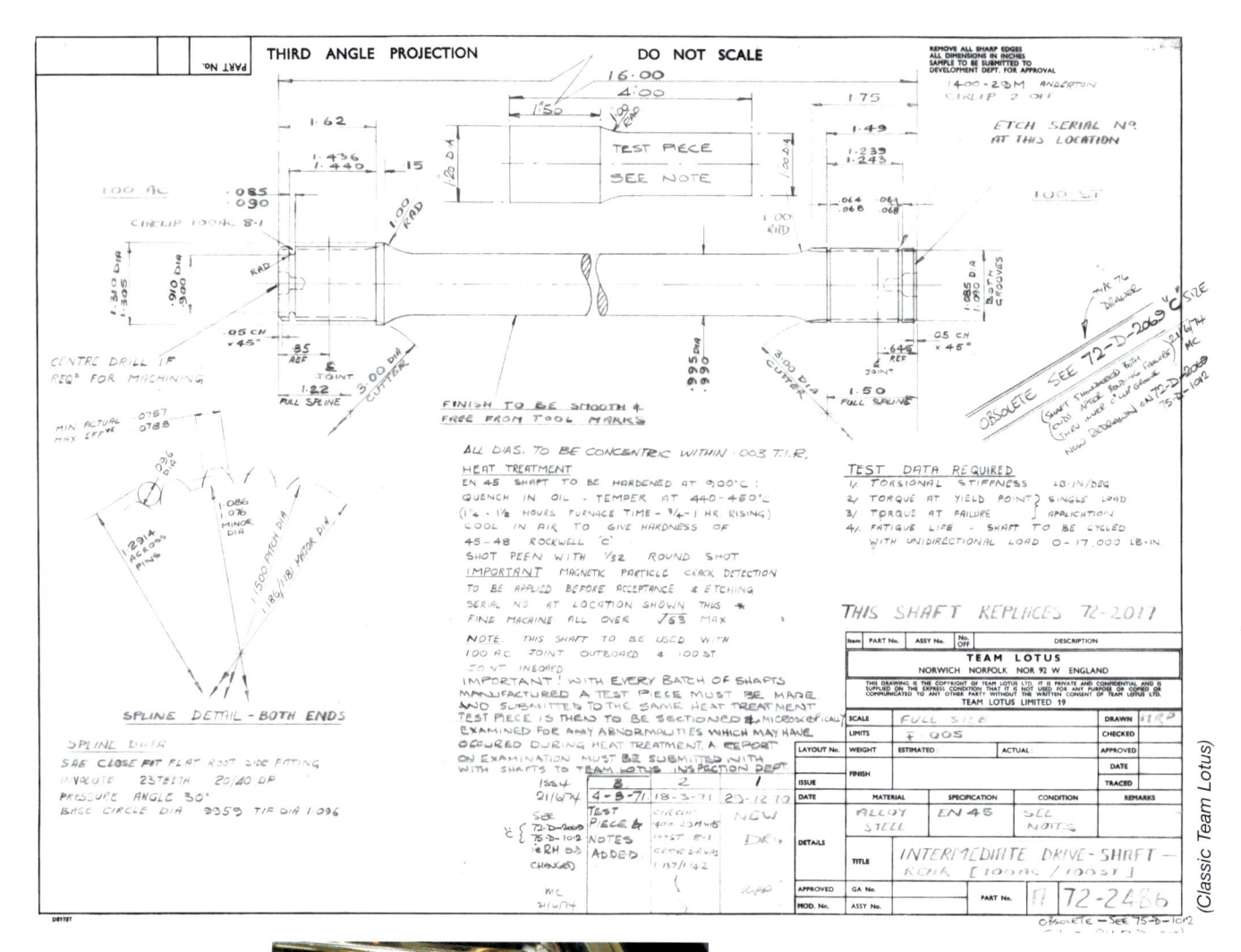

RIGHT: The main electrical cut-off master switch is located on the rollover hoop. Pull is for off.
(Author)

RIGHT: An original period fuel filler cap, now rendered obsolete for historic racing.
(Author)

top link that replaced the rear upper wishbone when the anti-squat was removed. The beam also carried the mounts for the rear anti-roll bar and the top of the rear shock absorbers.

Early in its life the chassis of the 72 was stiffened with cross-bracing in the rear of the tub and stronger suspension pickups.

Minor changes were made to the car for 1971, including improved mountings for the mirrors and vents in the side of the nose to direct air to the inboard brakes instead of the two original NACA ducts.

The regulations for the 1972 season required external 16-gauge sheet fuel tank protection in preparation for deformable structure regulations scheduled for the following year. This led to a reskinning of the cars then in use. When the deformable structure rules came in 12 months later the tubs were unstitched and rejigged. Double-skinned crush pads formed into integral radiator pods replaced the separate pod moulding.

FAR LEFT: The cockpit at launch.

MIDDLE AND LEFT: Cockpit comparisons between 72E/5 and 72/8. Unlike the rebuilt 72/6, the fire extinguisher is exposed and there's no room for the battery. *(Author)*

BELOW: Dashboard stripped from 72/3... *(Simon Hadfield Motorsports)*

BOTTOM: ...and 72/6, both prior to rebuilding. *(Author)*

The change in rules also limited fuel tank capacity to 250 litres (55½ gallons). This was divided so that no more than 80 litres could be carried in a single tank. The minimum weight of the cars was also increased for that season from 550kg to 575kg.

In 1975 a long-wheelbase version of the car was introduced. To achieve this an oil tank was inserted between the rear bulkhead and the engine. This, it was thought, placed an additional 25lb (11.4kg) on the front wheels. Weight distribution was now 34/66%. A new wing mounting also had to be designed because of this.

Cockpit

A large Perspex moulding around the cockpit protects the driver from the elements. The livery is painted on to this, leaving a clear windscreen at the top. The height of the paint line varied over the seasons.

Cockpit temperatures were improved over the Type 49 as the 72's oil tank is sited in the tail, instead of in front of the driver's feet. Consequently the exhaust air from the side-mounted radiators of the 72 no longer warms the driver, unlike the air that passed through the nose-mounted radiator of the 49. Moving these

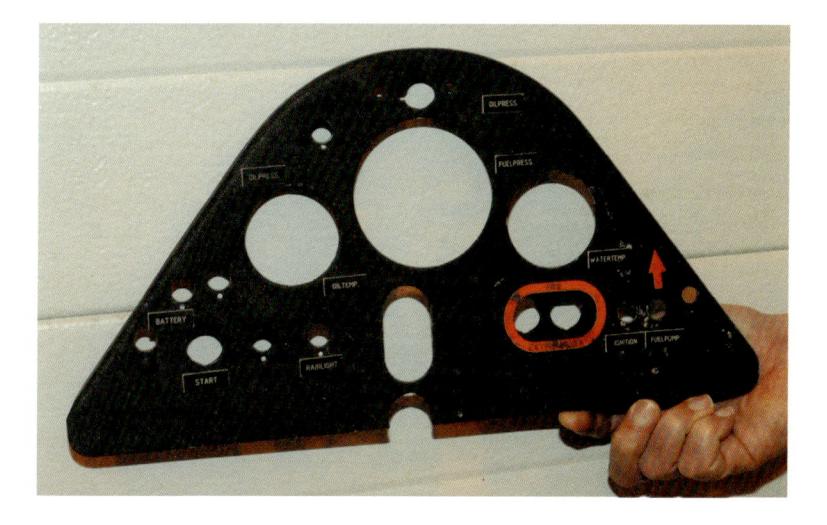

59

ANATOMY OF THE LOTUS 72

ABOVE: 72/6's dash makes use of dials from Stack and Race Tech. *(Author)*

RIGHT: Fire extinguisher button on what is obviously Classic Team Lotus's 72E/5. *(Author)*

RIGHT: The Perspex moulding that surrounds the cockpit had a varying paint line during the life of the 72. The Brabham BT33 in the background in Hoole Racing's workshops is the very car that ran out of fuel on the last lap of the 1970 British Grand Prix enabling Rindt to sweep past to victory. *(Author)*

components also contributed to the 72's greater rearward weight bias.

There are far fewer controls than a modern racing car. Even the brake balance isn't cockpit-adjustable – this has to be done by the mechanics by removing the nose box. The only controls that the driver has are the steering wheel, gearshift and the three conventional pedals. The gearshift mechanism is a rod that runs from the cockpit. A six-point harness is fitted.

ABOVE: Modern Momo steering wheel in the rebuilt 72/6. *(Author)*

BELOW: The gearshift operates by means of a rod that runs from the cockpit. *(Author)*

TOP AND ABOVE: Comparison between 72E/5 and 72/6 shows that the latter now has an additional steel rollover bar around the dashboard to meet current FIA regulations. The rebuilt car also features an alarm light perched on the top of the dash. *(Author)*

RIGHT: Willans shoulder belts on 72/8. *(Author)*

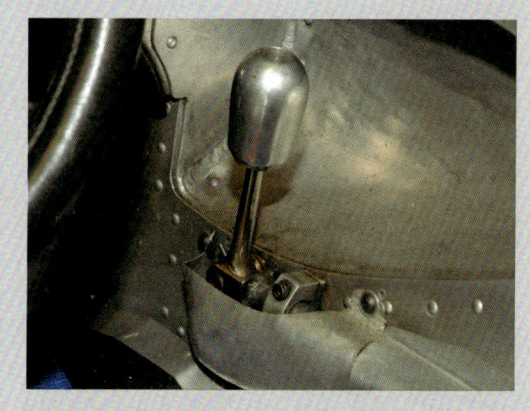

61

ANATOMY OF THE LOTUS 72

RIGHT: At the rear, a link and a lever (1) from a pyramid (2 – rear camber adjuster) attached to the top of the upright operates a compound torsion-bar spring (3). Note the twin radius rods (4) and twin lower parallel links (5), along with the anti-roll bar (6) operating via a drop-link (7) on the upright rear lower mounting.
(Author)

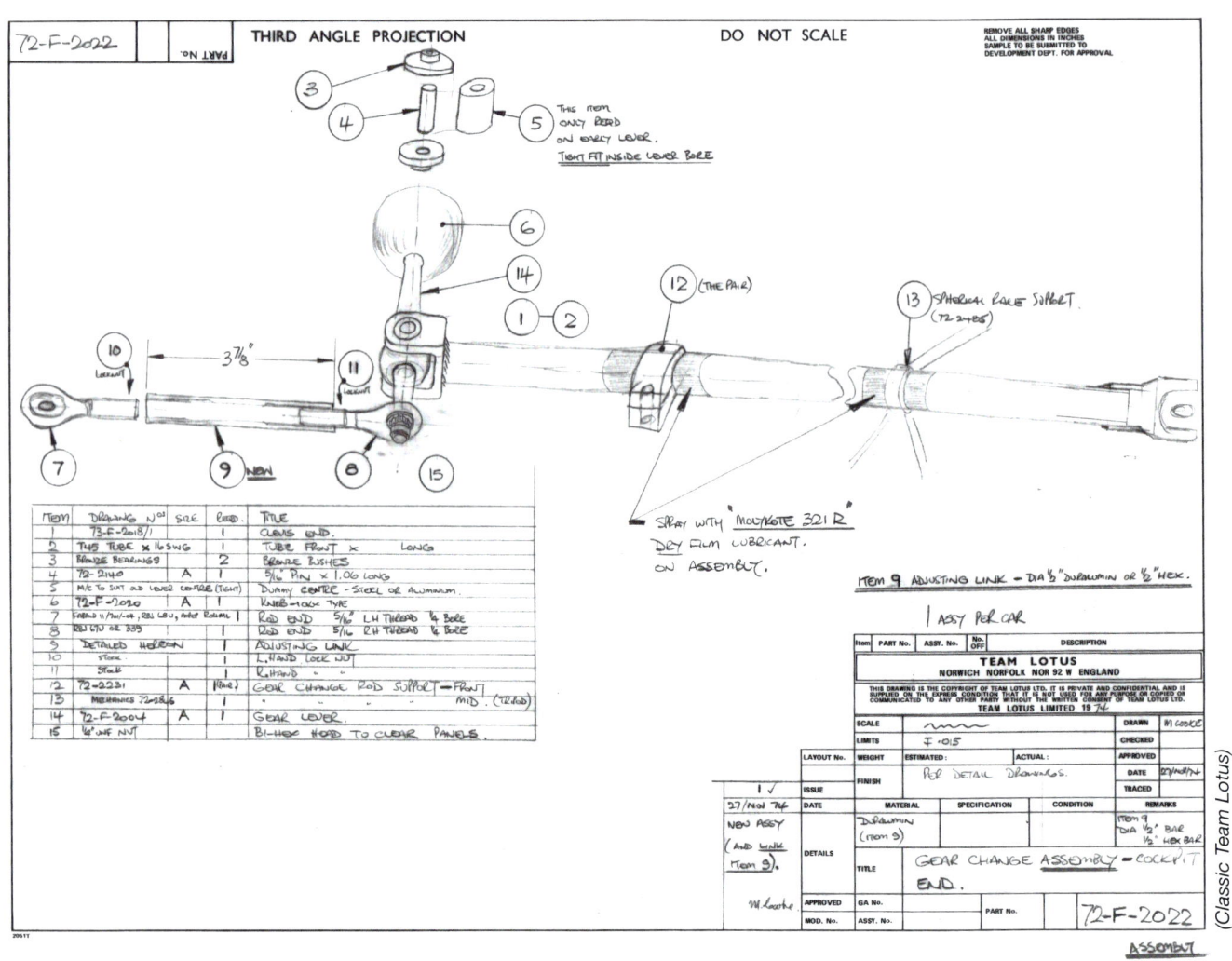

(Classic Team Lotus)

Suspension

Instead of the traditional coil-spring and damper set-up used in Formula One at the time, Team Lotus chose a layout that made use of torsion bars, which are attached to the wheel upright by a complex linkage. This gives rising rate characteristics, which was something that Colin Chapman wanted, although Maurice Phillippe was unconvinced. Thus it is soft under normal conditions but stiffens near the limits of travel, rendering it free from the lack of control inherent in soft springs. The bottoming when the fuel tanks are full that would occur with conventional soft springs is, therefore, avoided.

The compound torsion bar springs feature an outer tubular sleeve internally splined at one end to mate with an internal solid bar that passes back through the outer sleeve. The outer is mounted rigidly on the chassis structure at its open end. From here the inner bar element protrudes to pick up a linkage attached to the wheel upright. This is actuated by the suspension's vertical movement. The more the suspension deflects, the proportionally lesser the rate of twist of the torsion bar spring becomes. The front torsion bar runs alongside the tank bay area next to the driver's legs, with the end protruding from the front bulkhead. The rear bar runs longitudinally and extends out of the back of the car either side of the gearbox.

The torsion bars are machined to a very fine tolerance, originally using gun barrel making equipment. Crowded roller-race bearings maintain minimum friction clearance between the outer sleeve and the inner bar. They're around half the length of conventional bars of a similar rate, occupying considerably less inboard volume than conventional coil springs. The first torsion bars used on the Lotus 72 were particularly skinny and the team went through a number of sizes during the car's inaugural

BELOW LEFT: A view of the rear torsion bar (arrowed) from below. *(Author)*

BELOW: Stripped down rear camber adjusters. As befits a Maurice Phillippe design, these perform three functions: adjusting the rear camber, acting as the 'rocker' or actuator for the rear pull rod, and controlling the position of the top of the upright, providing a degree of toe control (although the adjustment is done by the bottom toe links). *(Author)*

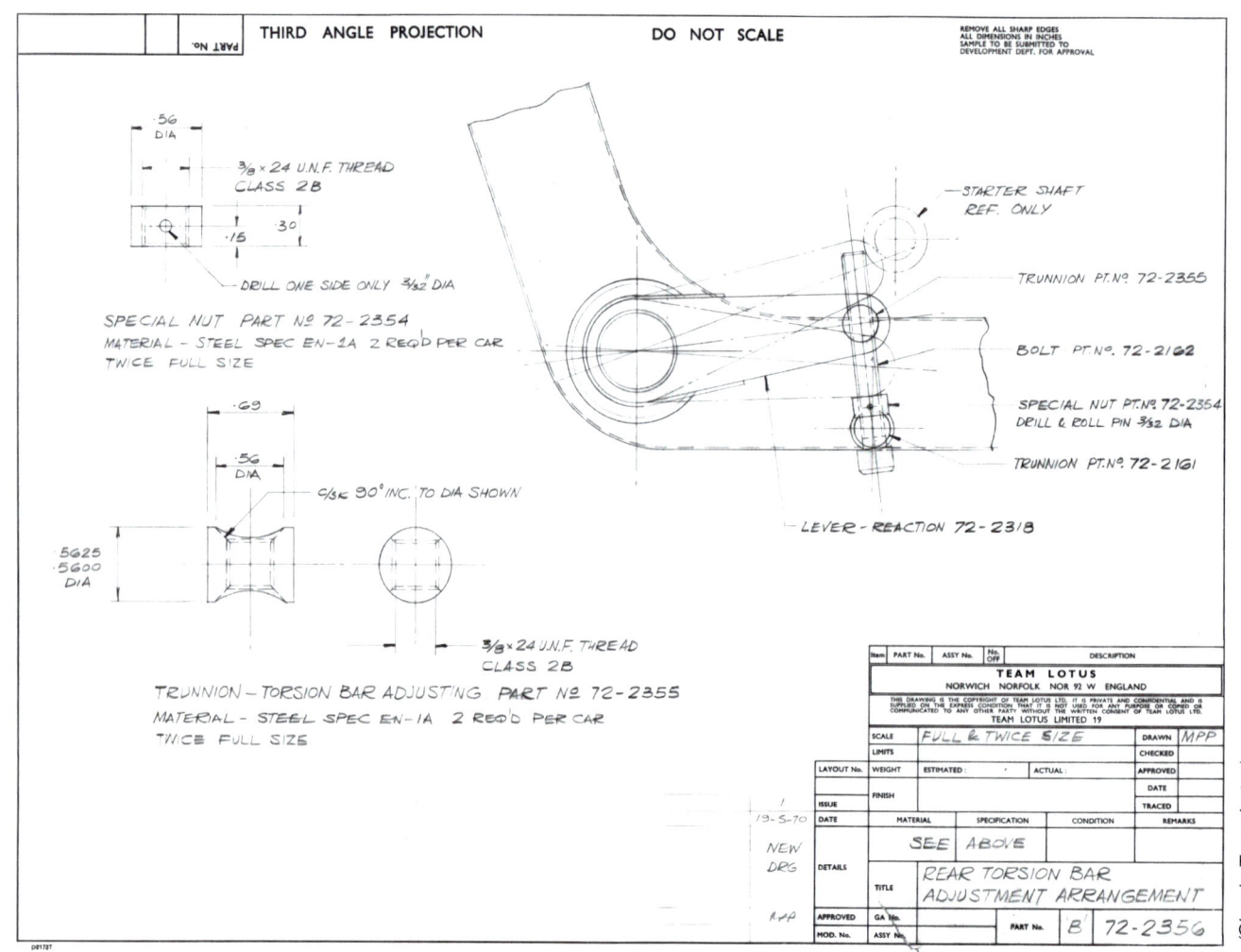

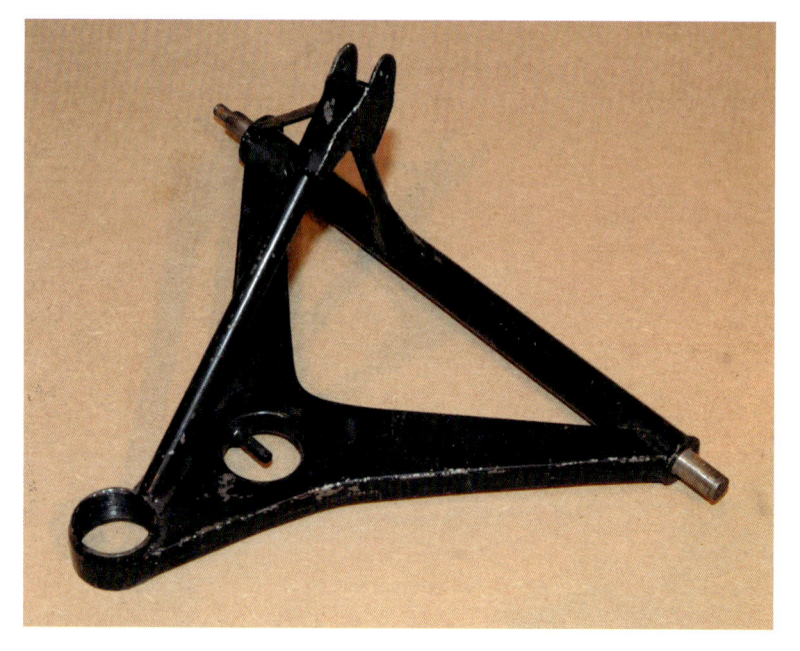

ABOVE: This upside-down shot of a front top wishbone shows the pull rod that activates the torsion bar. *(Author)*

season before settling on those coded white that were used for the rest of the car's life.

In the Type 72's final year, 1975, steel cable torsion bar actuation was tried, which operated only on bump when the cables came under tension. The flexible cable was thought to permit greater movement and prevent the inside rear wheel from lifting. One of the cables snapped in practice for the Brands Hatch Race of Champions, causing the left rear suspension to collapse. However, the fixing of the ends of the cables was improved in time for the International Trophy at Silverstone.

For the French Grand Prix that year helper coil-springs were wrapped round the front damper barrels to assist the torsion bars. This was because weight distribution had been altered by outrigging the engine around 5in (127mm) aft of the tub on a tubular framework. By this time the ageing cars were suffering all kinds of troubles, and for the British Grand Prix

THIRD ANGLE PROJECTION DO NOT SCALE

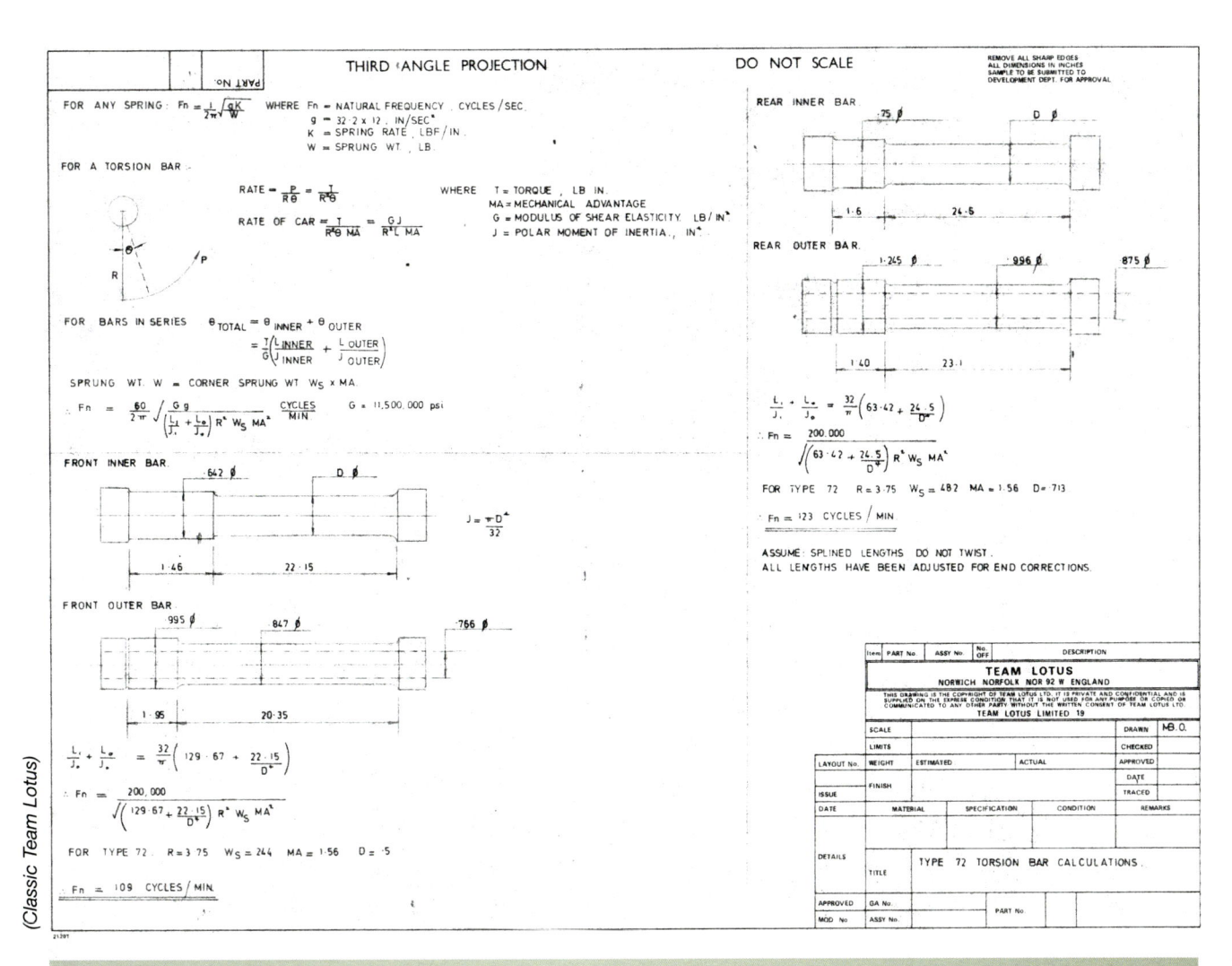

FOR ANY SPRING: $F_n = \frac{1}{2\pi}\sqrt{\frac{gK}{W}}$ WHERE F_n = NATURAL FREQUENCY, CYCLES/SEC.
g = 32.2 × 12, IN/SEC²
K = SPRING RATE, LBF/IN.
W = SPRUNG WT., LB.

FOR A TORSION BAR:

RATE = $\frac{P}{R\theta} = \frac{T}{R^2\theta}$ WHERE T = TORQUE, LB·IN.
MA = MECHANICAL ADVANTAGE
RATE OF CAR = $\frac{T}{R^2\theta \cdot MA} = \frac{GJ}{R^2 L \cdot MA}$ G = MODULUS OF SHEAR ELASTICITY, LB/IN².
J = POLAR MOMENT OF INERTIA, IN⁴.

FOR BARS IN SERIES $\theta_{TOTAL} = \theta_{INNER} + \theta_{OUTER}$
$= \frac{T}{G}\left(\frac{L_{INNER}}{J_{INNER}} + \frac{L_{OUTER}}{J_{OUTER}}\right)$

SPRUNG WT. W = CORNER SPRUNG WT W_S × MA.

∴ $F_n = \frac{60}{2\pi}\sqrt{\frac{Gg}{\left(\frac{L_i}{J_i}+\frac{L_o}{J_o}\right)R^2 W_S MA^2}}$ CYCLES/MIN G = 11,500,000 psi

FRONT INNER BAR

.642 ∅   D ∅
1.46   22.15

$J = \frac{\pi D^4}{32}$

FRONT OUTER BAR

.995 ∅   .847 ∅   .766 ∅
1.95   20.35

$\frac{L_i}{J_i} + \frac{L_o}{J_o} = \frac{32}{\pi}\left(129.67 + \frac{22.15}{D^4}\right)$

∴ $F_n = \frac{200,000}{\sqrt{\left(129.67 + \frac{22.15}{D^4}\right)R^2 W_S MA^2}}$

FOR TYPE 72 R = 3.75 W_S = 244 MA = 1.56 D = .5

∴ F_n = 109 CYCLES/MIN.

REAR INNER BAR

.75 ∅   D ∅
1.6   24.5

REAR OUTER BAR

1.265 ∅   .996 ∅   .875 ∅
1.40   23.1

$\frac{L_i}{J_i} + \frac{L_o}{J_o} = \frac{32}{\pi}\left(63.42 + \frac{24.5}{D^4}\right)$

∴ $F_n = \frac{200,000}{\sqrt{\left(63.42 + \frac{24.5}{D^4}\right)R^2 W_S MA^2}}$

FOR TYPE 72 R = 3.75 W_S = 482 MA = 1.56 D = .713

∴ F_n = 123 CYCLES/MIN.

ASSUME: SPLINED LENGTHS DO NOT TWIST.
ALL LENGTHS HAVE BEEN ADJUSTED FOR END CORRECTIONS.

TEAM LOTUS
NORWICH NOR 92 W ENGLAND

TITLE: TYPE 72 TORSION BAR CALCULATIONS

(Classic Team Lotus)

LEFT: Steel cable torsion bar actuation was tried in 1975. As 72/8 has spent most of its life in the Donington Collection it remains more or less as it was when it last raced that year, and thus retains this system. *(Author)*

ABOVE: An inner torsion bar with muff coupling at one end. The torsion bars were designed to work as a pair and are therefore asymmetrical. *(Author)*

(Classic Team Lotus)

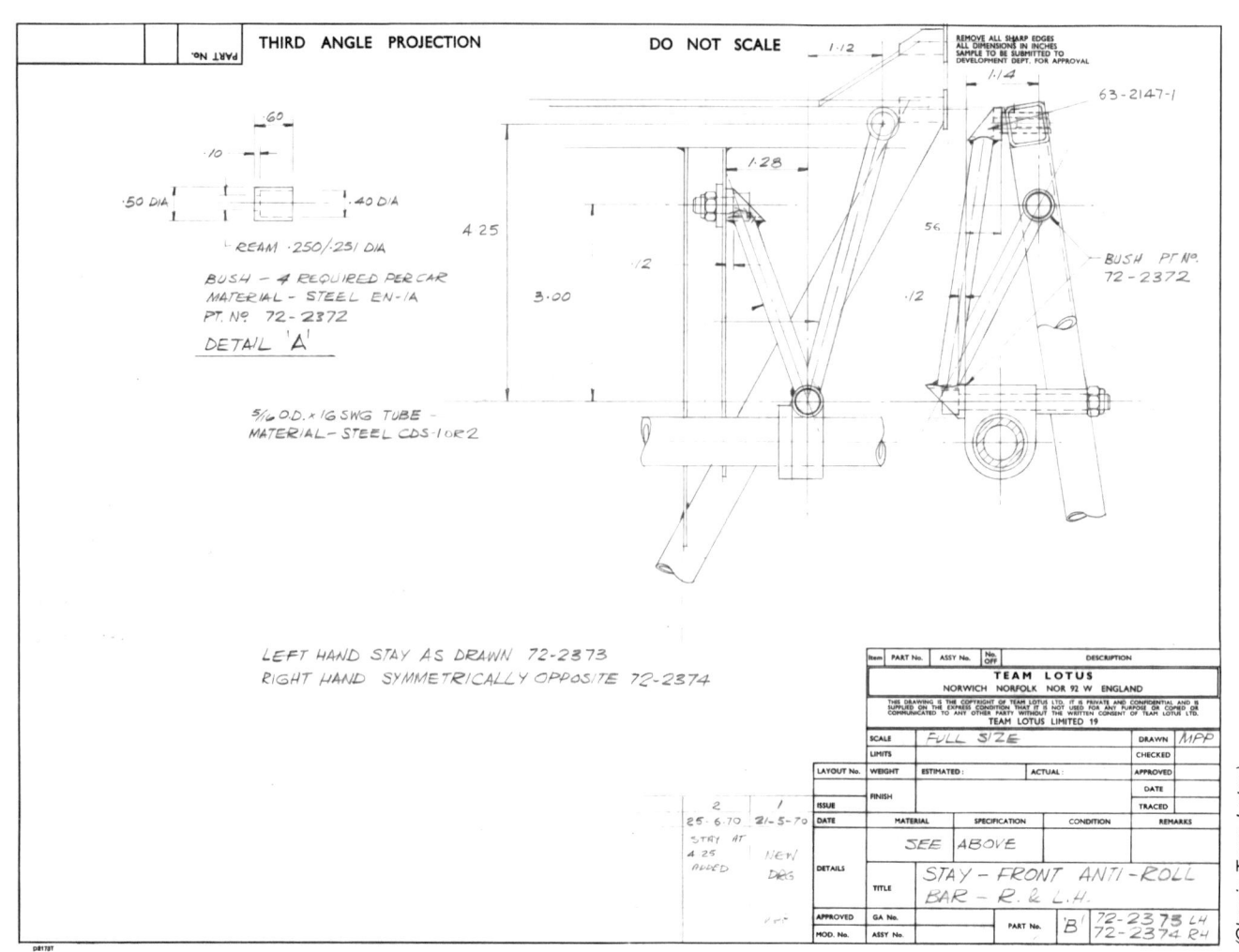

66
LOTUS 72 MANUAL

(Classic Team Lotus)

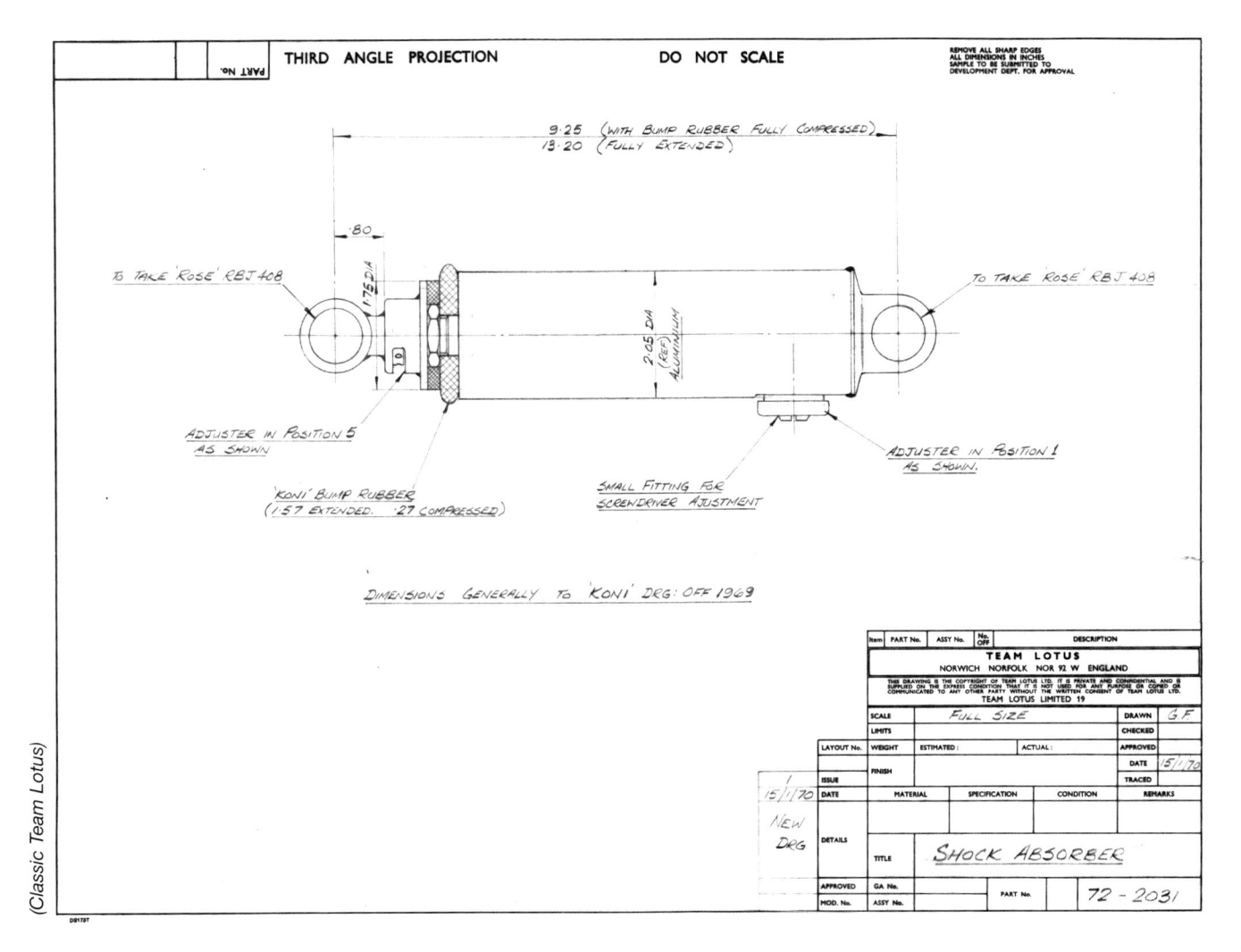

two of them had their torsion bars replaced by pure coil-spring suspension while a third car ran with 1973 suspension.

Conventional upper and lower wishbones were initially used for the suspension location at both ends of the car. The front ones were fabricated from nickel chrome-molybdenum sheet, the rear from steel tube. The front wishbones are mounted on a front subframe. Cast magnesium alloy uprights were initially mounted on to the wishbones. At first the forward pickup points of the front wishbones were lower than the rear points, thus providing anti-dive characteristics. Likewise, at the rear of the car the forward pickups were higher than the rearward ones, thus giving a pronounced anti-squat. The Lotus 49 had been notorious for the acute way in which its nose had pitched down under braking, while under power its tail had pitched down. The 56 IndyCar, though, had been noted for its low pitch characteristics, which, it was hoped, the anti-dive, anti-squat of the 72 would be able to replicate.

In this form the car had major handling problems, and changes were made before the 72 could be entered for a second World Championship Grand Prix. Rindt's car, 72/2, had both the anti-dive and anti-squat removed, while, 72/1, which was driven by Miles, just had the simpler rear-end conversion. Deletion of anti-squat just meant that new rear subframes had to be built. The removal of the anti-dive was a far more complex business. The change to the front subframe and pickups meant that the side skins no longer fitted. They were unstitched and the monocoque reskinned around revised bulkheads. It was such an extensive rebuild that only the rear cockpit bulkhead and engine mounts survived from the original. When a second parallel suspension car, 72/3, became available 72/1 was also completely rebuilt.

Inboard-mounted Armstrong dampers were,

OPPOSITE: Anti-squat was provided by the single rear radius rod, which was located on the cam cover and angled sharply upwards. *(Ford)*

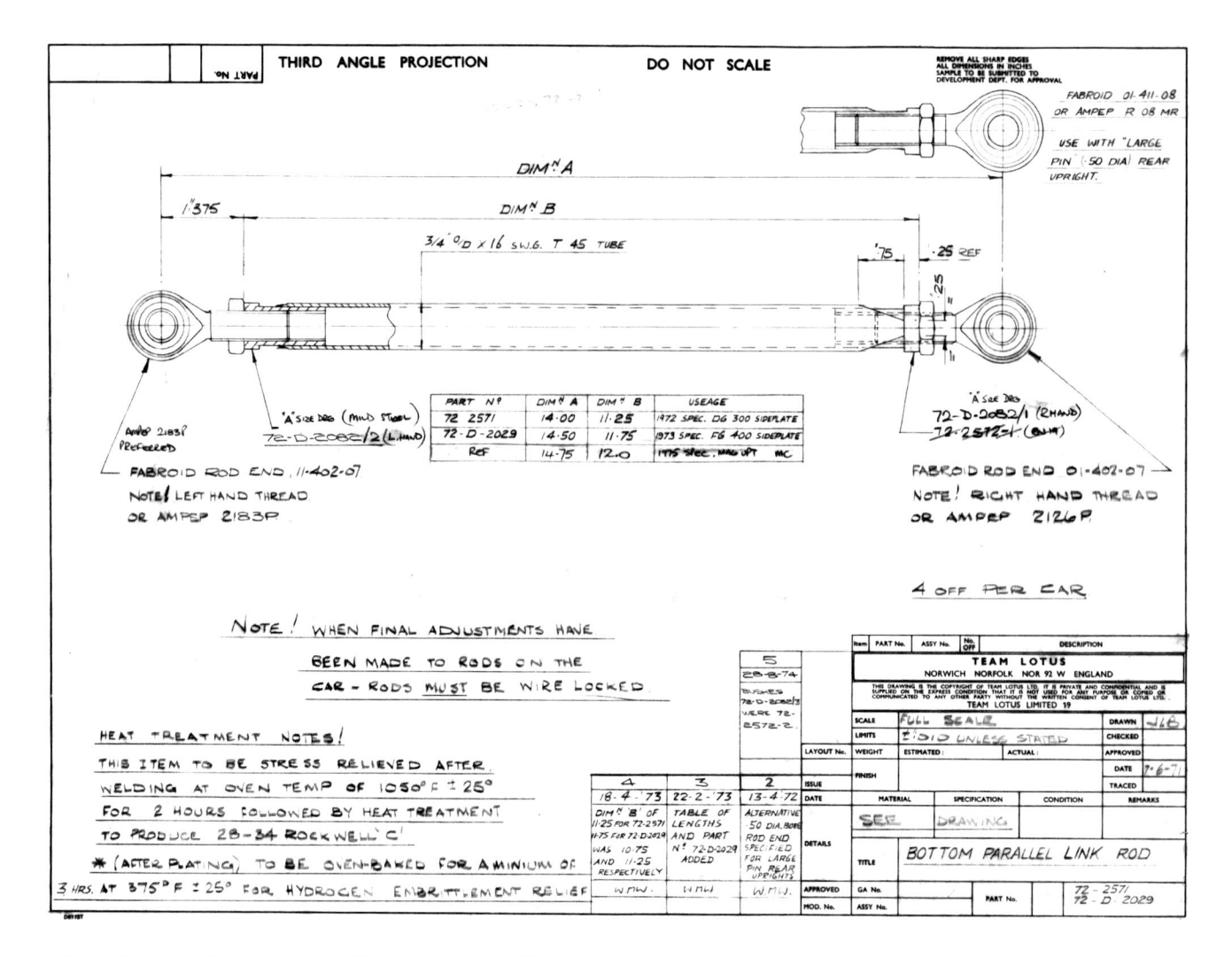

(Classic Team Lotus) at first, fitted front and rear. These were changed to Koni dampers that offered greater adjustability, having a rebound adjuster as well as a bump adjuster, the rebound adjuster being on the top of the shaft. The rear dampers were re-sited early in the life of the 72 to move them away from the hot air coming from the side radiators.

New suspension geometry was fitted to 72/5 to match the low-profile Firestone tyres introduced in 1971. Twin radius rods on either side replaced the single rod. Parallel links replaced the bottom wishbone to control toe-steer. (It had been discovered that the rear lower wishbone had been bending as the inboard end of the front leg was mounted on to the engine, and the rear leg on to the gearbox, and as these two major components heated up and expanded at different rates they therefore distorted the wishbone. The two lower parallel links, being independent of each other, negated this problem, but then required the addition of the second, lower radius rod due to the loss of the cross-bracing of the wishbone.) The rising rate suspension was also removed from the rear before the 1971 US Grand Prix. It no longer seemed to be an advantage and was suspected of adding to the new, low-profile tyres' vibration problem. Suspension revisions continued through 1972.

Further retuning was required the following year with the change from Firestone to Goodyear tyres. By this stage rival designs had more even weight distribution. Lotus countered by experimenting with wide-track suspensions and stiffer torsion bars springs to produce a greater load on the front tyres. At the 1974 French Grand Prix an even wider track, by more than an inch either side, was used. In order to reduce frontal area, the narrow-track version was also revised for Monza that year, staying in place until the US Grand Prix.

Among the modifications made to the 72

LEFT: Twin radius rods replaced a single rod to match the low-profile Firestones introduced in 1971. *(Author)*

BELOW: Koni dampers replaced the original Armstrongs. *(Author)*

during its final season were a lowering of the front suspension in Argentina. This involved adapting front suspension damper units with 2in (50mm) spacers made from sawn-off jack handles. Small, die-opening springs were fitted to the spare car for the French Grand Prix to stiffen the front suspension.

Brakes

The disc brake layout was designed for minimum unsprung weight and to keep the heat into the hub/wheel/tyre assemblies to a minimum. The brakes were mounted inboard, the fronts on the front subframe and the rears on the gearbox sideplates, a factor that dramatically reduced the unsprung weight. This was an important part of the car's initial design as it meant softer tyres could last longer, while such elements as uprights and wishbones could be smaller as they didn't have to carry the weight of the discs and calipers. The front brakes work on the wheels through shafts specially made up with Hardy-Spicer and Lobro driveshaft joints.

The originally solid Girling discs were cooled by airflow that entered through flush NACA ducts formed in the nose cowl and exits via

69
ANATOMY OF THE LOTUS 72

RIGHT: Close-up of the brake shafts running to the hubs and the solid inboard discs at launch. *(Ford)*

ABOVE: The front brakes are mounted inboard on the front subframe… *(Author)*

RIGHT: …while the rear brakes are located on the gearbox sideplates. *(Author)*

moulded chimneys on the upper surface of the same cowl. At the 72's first race ventilated discs replaced the solid ones on Rindt's car when an insulating spacer overheated and disintegrated.

The NACA ducts on the top surface of the nose were quite quickly replaced by sculpting the vertical sides of the nose cowl, beneath and behind the front wings, to guide the required cooling air to the inboard front brakes.

Drilled discs were fitted for the 1974 British Grand Prix and by the 1975 Brazilian race larger front discs were in use. These required even greater cooling; consequently late in the 72's career external scoops appeared on the top surface of the nose cowl, just outboard of the cooling air exhaust chimneys.

The inboard mounting of the rear brakes also relieved the suspension of major braking loads, which enabled only upper radius rods to be fitted at the rear. (As described above, a second, lower radius rod was added to each side at the rear when the lower wishbones were replaced by parallel links.)

Following a front brake shaft fracture in the 1970 Austrian Grand Prix the hollow shafts were replaced by solid ones for the rest of the season and were so at Monza. However, the team reverted to drilled brake shafts for the 1971 season.

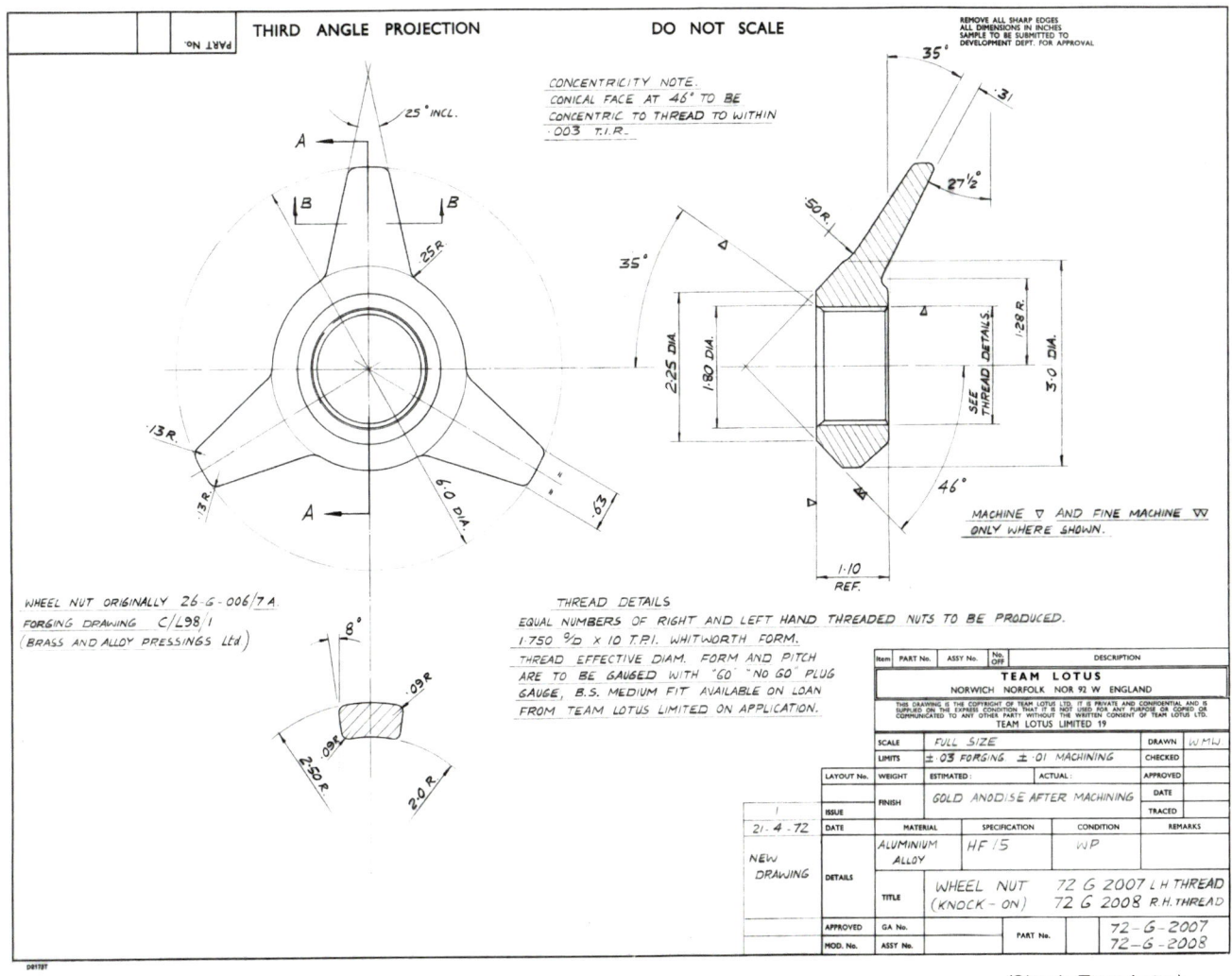

(Classic Team Lotus)

The front brakes were fine during the early days of the Type 72. However, aerodynamic downforce increased considerably during its lifetime as a result of larger and larger wings.

In an attempt to maintain competitiveness a host of minor changes were made to the 72 in its final season. Included were larger and stronger Girling calipers, a different design of straps to mount the discs, and stronger brake shafts. During 1974 the cars had been suffering from spongy brakes, and these were attempts to overcome the problem.

Wheels and tyres

The initially cast wheels were held on by a huge spinner and a safety clip. At first the sizes were the same as the Lotus 49C, with 13in diameter fronts and 15in rears and

LEFT: The unique front brake mounting system viewed from the inside. *(Author)*

RIGHT: A modern 100% copy of the front hub. *(Author)*

BELOW: The rear upright arrangement is fairly standard. However, note the pull rod adjustment for the torsion bars. *(Author)*

respective rim sizes of 10in and 15in. Rindt also tried 17in rears, which generated too much rear-end grip and caused excessive understeer. For the 1971 US Grand Prix 13in rears were fitted with higher profile tyres. For the following season 13in fronts and 15in rears again became the norm.

When the Type 72 was launched Team Lotus had a strong relationship with Firestone, with tyres being tailor-made for the team. Because of its inboard brakes the 72 had a low unsprung weight. This meant that it could use softer tyres with less rigid sidewalls and a steering geometry that put less work into the tyres. The brake layout, the minimum overall weight and the smooth, pitch-free riding characteristics initially exploited softer tyres. What had been virtually qualifying tyres could now go a full race distance. The inboard location of the brakes improved such tyres' working conditions.

Firestone introduced a new low-profile tyre for 1971, which led to suspension modifications and different diameter wheels. The lower the profile, the faster the tyres went. The faster they went, the more vibration became a problem. The uprights were changed to fabricated steel as the earlier magnesium ones had been suspected of twisting. With the withdrawal of Firestone, Team Lotus changed to Goodyear tyres for 1973. Its tyres were far from ideal for a car designed with rearward weight bias and low unsprung weight – Goodyear engineers were used to cars with the weight bias further forward. Downforce and some geometry changes initially went partway to masking the problems. Colin Chapman's relationship with Firestone was probably more important to what the car did, and why, than anything else, so once Goodyear – which made bespoke tyres for Formula One rather than for any specific team – became Team Lotus' supplier then any advantage was lost.

Development had now made the uprights heavier than comparable magnesium castings. New castings were made, only for Goodyear to change its tyre size. Large, ugly stopgap uprights had to be brought into play and appeared to work well. However, magnesium uprights were to prove overweight yet again, so then it was back to fabricated steel.

For 1974 Goodyear reverted to tall, 28in overall diameter rear tyres, and year-old uprights had to be fitted to provide alternative pickup points and match the tyres. By then Goodyear's tyres were better suited to rival teams and the company couldn't afford to tailor its product just for Team Lotus. The rubber now on offer was just too stiff. The 72s no longer handled well and it was only when the car had been consigned to history, and the notion of inboard front bakes at last rejected, that Team Lotus could make its Grand Prix cars handle again.

LEFT AND FAR LEFT: Wheel taken from 72/3 prior to restoration. *(Simon Hadfield Motorsports)*

FAR LEFT: 72/8's wheels feature an all-gold finish. *(Author)*

LEFT: Avon Tyres is the sole supplier of tyres for Lotus 72s competing in historic racing. *(Author)*

During 1973 and 1974 the team also suffered three failures of the 15in MelMag wheels now fitted, and it was decided to revert to cast 13in wheels. This meant that the Type 72 could no longer be fitted with tyres that used the latest Goodyear compounds.

The light and rigid MelMag wheels were essentially two saucers with a central boss, the whole bonded together. They could not, though, be tested without destroying them, and after Ronnie Peterson had an accident at the Nürburgring it was found that a wheel hadn't been glued correctly. Team Lotus successfully took Magnesium Electron – the manufacturer of MelMag wheels – to court over this, although, as team manager Peter Warr pointed out, this wasn't done maliciously but was simply an attempt to recover money spent on the programme.

Major changes had to be made to the 72s to try and cope, and for the 1975 Brazilian Grand Prix the cars ran with new rear uprights that gave further revised geometry. However, the new tyres demanded heavier loadings and the 72 just couldn't heat them sufficiently.

Tyres for the Type 72s used in historic racing today come exclusively from Avon Tyres Motorsport, the competition tyre department of Cooper Tire & Rubber. Using its A11 compound, this supplies the control crossply slick tyre for all the Formula One cars from this period still racing. The Avon tyres are largely similar to the original sizes, although it's difficult to match the large rear tyres with which the car finished in 1975. Classic Team Lotus's 72/9, which hasn't been run since it retired from Grand Prix racing, still retains its Goodyear tyres from that period.

73

ANATOMY OF THE LOTUS 72

The Cosworth DFV engine

The Lotus 72 was designed for exclusive use with the compact and rigid four-cam, 3-litre Cosworth DFV V8 engine, which is utilised as a stress member and is bolted against the monocoque rear bulkhead. Suspension loads are carried on sandwich plates assembled into the Hewland FG transaxle casing. At the top of the engine, an alloy plate from the cam covers is bolted to ear-like brackets on the upper corners of the tub. At the bottom, the DFV is held on by two large bolts. Around 3,350 individual parts are involved in its manufacture.

The Cosworth DFV suffered from torsional vibration problems, which were still leading to breakages in 1970, the first year of the Type 72. This was virtually eliminated the following season when designer Keith Duckworth introduced a unique quill hub arrangement in the second compound gear. There were many subtle changes between the DFV's first appearance at Zandvoort in 1967 and 1982, the year it won its final world title. During that time power rose from 400bhp at 8,500rpm to over 500bhp and the ability to run to 11,000rpm.

The original rule which said that all DFVs had to be sent back to Cosworth for rebuild or repair was relaxed by 1971, although Cosworth continued to look after the new 1971 units. Team Lotus used JW Automotive to maintain its DFVs. By 1974 the cost of a new DFV, now

BELOW: The inner workings of an early Cosworth DFV are clearly laid out in Theo Page's cutaway drawing. *(Ford)*

delivering about 475bhp, had risen to £9,000, having been £7,500 when first introduced. The increase in horsepower over this time had mainly been due to a progressive increase in the rev limit, as there were no significant changes to the ports, valves or cam profiles.

Block

The DFV features an asymmetric light aluminium block with a five main bearing crank. These were cast in Cosworth's own foundry in Worcester, where the company employed a special casting process that enabled it to produce an aluminium block that matched the strength of a cast iron one. The block extends from the decks to the centreline of the crankshaft, the lower half of the crankcase being integral with the sump casing.

Three main bearings are formed by the sump and two by caps, although early versions were formed by five sump bearings. Included are front bearing, centre bearing and rear bearings; the main caps are the sump. The caps are aligned with one dowel either side and are tightened regularly so that the gap between cap and block remains square. When this is achieved the dowels are locked, the feeler gauge is slid out and both sides are slowly torqued. A hole underneath the metering unit allows for any leakage (such as fuel or water) going through the right-hand cylinder bank.

(Classic Team Lotus)

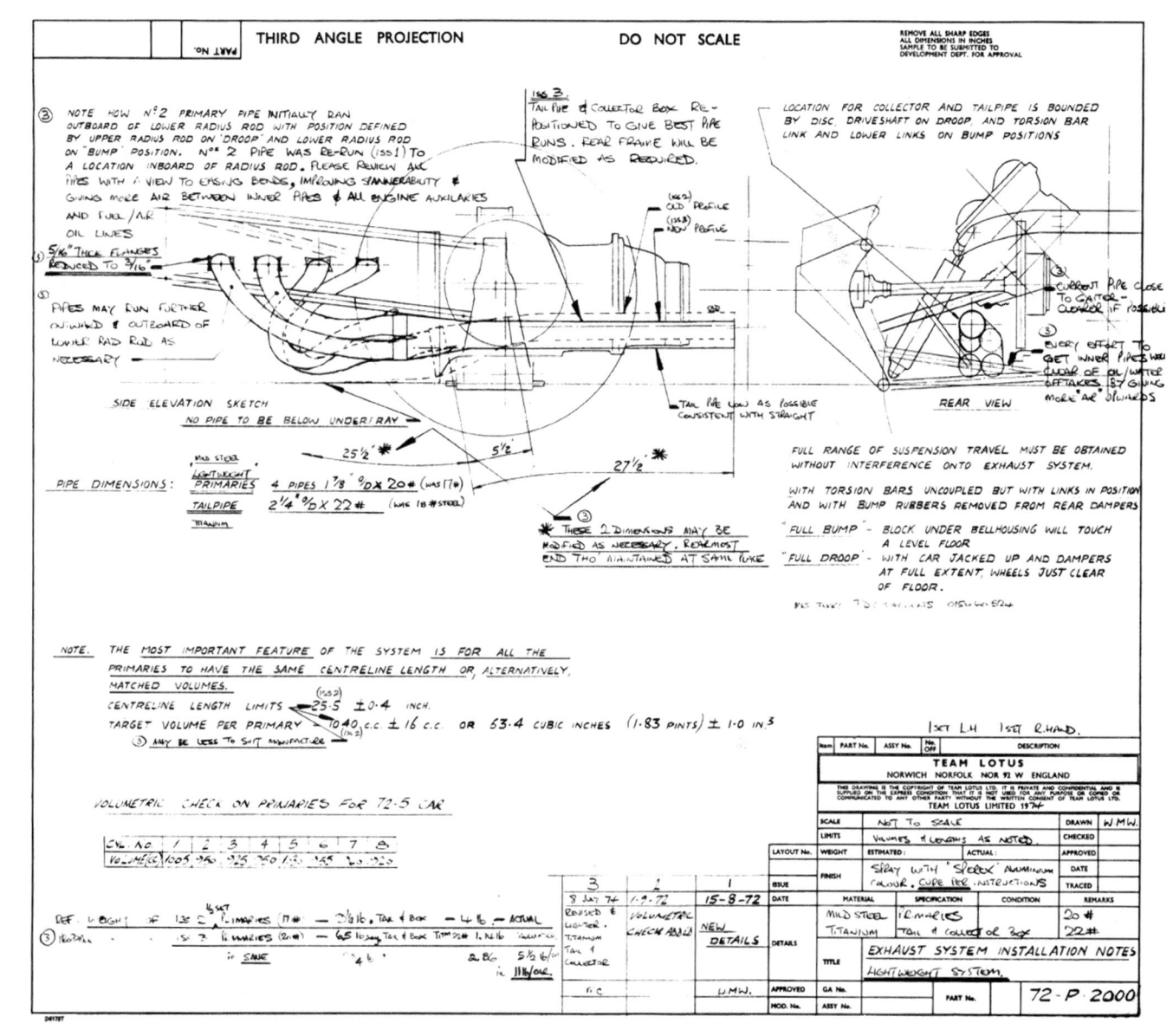

ABOVE: **A batch of DFV crankshafts. Early ones were machined from steel billet, but after serious production had begun nitrided forged steel versions were used instead.** *(Ford)*

Cylinder liners

The originally wet cast iron liners in each of the cylinders are in constant contact with water. The inner bore is perfectly straight. The outside of the liner has two O-rings at the bottom, while the top flange rests on the counter bore. The block should be cleaned and prepared prior to fitting the liners and all marked for the correct position within the block, which should be heated to 150°C to receive the liners. The liner must be a certain distance from the top of the block. Sealing between the cylinder head and the block is secured by a Cooper ring located in a recess formed between the liner and the block. Grooves machined on top of the block at the edge between the liner give an indication of leaks. In the event of a blow-up, the liners can be changed by keeping the standard bore and machining its location in the box to accept a bigger external diameter liner.

Crankshaft

The steel forged crankshaft is of a single-plane shape, mounted as low as possible to keep the centre of gravity low. At one end a boss takes the flywheel with eight $3/8$in UNF bolts. On the other is the location for the timing gear. The crankshaft revolves in five steel-backed main bearings with lead indium wear surfaces, numbers two and four holding it in position. It has five journals, four pins and two con rods mounted on each pin next to each other. On the timing gears side, the crank gear drives the series of gears; the main gear is secured via a press-fit and located on one dowel. The oil system on each end of the crankshaft is achieved by a conventional oil seal secured on the flywheel side by a retaining ring. On the front of the engine, the oil seal is pushed in the front timing gear cover and secured by three screws.

Con rods
The connecting rods are steel forged, split across the big ends at 90° to the rod shank, the outside being shot-peened for extra strength. In the little end there is a mixture of soft metal alloy. On the big end there is a plain shell bearing held by a cup and two ⅜in UNC high tensile bolts. The tightening of the con rods is conventional.

Pistons
The forged light aluminium pistons are retained on the con rod by a gudgeon pin, which is retained by two circlips. Between pin and circlips are dished synthetic washers known as Belleville washers. The piston crown is pocketed to give clearance to the valves. Three piston rings are used, two compression and one oil control ring.

Cylinder head
The light aluminium cylinder heads have aluminium, bronze and copper nickel valve seats and guides. The heads are interchangeable between the cylinder banks. The inlet ports are inclined towards the centre of the engine on both cylinder banks, the exhaust ports to the outside. The ports to each combustion chamber merge into a single inlet tract inside the head. On the front of the cylinder is an idler gear that drives the camshaft gears mounted on a roller bearing on a steel pin that protrudes from the cylinder head. All the valves are assembled with double springs. These are held to the valves by a top cap with two collets. The valve stem is sealed to the guide by a rubbery seal held against the valve stem by a spring. This, in turn, is held on to the guide by the bottom spring platform. Ten studs hold the cylinder head to the block, four smaller studs on each outside edge. Inlet valve size is 1.36in (34.5mm) and exhaust valve size 1.14in (29mm).

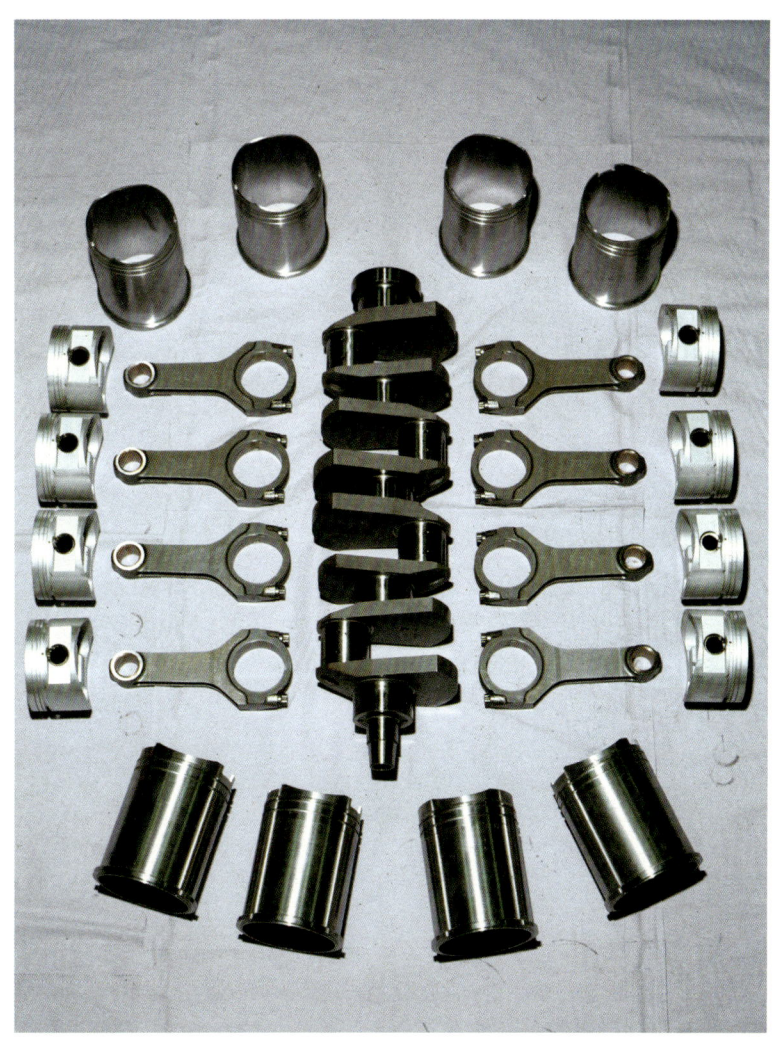

Cam carrier
The cam carrier is retained by ten pairs of studs, that also retain the cam bearings, and eight cap screws. The cam carrier carries the tappet pistons and camshafts in its own assembly. A small shim is located between the valve stem and tappet bucket. Both shims and buckets are made from steel.

ABOVE: Cosworth DFV crankshaft, pistons, connecting rods and cylinder liners. *(Ford)*

LEFT: Team Lotus initially used Autolite plugs for the Type 72. However, this changed to Champion for 1972. Despite the fact that 72/6 still carries Champion decals to ensure that it retains an authentic colour scheme, CGA makes use of NGK plugs. *(Author)*

RIGHT: The eight inlet trumpets are each mounted on two O-rings and retained by a steel ring screwed to the manifold top. *(Author)*

Camshaft

The steel camshaft rests on plain shell bearings and five caps, which are numbered to avoid being incorrectly replaced. While the inlet and exhaust cams are the same shape, they can't be wrongly installed because of the distance between the lobes due to the different diameter of the inlet and exhaust valves. At the front end and rear of the front bearing is a shoulder that prevents the camshaft from moving. On the back of the engine is a magnesium plate held to the cylinder head by four ¼in UNC bolt cap heads and a $5/16$in UNC cap head with a big washer. Another magnesium plate is bolted to the cam carrier in like fashion. These seal the rear of the cylinder head and the cam carrier.

The cam cover is cast in magnesium and bolted to the carrier by 22 $10/32$in UNF cap heads around its edge and ten $5/16$in nuts and washers down its centre. The front part of the cover is designed to form part of the engine mounting. Four $5/16$in bolts secure an engine plate to the cover, which is bolted to the chassis by a single $3/8$in UNF bolt. An aluminium mounting block is located at the bottom of the sump and bolted to the chassis by two $3/8$in studs.

To lubricate the cam, an oil passage passes through the cylinder head from the block to the centre camshaft bearing. The camshaft being hollow, this allows the oil to pass to the other bearings as well.

Throttle slides

The throttle slides rest on a series of rollers and ball bearings, the guillotine travel being limited by plastic stops. The guillotine is returned by two springs located on the back of the manifold and supported by two plastic plungers. These springs are aided by two additional ones that are mounted to suit different throttle/pedal arrangements.

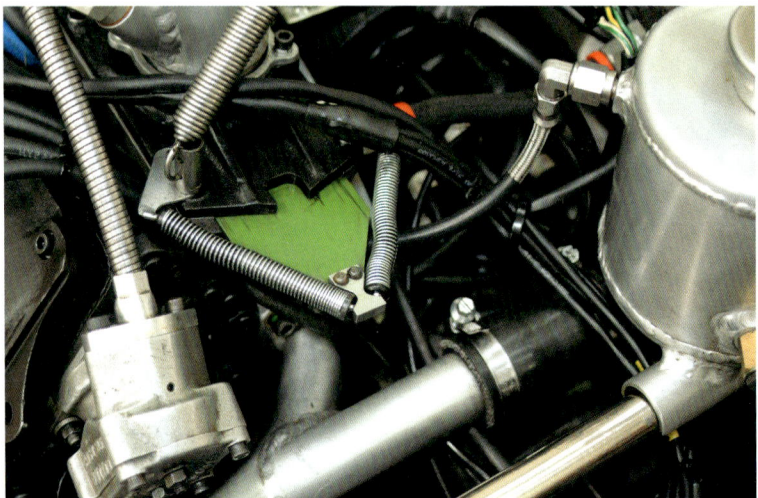

Inlet trumpets

The conical-shaped inlet trumpets are supported by the manifold top, as is the throttle control rod. They're mounted on two O-rings and retained by a steel ring that's screwed to the manifold top. The fuel injector is located in the trumpet.

Metering unit

The metering unit and the electrical assembly – which were nicknamed 'The Bomb' at Cosworth – are connected to a small gearbox that obtains its power from the second compound gear via a quill shaft. This means that the timing of the ignition and fuel injection can be accurately set in relation to each other. The unit is located inside the V, the front of the metering unit being supported by an aluminium mount bolted to the block.

Looking from the front, the layout of the timing gears follows the shape of the engine. The crankshaft gear drives the first compound gear, which in turn drives the second compound gear. This provides the take-off point for the metering unit/ignition assembly drive and carries on the timing gear to the camshafts via idler gears. The second compound gear is a complex assembly made up of a hub incorporating 12 quills. At the end of the line are the camshaft gears, bolted to the camshaft by three cap screws. These gears are enclosed by a cast magnesium cover on the engine, and

BELOW: The primary method of returning the throttle back to the closed position. To the left is the fuel pump drive cable. *(Author)*

also two smaller magnesium covers on each cylinder head assembly. On each corner of the cast cover is a pulley on which runs a toothed belt that's driven by the second compound gear. These provide the power for the engine's ancillary equipment. On the left-hand side is the mechanical fuel pump, the water pump for the left-hand bank and the oil pressure pump. On the right side is the water pump for the right-hand bank and the scavenge pump. Between the rear of the water pump and the front of the scavenge pump is a small clutch assembly which will slip at a pre-set load, thus preventing damage to the rotors and front drive belt when the oil is cold.

Water pumps

The two centrifugal water pumps, one each side of the crankcase, are identical in construction apart from the fact that they're left- or right-handed and therefore cannot be interchanged. The impeller is contained in the aluminium housing of the pump body and its shaft is supported by two ball bearings. Water from the pumps is passed through an aluminium tube secured to the block by a cast aluminium elbow. The tube is sealed to the elbow and to the pump outlet with rubber O-rings.

Oil pressure pump

The oil pressure pump body is mounted to the engine. It contains the rotor, pressure relief valve and oil filter in one assembly. The pumping mechanism is a conventional eccentric rotor type. Oil is passed from the pump to the engine via a pipe, excess oil from the pressure relief valve being bled into the scavenge system. The pump receives its power through an Oldhams coupling from the rear of the left-hand water pump.

Engine oil system

Oil is drawn from the tank into the oil pump, where it's pressurised and then pumped through the filter into a cylinder block via a steel tube. It passes through oil ways in the block to the crankshaft assembly, the cylinder heads and camshaft assemblies, with a small amount being directed on to the compound gears through a small jet. It returns to the sump and is scavenged and returned to the tank via oil coolers. The oil tank is vented to a catch tank. The approximate consumption for a Grand Prix was about six pints.

Water system

The water pumps are connected by a passage in the sump that enables water to be introduced into either pump. It's driven by the impellers in the cylinder block, passes around the liners and through the cylinder head, and leaves the engine through an outlet at the rear of each head. It returns to the pumps having been cooled through the radiators. A thin aluminium cover protects the belt and pulley arrangement.

Fuel system

An electrical high-pressure pump sucks five-star petrol through a filter, which goes to a non-return valve or bypasses the mechanical engine fuel pump, then to another filter and the metering unit that distributes it to the cylinder through injectors.

LEFT: The rear of a Cosworth DFV following removal from 72/3 shortly after the car was purchased by the Schryver brothers. *(Simon Hadfield Motorsports)*

BELOW: The left-hand underside of the car reveals the oil pump behind a couple of cold-water return pipes to the radiator plus brake and clutch and oil pressure lines. *(Author)*

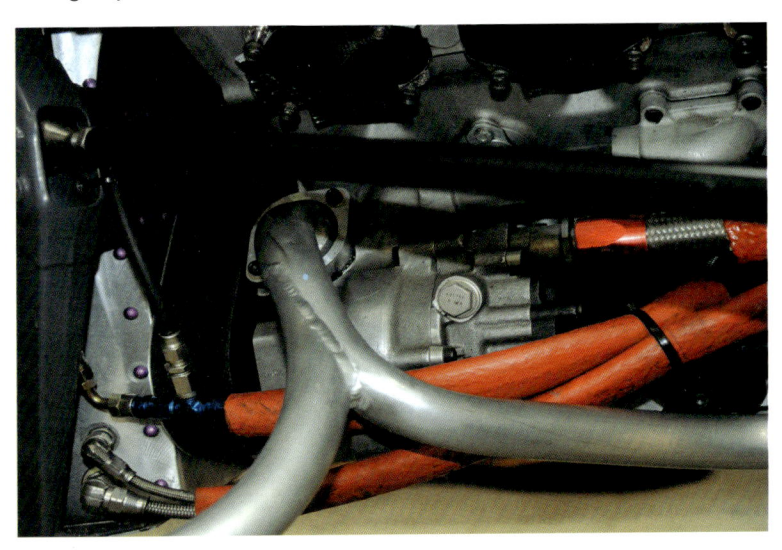

ABOVE: The right-hand side of a Cosworth DFV illustrating how the water and oil scavenge pumps were low down on the side of the engine. *(Ford)*

ABOVE RIGHT: Fuel pressure relief valve on 72/8. *(Author)*

Fuel injection system

Use is made of the indirect Lucas shuttle metering system. A separate electric pump is mounted on the chassis and governed by a dashboard switch. This sucks the petrol from the tank, sending it around the system. The petrol is pressurised because of its flow and by a relief valve designed to keep the pressure at around 110psi. The fuel is fed to a metering unit, which combines a metering distributor with a mixture control. A piston, driven by the shaft, coming from the distribution located inside the metering, sends the correct amount of fuel at the precise moment to each cylinder. The amount injected is determined by the travel of a small free piston or shuttle operated by the fuel pressure. The mixture control assembly comprises a fuel cam mounted on the front of the unit and liaised to the slide by a rod. When opening, the slide determines the travel of the shuttle, sending the quantity of fuel to be injected. The engine also receives the exact amount of fuel to match the quantity of air admitted. The metered fuel reaches the cylinders through injectors located on the outside of the trumpets, which atomise the fuel as it enters the air stream. The shuttle or fuel cam is mounted on an eccentrical pin going through it.

This has five positions and is set in full rich position when cold. A different set of fuel cam profiles is available to suit varying racetracks.

Cosworth DFV engine specification

Configuration: 90° V8.
Capacity: 2,993cc.
Bore: 3.373in.
Stroke: 2.555in.
Compression ratio: 11:1 (approx).
BHP: 480 (approx) at 10,500rpm.
Torque: 245lb/ft at 8,500rpm.
Valve lift: 0.410in (less tappet clearance).
Timing: Inlet 102° MOP.
　　　　　Exhaust 102° MOP.
Firing order: 1-8-3-6-4-5-2-7.

Cylinder configuration:

	Front	
5		1
6		2
7		3
8		4
	Rear	

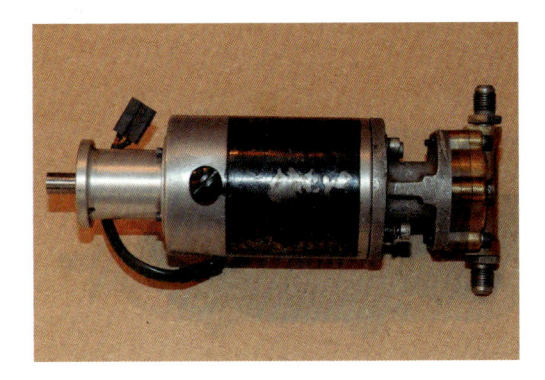

LEFT: Earlier electro-mechanical fuel pump taken off 72/6 prior to rebuild. *(Author)*

Cylinder block: Cast aluminium alloy. General assembly is bearing type.

Wet liners: Cast iron steel in constant contact with water.

Crankshaft: Steel. Turns on five main bearings. Positioned between block and sump.

Con rods: Forged steel (shot-peened).

Pistons: Forged aluminium with two compression rings and one oil control.

Ancillary system: Two water pumps, one per side. One oil pressure pump. One scavenge pump.

Cylinder heads: Cast aluminium alloy, two 1.14in exhaust valves x two 1.36in inlet valves per cylinder assembled with double springs. One spark plug per cylinder located in the centre of the combustion chamber.

Inlet manifold: Cast aluminium alloy inlet trumpets press-formed steel with injector location.

Cam carriers: Cast aluminium alloy takes the tappet piston and camshaft.

Throttle slides: Steel sliding on a series of ball bearings and rollers returned by two guided springs.

Camshafts: Four steel, each turns on five bearings.

Cam covers: Magnesium casting.

Injection systems: Lucas indirect injection shuttle metering system. Pressure 110psi approx. Injection timing at 30° ATDC.

Ignition system: Lucas OPUS ignition with Thyristor engine speed limiter. Lucas alternator.

Spark plugs: Champion R56 or equivalent.

Weight: 165kg.

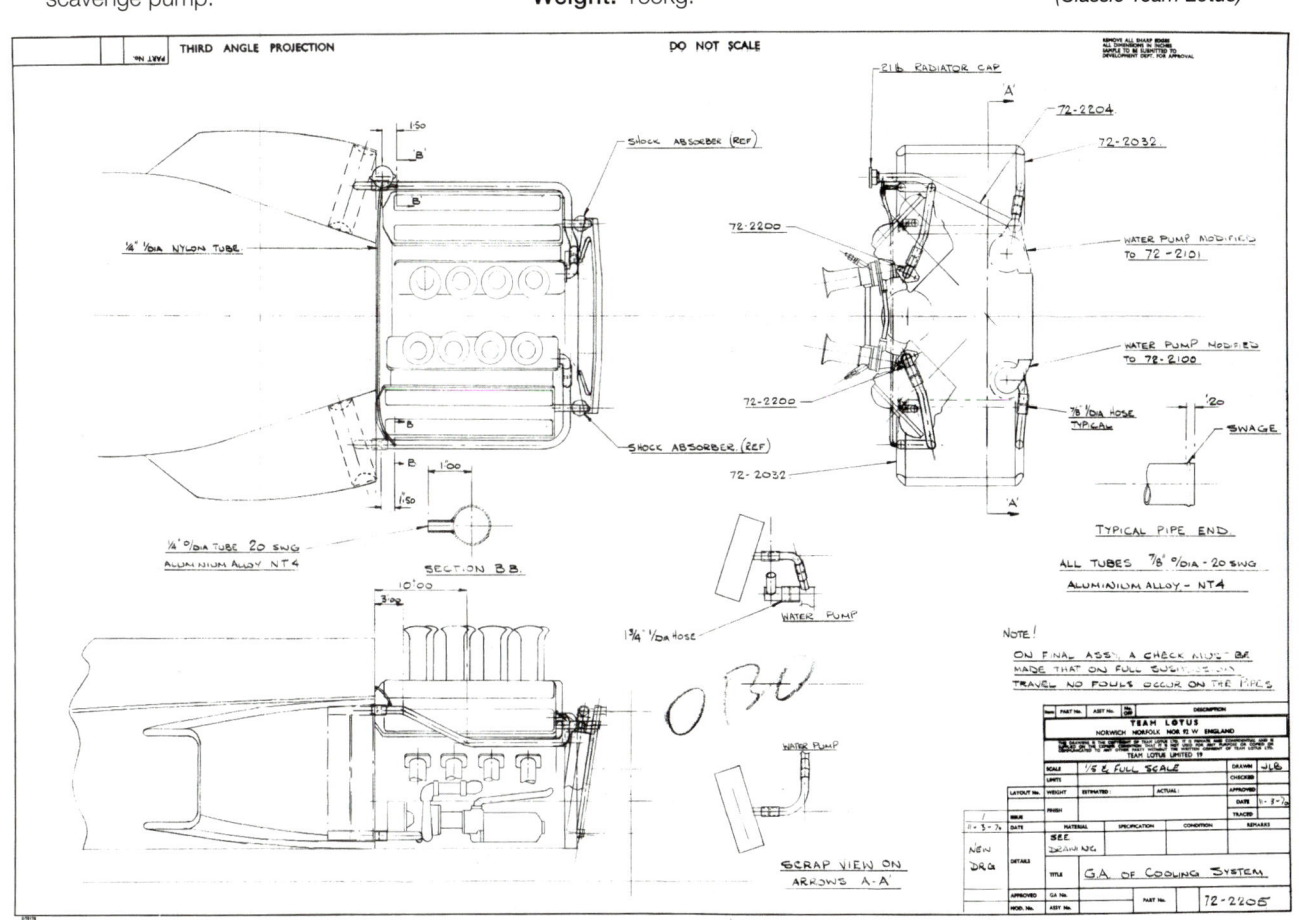

(Classic Team Lotus)

RIGHT: The original-specification fuel pump on 72E/5. *(Author)*

FAR RIGHT: 72/6 uses an electro-mechanical pump whereby at low rpm (ie starting up) an electric pump operates within the same body as the mechanical pump. When the rpm is high the electric portion is switched off and a clutch engages the mechanical pump. *(Author)*

RIGHT: Period exhausts would have been made from mild steel. However, 72/6 now uses handmade 321 stainless steel exhausts from Alunox. Several systems will be used during the course of an historic racing season depending upon the nature of the circuit and advice from the engine builder, in this case Langford Performance Engines. *(Author)*

FAR RIGHT: The Lotus 72's Hewland FG400 replaced the company's heavy DG300 after just two races. *(Author)*

Hewland gearbox

At launch the Lotus 72 was fitted with a five-speed Hewland DG300 gearbox (DG stood for 'different gearbox'). Introduced in 1966, this was the Maidenhead company's first gearbox for the 3-litre Formula One. During the period of this formula, all the Formula One manufacturers – with the exception of Ferrari and Alfa Romeo – used Hewland products at some time. The DG300 was soon regarded as too heavy. At the same time Hewland's FT200 gearbox, which had been developed for the 1.6-litre Formula Two, was considered to be too light for the power and torque of Formula One. The result was that the two were married together in a slightly different casing for F1, thus creating the straightforward and lighter cam and pawl FG400. Many of the FT200's internals were retained, including the gears with larger DG final drive parts.

After its first two races, 72/2's DG300

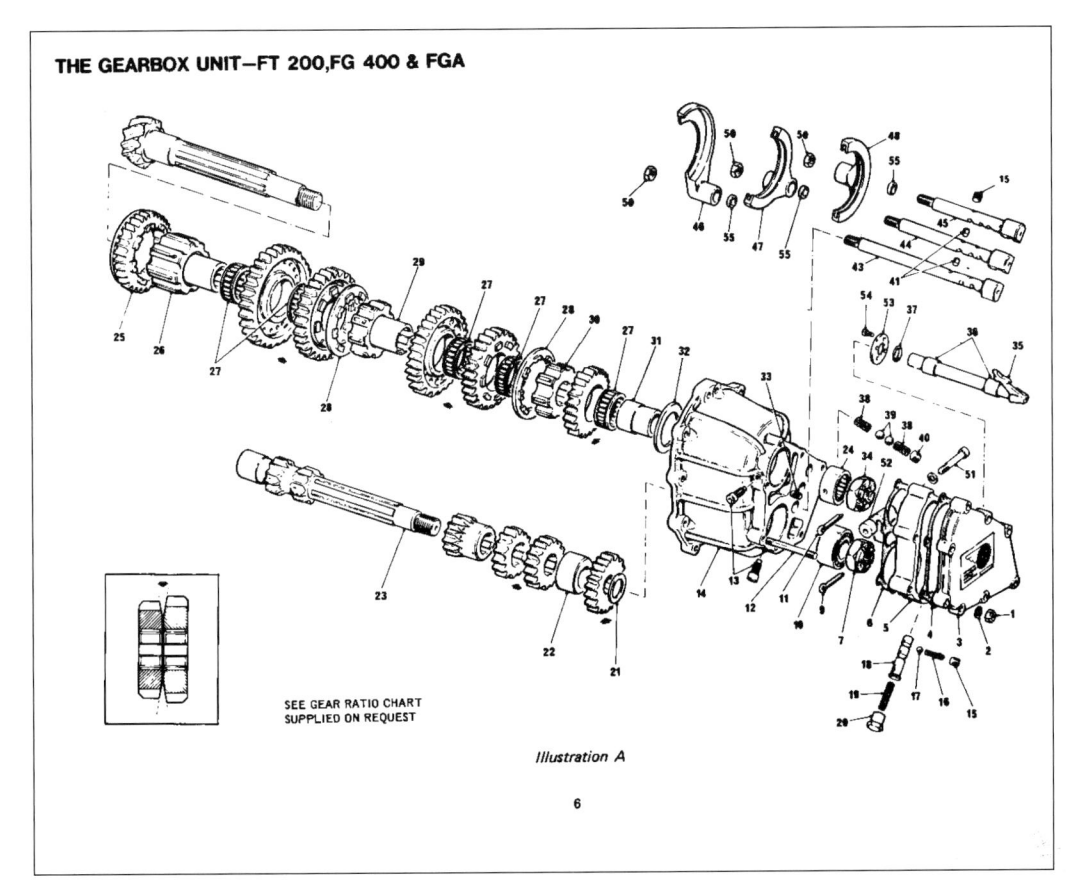

LEFT: The gear clusters and selectors of the Hewland FT200, FG400 and FGA.
(Hewland Engineering)

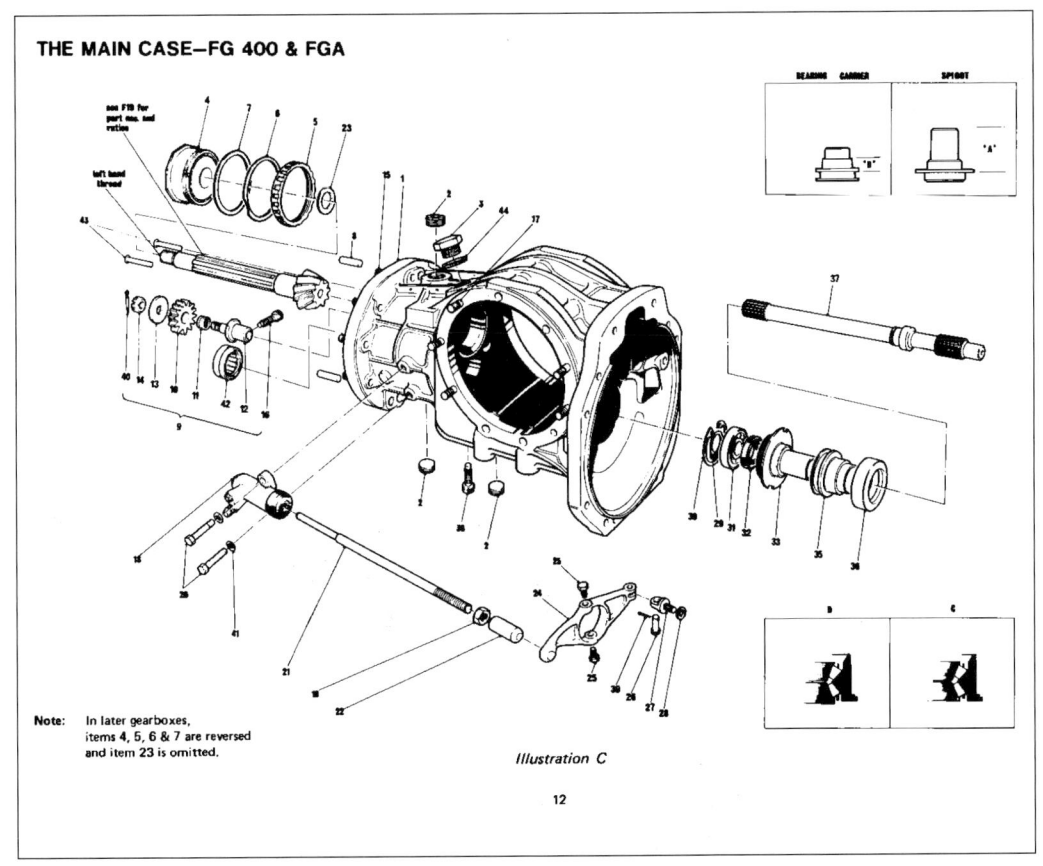

LEFT: The main case of the Hewland FG400.
(Hewland Engineering)

ANATOMY OF THE LOTUS 72

was replaced by a FG400. Although 72/1 retained its DG300 gearbox all subsequent 72s were built with FG400s. During the Lotus 72's life as a Grand Prix car the amount of tractive effort caused by the rearward weight bias and the size of the tyres caused problems with crown wheel and pinion and gears.

Hewland FG400

Specifications:
Drive weight (approx): 110lb.
Oil capacity: 2 litres.
Type of oil: SAE 80 or 90.

Torque settings:
Pinion nut (LH): 115ft/lb.
Layshaft nut (RH): 80ft/lb.
Crownwheel bolts: 75ft/lb.
All 5/16in UNF nuts: 20ft/lb.

The reliable AP clutch used on the Lotus 72 is an early form of hydraulic clutch. The slave cylinder is mounted on the outside face of the rear of the gearbox. An electrically actuated clutch activated by a knob on the gear lever was tried at Silverstone during unofficial practice before the 1973 International Trophy. This feature would reappear on the Type 76.

RIGHT: The Hewland FG400 gearbox of Classic Team Lotus's 72E/5. (Author)

RIGHT: The best features of the DG300 and FT200 gearboxes were married together in a slightly different casing to create the FG400. (Author)

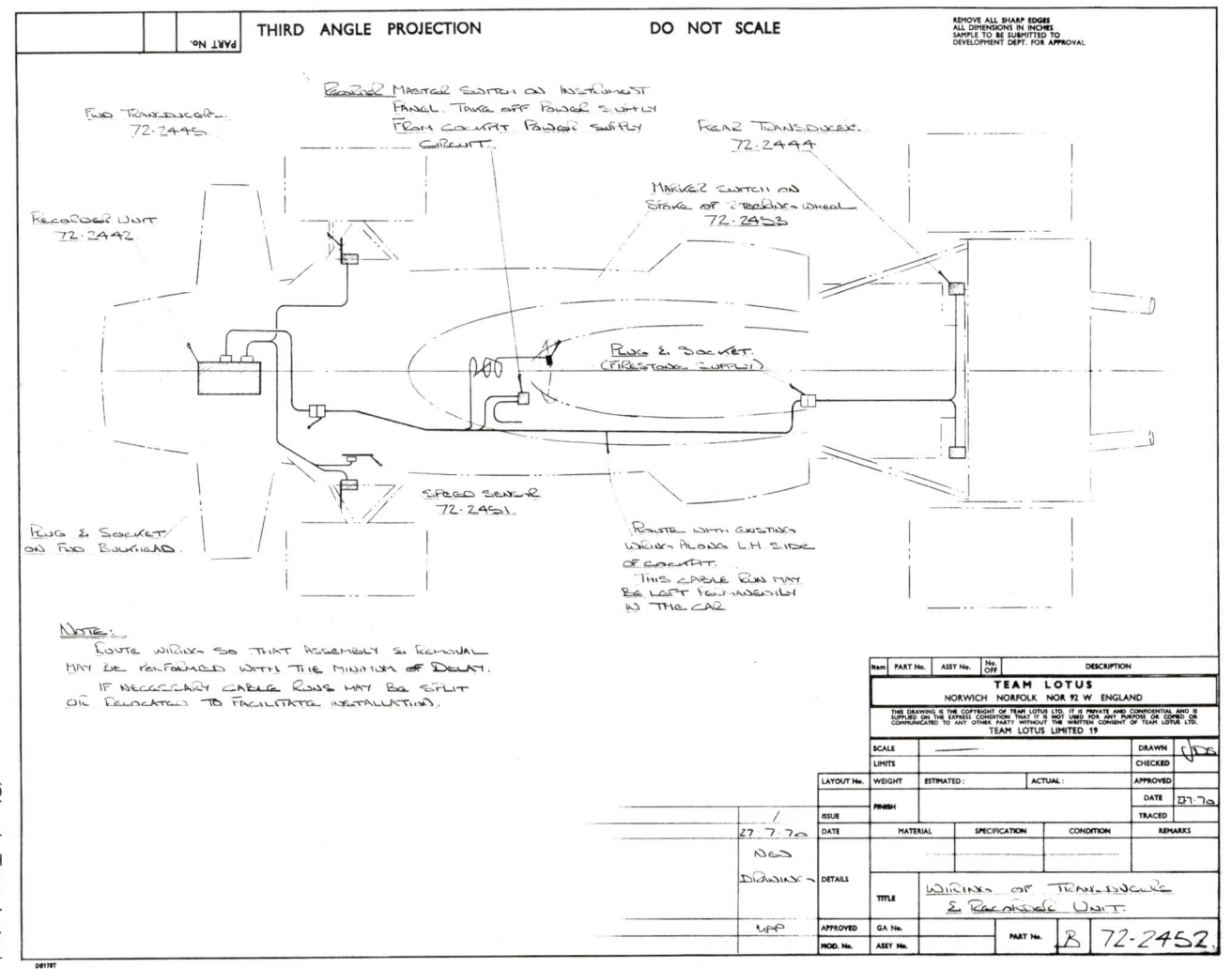

Electrics

Between the metering unit and the distributor assembly is located an alternator of sufficient power to keep the battery charged. The current regulator is incorporated inside a box that contains the complete electronic ignition system. This is located at the back of the inside of the vee of the DFV. It can be changed by disconnecting the wiring coming from the unit and undoing three clips.

LEFT: The current regulator is incorporated inside an aluminium box, which contains the complete electronics system. It is located at the back of the inside of the V and can be easily changed by disconnecting the wiring coming from the unit and undoing three clips. *(Author)*

FAR LEFT: An 'off the shelf' starter motor from ARC Racing is fitted to 72/6. *(Author)*

GTX GTX GTX
GOOD YEAR
John Player Special
John Player
John Player Special
John Player Special
15
BUCKHAMS

'By the time I got the 72, it was five years out of date.'

Brian Henton
John Player Team Lotus driver 1975

Chapter Three

The driver's view

The 18 drivers who raced the Lotus 72 during the 1970s usually had strong views, sometimes conflicting, about the car. It took two, Jochen Rindt and Emerson Fittipaldi, to the World Championship while it had very different effects on the careers of others. Four decades on, there are those who still have vivid memories of their time with the car that Fittipaldi remembers as the best that he ever drove.

(Ford)

It's perhaps not surprising that those who won Grands Prix with it regarded the Lotus 72 as a special car to drive. In his biography of Jochen Rindt, Heinz Prüller quoted the Austrian as saying at the time he won the Dutch Grand Prix, 'Sometimes I think the Lotus 72 really is a super car.' At a Silverstone test he had observed, 'Driving it is quite sensational and quiet different from other cars.' At Spa he told Alex Soler-Roig, 'The Lotus 72 which you're getting into this afternoon is the most fantastic car you have ever driven.'

Against this it has to be noted that in his biography of Rindt, Alan Henry reported him as saying he would never 'get into that bloody car again', but then that was in Spain when it was in its original form. Jackie Stewart is quoted as saying that Rindt 'definitely did not like the Lotus 72', although he was known to have wound him up about its fragility, pointing out, as his mechanic Eddie Dennis recalled, such things as its quarter-inch bolts. Given its troubled first season, it's perhaps not surprising that Rindt was ambivalent about the car in which he scored the majority of his Grand Prix victories. However, he never criticised the 72 to Dennis.

Those who've raced it in historic events also recall the 72 fondly. While emphasising that he wasn't a full-time racing driver, David McLaughlin – who competed with 72/6 – observed that the car was fairly easy to drive. 'It was so soft that it had a lot of feel.'

Emerson Fittipaldi

Jochen Rindt's successor as Team Lotus's number one, Emerson Fittipaldi became acquainted with the Lotus 72 only towards the end of its birth pains and his views are anything but inconsistent. There were times when he and the Lotus 72 seemed to merge into one machine. Even today he speaks fondly of the car, placing it on a pedestal above all others, and there's no doubt that he was one of those who helped develop it into a world-beater.

'The first time that I drove the car really fast was at Watkins Glen after the tragedy at Monza,' he remembered. 'When we went to Monza I crashed one 72 on Friday going slowly. I missed the braking point going into the Parabolica. It was a brand new car, the one that Jochen was going to drive the next day.

'It was a new concept of car for me, so very different from the Lotus 49. It had a very critical set-up. It was lighter than the 49 with different weight distribution and very sensitive.' Fittipaldi also stated that the type 72 was a much harsher car to use than the 49, and quicker to change direction. 'The 72 was a fantastic car to drive. It was the best racing car that I drove during my long racing career.

'In 1970 Jochen won the World Championship and I was immediately fast with it at Watkins Glen and won my first race. In 1970 there was still a little bit of tread in the tyres but in 1971 the tyres were completely slick for the first time. Then the car lost a lot of performance because the slick tyres created more grip, and we couldn't get the car to work. The slicks generated so much more grip that the 72's suspension wasn't strong enough.

'Then Maurice and Colin worked together on the flexibility of the car. We had problems with the bump steer and toe-in under power, and under braking the tyres would toe-out. The whole suspension was moving. It took us about six months to get the car working but by the end of the season it was really beautiful. The suspension was now much more rigid. It was reinforced and the progressive rate on the rear suspension changed for the Rothmans World Championship Victory Race at Brands Hatch at the end of 1971. This was the first, good indication that the Lotus 72 was back again. It was again an extremely competitive car. From that point on through 1972 and 1973 it was a magic car to drive. Colin was a master at designing a car and a master at setting it up.

'The progressive torsion bars were very difficult to adjust to different types of surface – the system was very critical. At the beginning of 1972 we used neutral, non-progressive suspension and that enabled us to make the car work on different tracks. The torsion bar was very critical for the velocity rates of the suspension. This made the car very consistent on different tracks. It was then that I won the championship. I would talk to the car and the car would talk to me; we could speak to each other.

'The Lotus 72 was a better car than the McLaren M23. The McLaren was a car which you had to work on to adjust from track to track. It wasn't an easy car to work on in this way. It was extremely good in really fast corners, but overall the 72 was, for sure, a better car than the McLaren.' The Brazilian also pointed out that the M23, which has to be seen as another great car of the 3-litre era, was a far simpler design than the 72.

'When I drove the 72 I had the confidence that I could give 110%. It was there when I needed it – in handling, in braking, the car was fantastic. When I drove it last year [2010] I felt the car was still too good to drive today. I found it enjoyable after so many years. I never drove the other Lotus Formula One cars, but I suspect that it was the best that Colin designed. The innovations that it had at the time were incredible – the torsion bars, the inboard brakes, the side radiators, the revolutionary wedge shape. It's still a beautiful-looking car.'

In practice for the 1970 German Grand Prix at Hockenheim, Jochen Rindt in his 72 towed Fittipaldi's 49 for three or four laps. The Brazilian observed how well the 72 put the power down coming out of the chicane. Rindt had to keep lifting to allow the 49 to keep up.

That year at Monza during practice Fittipaldi's 72 was so new that, he was to observe, it still wasn't really finished when it got to the track. After about three laps with no front wing, Chapman called him in to take off the rear wing as well. Not knowing the car at all, he agreed. He was still bedding in the brakes and didn't at this stage know the braking points yet. As a result he had an accident at the Parabolica. However, at his next race, the US GP, he declared he very much liked the car. It was not very forgiving but he could drive it on the limit.

In 1972 Fittipaldi wrote that the car was superior, or at least equal, to the McLarens, Tyrrells and Ferraris of that time. He observed that it scored particularly well under braking and in putting the power down coming out of the corners.

RIGHT: Emerson Fittipaldi on the grid for the 1973 Race of Champions. 'I had the confidence I could drive it 110%.' *(Author)*

ABOVE: **The Lotus 72 is burnt into John Miles' memory.** *(Ford)*

John Miles

A major feature of the Lotus 72 at launch was its anti-dive and anti-squat, aimed at eliminating pitch under braking and acceleration. This was achieved by inclining the front and rear suspension mounting points upwards, thus pointing longitudinal thrust vectors towards the car's centre of gravity. John Miles, as main tester for the 72's early development (Rindt appeared little interested in testing), as well as one of the two drivers who raced it in this configuration (indeed, his car retained the anti-dive for a few races after both anti-dive and anti-squat had been removed from Rindt's), is ideally placed to explain why this turned out to be a bad idea. 'If only I knew then what I know now, I could have said at the design stage that this was madness, although I doubt that, as a young "whippersnapper", I'd have been taken notice of. We had to find out the hard way,' he recalled.

'This car is so burnt into my memory that I'll remember its early days for ever. Chapman is considered to be a genius, but there was a lot of stuff that he didn't know. Once he latched on to some breakthrough, there was no compromise ... He threw everything into it.

'Apart from its fragility, the prime reason for the car not performing in Spain and at the Silverstone International Trophy was, as is well known, the extreme amount of anti-dive and anti-squat. As I said, the objective was to eliminate pitch completely under braking and acceleration, but you rarely get something for nothing in a suspension system. Looking back, it surprises me that Chapman and Phillippe hadn't thought hard enough about the negative influences of such extreme measures.

'The car has in-board brakes. Because the braking is via the driveshaft, the deceleration forces appear at hub height, which means that the car could have had parallel suspension (as it subsequently did) and still have a considerable amount of anti-dive acting on the centre of gravity, whereas outboard brakes would imply ground-level deceleration forces acting on the mass and a thus a bigger pitching moment.

'On paper it was a very elegant design, except for this massive amount of anti-dive. The top arm was inclined down at the front by about 12°. Once you get to 100%+ anti-dive, you could, when braking at over 1.0g, momentarily take the front springs off the car, because what you're doing is jacking the front up via the angled linkage. In effect you have no suspension. Down a straight the car would feel quite normal, but when you put the brakes on the body was completely locked, with no resilience in the suspension and no feel. The tyre contact patch wants to be connected to a suspension system, not to a jack. As soon as you put the brakes on the front felt like it was on stilts.

'A further issue regarding anti-dive is that you drag the hub centre forward when braking, especially when it's done by leaning the top arm forward. This drags the tyre's contact patch with it, which means that you not only have "rigid" suspension, but you're accelerating the body rearwards, producing a high transient load at the contact patch, which in turn doesn't favour smooth breakaway.

'As soon as you put the brakes on you were either skidding at the front with no feel and smoke coming off the tyres, or you were slowing down but not conscious of much braking bite. Front wheel locking was so sudden that you couldn't modulate the brake pressure to bring back traction.

'There was also the rising rate torsion bar suspension system, again designed to inhibit pitching and the need for bump stops. It was very clever but very fussy to set up. Having included this feature in the design one wonders why Chapman went to the extreme antis.

'In essence, the rear end behaved in a similar manner as the front due to the extreme anti-squat. When you put the power down the rear suspension felt "locked", because most if not all the pitching resistance due to rearward weight transfer was going through the angled suspension linkage, not the springs. Throttle up, and the rear suspension simply went "rigid", with poor traction and feel.

'After the *Daily Express* Silverstone meeting there was a lot of frantic activity to make the front and rear suspension "parallel". The front end was a major carve-up and modifications had to be done in stages between GPs. There were some very good fabricators at Team Lotus who were working day and night. It was frantic all that season and was still so at Monza, where the guys were absolutely exhausted, plus they had to deal with a third car for Emerson. From where I stood it seemed rather chaotic.

'The brake shaft failure I had in Austria the weekend before Monza threw me across the road. Then came Jochen's accident at Monza. You can never say for certain that a right-hand brake shaft broke, causing Jochen to turn left into the barrier before the Parabolica, but I don't know what else could have caused such a violent movement. I certainly don't believe Jochen would have lost control in such a major way without a breakage because his driving was of such a high calibre.'

Chapman had instructed Miles to drive the Type 72 without the wings at the end of Friday practice. As far as Miles was concerned, the car was undrivable. 'We had no idea what the aero balance was. I got to the Curve Grande on my first lap and the thing just snapped into

BELOW: Miles in practice for the Spanish Grand Prix, where 72/1 appeared in its original specification. *(Sutton Images)*

oversteer. I then just cruised round to the pits. Having had the bust-up with Chapman about running with no wings, I could see the writing on the wall.

'The Lotus 72 was like a difficult, troublesome child that grew into a high-achieving person. The soundness of the basic concept was proven by the length of time that it was raced as a competitive car. I dare say that if you drove a 72 in 1973 it was equally well sorted as the 49 was when I drove it in South Africa.

'I never really became part of the Formula One circus. Once you were in a Formula One Lotus, your destiny was in Chapman's hands, and there seemed something rash about the Lotus approach to F1 at the time. But overall I had a great time, especially when I was left to my own devices in Formula 3, sports cars, and even in the Lotus 63 4WD Grand Prix car, because nobody else wanted to drive it until it was wet at Watkins Glen. I didn't think it was quite as bad as other people thought, until more and more drive torque went to the rear axle, which simply made it into an awful rear-wheel-drive car!'

BELOW: Reine Wisell explains the Type 72's handling at Zandvoort. *(Ford)*

Reine Wisell

'At the time I drove it, the Lotus 72 was outstanding,' recalled Reine Wisell. 'But there was a lack of money and the team preferred to give everything to Emerson. In 1971, they sold my car [to Dave Charlton], I was told to drive the turbine and I said something to Colin Chapman, which he didn't like.

'I had had experience of Formula One before I joined Lotus. I was offered a drive with McLaren before Bruce died. My first F1 outing was with them in the Silverstone International Trophy when I was fifth. Coming third in my first Grand Prix meant nothing really.

'At Watkins Glen in 1971 I said that I had no brakes before the race but I was still sent out. After pumping up pressure in some of the corners there was no pressure left. I managed to put the car into the barriers at a good angle and walked back. The driver was nothing, it was the constructors championship that mattered.'

'When Colin called me up at the end of 1972 to drive again in Canada and America I was under contract to Marlboro and he was with John Player and it was a big mess. He gave me that [second] chance. However, I was critical of Emerson Fittipaldi as a teammate. During one practice my car was called into the pits and the wheels taken off until Emerson set a quicker lap. When Emerson then left and went to McLaren, Colin asked if I would team up with Ronnie Peterson for 1973 and I said no. He was very surprised. I don't think anyone had said no to him. I'd lost too many friends, and I'd lost interest.'

In 1996 Wisell was reunited with 72/3 at Anderstorp. Michael Schryver had entered the car for a Thoroughbred Grand Prix event there, and during a preview for the local press the Swede drove the car for around ten laps, wearing, recalled Simon Hadfield, his old overalls. 'The car was just like it was at the beginning of the 1971 season,' said Wisell.

Tony Trimmer

Tony Trimmer, who drove one of the factory Lotus 73 Formula Three cars in 1972, carried out extensive testing of the 72 on Lotus's own track at Hethel that year. Much of this was aerodynamic work and he has vivid memories of driving the car to which numerous tufts of 'knitting wool' had been taped. 'Alongside ran another car with a cameraman recording what the airflow was doing. The days of the wind tunnel were still to come.'

These were, as Trimmer recalled, the early days of the 72 and, he said, 'it still had a rather prehistoric wing. Nevertheless, it was extremely quick in a straight line and, with its inboard front brakes, it was absolutely fabulous under braking. I was also impressed by its straight-line stability. These were the places that it shone. Its handling was also up to par for its day but it was in these three areas it had an advantage.'

Like Fittipaldi, Trimmer went on to drive a McLaren M23, but unlike the Brazilian he preferred this to the 72. 'As far as I'm concerned the McLaren was an exceptional car, but then it probably suited my style of driving. The 72 also improved in the years after I'd driven it.'

Trimmer was only to race the 72 at the

ABOVE: It may be that Ronnie Peterson is asking fellow Swede Reine Wisell what the Lotus 72 is like to drive at the 1971 Race of Champions. Two years later he would find out. *(Ford)*

BELOW: Tony Trimmer tested the Type 72 but raced it only once, at the 1971 Race of Champions. *(Ford)*

Brands Hatch Race of Champions. He was also entered for the German Grand Prix at Hockenheim. David Walker was scheduled to drive the 56B turbine car at that event but blew up the turbine at the back of the circuit – right in front of Trimmer, showering him with red hot bits of turbine blade. What was worse for Trimmer was that Walker then took over his 72 for the race. 'A shame,' he recalled, 'as practice had indicated this to be my best performance so far.' Trimmer was to try and qualify for a further six Grands Prix at the wheel of the Maki and the privately-entered Surtees and McLaren of Melchester Racing, but Hockenheim with the 72 was probably the nearest that he got to a World Championship grid. Today, though, he can proudly point to the fact that 1972 was the season that Fittipaldi became World Champion and that he helped with the development of the car that year.

Brian Henton

'By the time I got the 72 it was five years out of date,' said Brian Henton. 'Chapman tested about 20 drivers. My forte was an ability to translate to the engineer or designer what was happening with the cars. I got in the car at Silverstone. There had been about three or four people before me telling him how good it was. When I returned to the pits he asked me how good I thought it was. "To be honest Colin, it's the biggest heap of shit I've ever driven."

'"You're the man for me," he said. "You've got the drive."

'The Lotus 72 had been a fantastic car and had won World Championships. There was probably no other car in history that had that longevity. What was really the death knell of the 72 was when the tyre on Mark Donohue's Penske-entered March exploded in Austria. Goodyear was then faced with a product liability problem in the States. Overnight it changed the construction of the tyres to a very stiff radial, which may have been fantastic on the cars that didn't have sophisticated suspension like the Marches, but it made the Lotus 72 into an also-ran. No matter what we did, even changing to conventional front spring suspension, we couldn't get the temperatures of the tyres up and thus more grip. If only I could have got hold of a Lotus 72 three years earlier.'

Living near Donington, Henton had often been roped in to test various Formula One cars. It was long before the days of test drivers being employed on the team. Thus he was able to compare the Lotus 72 to a number of its competitors. 'The thing that made the 72 stand out was the fact that its steering was so light. In terms of physical effort it was very easy to drive. The problem that we had, though, when I was racing it, was that it had very low grip levels because it couldn't really work the tyres. My number one, Ronnie Peterson – one of the best drivers of his era – was fighting for lowly places on the grid. The trouble was we were overdriving it. The lowest point was in Austria. Ronnie crashed in practice and took the spare, and I then crashed when Mario Andretti blew his Ferrari's engine and I hit his oil. That meant we only had one car left for the race.

'I remember going to Snetterton with a massive load of bits – front suspensions, rear suspensions, different wings – and bolting them all on, just trying to mask the problem that we had with the tyres.'

Henton's first Grand Prix was the rain-affected and ultimately chaotic race at Silverstone, where his car had coil springs in place of the torsion bars. 'At one time in the British Grand Prix I thought I was doing quite well. Then it was the most bizarre thing that I've ever seen. I got down to Stowe and then started spinning all the way from Stowe to the next corner, Club, passing about five cars stuffed in the bank and watching James Hunt running for his life, as I got nearer and nearer. Then there was the inevitable crunch as I went into the barriers, and I thought, "If only I could have made it round Club I might have even been on the podium." Henton was actually a couple of laps back when the red flags came out, but as nine of the cars classified ahead of him weren't actually running at the finish you see his point.

'In America, Ronnie drove the race of his life and got me the biggest bollocking from Peter Warr. During the race I'd received a sign saying "Scheckter – Hold". You didn't have to be a mind-reader to realise that Scheckter was coming round in front of Ronnie and they wanted me to hold him up as they came to lap me. I did for a lap, which was quite a long time at Watkins Glen. At the reception after the race Peter Warr had a real go at me for holding up Scheckter. I almost fell off my chair. "You told me to," I said. "No I didn't," he replied. "Then why did you put that sign out?"

'Seven days later it was announced that Peter Warr was to join Wolf Racing, and who would their driver be the next season? Jody Scheckter.'

Historic racing

The surge of interest in historic racing brought a number of Lotus 72s back into competition. In 1992 Michael Schryver won the then Thoroughbred Grand Prix Championship with 72/3. However, such is the understanding of their value and their place in history that, although one did race towards the end of 2011, it was possible that none would race the following year.

Among those who raced a Lotus 72 in the days when it was more common to do so was Sean Walker, a former BRDC Silver Star winner who has enjoyed a career in a wide variety of modern single-seater and sports cars as well as historic machinery, and is one of the very few privileged people to have raced a Lotus 72 – and not just any 72. Walker has family ties with the Chapmans, as his father, Ian, ran one of the most successful independent Lotus entrants of the late 1950s and early 1960s and was a close friend of Colin. At one point Ian Walker Racing was entrusted with the running of the factory Lotus 30 sports car.

Walker senior was talking to John Player about possible sponsorship shortly before he decided to close his team, and suggested to Chapman that he might like to pursue the company. The result was the Gold Leaf livery that first adorned the Lotus 49s and also,

BELOW: Brian Henton told Colin Chapman exactly what he thought of the 1975 Lotus 72. *(Sutton Images)*

ABOVE: Sean Walker now heads FAI Automotive, the automotive parts supplier established by his father, Ian. *(Author)*

during their first two seasons, the type 72s. It was therefore fitting that his son should be given the opportunity to race 72E/5, one of the most famous of all the 72s and still in the possession of the Chapman family.

When Ian and Sean heard that Clive Chapman was to launch Classic Team Lotus, they thought, as Sean put it, 'to complete the circle a little'. The result was that they acquired a Lotus 87B, and during 1994 and 1995 Sean contested 12 races, winning five. The car was sold at the end of 1995 but Sean was later to shake down Classic Team Lotus' Type 49 and Type 77, the latter being that which Mario Andretti used to win the 1976 Japanese Grand Prix in monsoon conditions. It also poured with rain when Sean drove it, but thankfully it had been restored with exactly the same settings as the day it triumphed at Fuji. Clive Chapman then asked him if he was interesting in racing in Historic Formula One again, but this time in the collection's running 72.

In 2001 the car had just been rebuilt, nothing having been done to it for some considerable time. Invited to 'do a few laps at Hethel', Walker was understandably hooked. 'It was far too good to not want to go out and do something in it. The whole day was very special. It was quite emotional.

'Getting into a car of that period is much easier than into a modern car. It's a bit like getting into an armchair, because there's more room. You next fiddle about with the mirrors. Starting is simply a matter of the master switch and then pressing the start button. At the start I stuck out a little too much and was being buffeted a bit, so we had to adjust the pedals.'

There was no further testing before the car was entered for a race at Silverstone, where there were 'a few niggling problems'. As Walker left the pits he felt the clutch slipping. As a result he held back off the start line, a wise move as the clutch now failed. In doing so, he avoided a massive accident when the leaders collided at the first bend.

That was it until a couple of years later when Clive Chapman suggested that Sean drive 72E/5 in the Monaco Historic Grand Prix. While jumping at the chance, Walker also suggested that they take in an event beforehand to iron out any potential problems. The ideal would be a twisty circuit that could perhaps ape Monte Carlo's confines. A round of the Historic Formula One championship taking place at Jarama in Spain seemed a good bet. The car went well in qualifying against far more modern machinery, and Sean was up to about seventh or eighth when unfortunately a throttle cable broke. 'The car felt great, fantastic. We didn't have to do many changes to it.' For a circuit with tight, twisty corners it seemed ideal, being much softer than a modern car. One of the things that you want out of a tight corner is great traction, and being relatively soft the 72 was, said Walker, ideal. It would be the same for Monte Carlo.

At Monaco the car was number one on the entry list, which meant the team had the first bay in the paddock. As far as Walker was concerned that meant they had no excuse not to be first out on the track. Having never raced round Monte Carlo before, he still finished the first practice in third place. Eddie Dennis, Team Lotus chief mechanic during most of the 72's time as a Grand Prix car, was working on the car, which Walker describes as 'a huge buzz'. (Dennis had already assisted Walker with his Type 87.) In the second session, 72E/5 had a problem with its metering unit, meaning that Walker was unable to put in a 'decent' lap. This was solved by the end of the session, but he was now down to fourth fastest.

Many historic Formula Ones use 'modern' short-stroke Cosworth DFV engines. However, Clive Chapman is a traditionalist and 72E/5 is fitted with a long-stroke engine built to the same specification as it would have been in the 1970s. That meant the car was probably giving away 45–50bhp to the other front-runners. It was only after practice that Walker learnt this. 'Eddie then told me not to beat myself up about not getting on to the front row because we were giving away so much,' because around Monaco in an historic car this was unlikely to make much difference.

'We lined up on the outside of the second row with high hopes,' recalled Walker. However, heading up towards Casino Square on the green-flag lap 'the electrics went'. All that had happened was that a fuse on the dash had popped out. Had Walker understood this he could have easily restarted the car.

Classic Team Lotus team manager Chris Dinnage said to Sean: 'I punched the fuse back in and it started first time. I don't know what's wrong with the car.'

'Could you repeat the first bit?' asked Walker.

He had thought it might have been the master switch so turned this on and off but had no idea about the fuses. 'It was just the fuse, and all I had to do was push it back in.'

Walker was to drive the car one more time, in a four-lap demonstration at Brands Hatch a few years later. Martin Donnelly was demonstrating a Type 79, and Damon Hill what had been his father's Type 49; illustrious company. There were also some amateur owner-drivers, and one of these, disregarding the instructions given at the drivers' briefing, had decided to do an extra lap. In doing so he hit the 72's front wheel and launched his car into the air. Luckily the only damage to the 72 was to the corner, but Sean recalled it could have been so much worse.

'The 72 is one of, if not the most iconic-looking of Formula One cars. I've driven six Grand Prix cars, including a later shakedown in the Classic Team Lotus 79, but it's the 72 that people remember when I talk about them, if only to say that they owned a Corgi toy "John Player Special". Even if they know little about Formula One, they know this car.

'I had a huge feeling of anticipation and privilege before getting into the car, but it was a warm feeling, it just felt right. It didn't disappoint. Within the first lap of driving the car it was just right. Sometimes when you're driving a car for the first time it takes a few laps to get to understand it. But within a lap the 72 was friendly; it was not going to bite.

'This may sound bizarre, but it reminded me of when I first started racing in Formula Ford. It felt just like a big Formula Ford, so it didn't feel daunting or frightening.' The last FF that Walker raced was a Van Diemen RF78, 'and it just felt like a more powerful version of that.' (Dave Baldwin, a director of Van Diemen in 1978, was a draughtsman at Team Lotus during the early days of the Type 72, and in the little Van Diemen can perhaps be imagined the lines of the earlier Grand Prix car.)

'It was a very friendly car, very forgiving. It has no vices and it did everything that you wanted it to do. It turned in well; you could put the power down. If the rear did break out it was easy to bring back in. There's no wonder that the car did so well for so long. If I hadn't driven the Type 79 a few years later I'd have said that it was the best Lotus that I'd driven. The only time I raced it properly – at Jarama – it proved itself good in a racing situation. You could place it very quickly without getting an adverse reaction. It was great if you were following somebody and wanted to dive out and out-brake them.'

BELOW: The close ties between Colin Chapman and Ian Walker make it particularly appropriate for the latter's son, Sean, to have raced 72E/5 in historic events. *(Sutton Images)*

'Not for them the mundane routine.'

Peter Warr
Team Manager,
Team Lotus 1969–89

Chapter Four

The mechanic's view

The type 72 was, for many of the hardworking Team Lotus mechanics, perhaps the most significant car that they were to work on. For their successors, who prepare the cars today, the pressure may be less, but there is still the same attention to detail. High-level servicing and pre-race preparations are essential to the 72s' future if the fans are to be able to continue to enjoy them.

(Sutton Images)

Two mechanics per car would be taken to each Grand Prix plus another mechanic for the spare car. In addition there would be the chief mechanic. A truck driver would also be available as to assist. The rest of the team at the racetracks would be the two drivers, the team manager – which was Peter Warr during the period in question – and Chapman himself.

There were three chief mechanics at Team Lotus during the Type 72's time, with Eddie Dennis the longest serving. Gordon Huckle, the first person ever to drive a 72, held the post during the 1970 season, having joined Team Lotus in 1966. He worked on Jim Clark's Lotus 49 and then the Type 62 sports car as driven by John Miles. He returned to the Formula One team for Rindt's championship year before standing down due to understandable exhaustion. During that year the regular mechanics for the two cars were Dennis, Herbie Blash (now an FIA observer), Derek Mower and Dave Sims.

Dennis took over from Huckle for 1971, with Mower and Sims leaving after the first two races to be replaced by Steve Gooda and Jim Pickles. While these worked on Fittipaldi's car, Rex Hart and Mike Coughtree were assigned to Reine Wisell's. They were joined later in the season by Stevie May. The following season Gooda and Pickles continued with the Brazilian, aided after the US Grand Prix by Trevor Seaman. Hart and May were assigned to Dave Walker.

A shuffling around of the mechanics at the start of 1973 saw Keith Leighton and Yoshuatsu Itoh join the Formula One squad. Leighton took over from Dennis as chief mechanic for the 1974 season. The pressures of working for Team Lotus meant that Leighton left during the Monaco Grand Prix and Dennis – in Monte Carlo as a spectator – found himself back in his old role, a position he retained until the demise of the 72. In all, about two dozen Team Lotus mechanics attended on the Lotus 72 at the racetracks between 1970 and 1975. The car, they're reported to have said, was 'a complex sod to work on'.

BELOW: Type 72s and the 56B receive attention in the paddock at the 1971 British Grand Prix. *(Ford)*

TEAM LOTUS FORMULA ONE MECHANICS 1970–75

Graham Bartels	Keith Leighton
Arthur Birchall	Stevie May
Michael 'Herbie' Blash	Derek Mower
Dougie Bridge	Jim Pickles
Ian Campbell	John Robinson
Bobby Clark	Trevor Seaman
Mike Coughtree	Dave Sims
Ian Dawson	Ake Stranberg
Eddie Dennis	Glen Waters
Dougie Garner	
Steve Gooda	*Truckies*
Rex Hart	Vic McCarthy
Gordon Huckle	Nick Norman
Yoshuatsu Itoh	

ABOVE: Team Lotus mechanics at work on a Type 72 in a pit garage at the Nürburgring, 1973. *(Sutton Images)*

BELOW: Eddie Dennis (right) and the mechanics class of 1971. Left to right: Stevie May, Dougie Bridge, Rex Hart, Mike Coughtree and Steve Gooda. *(Ford)*

Eddie Dennis

'I was never apart from the Lotus 72,' recalled Eddie Dennis. 'It was more complicated for sure with its torsion bars and inboard brakes, which were time-consuming to work on. The front torsion bars were particularly difficult to work on because they were tucked inside where the fuel tanks were. In later years when the car had a deformable structure, that made it even more difficult. You had a small amount of range before you had to take the torsion bar out and rotate it to get a different angle on the links. The rear torsion bars were much easier to work on. In the early days we didn't know which torsion bars to use – we had a range of about four or five. They were fitted the wrong way round the first time and the car was getting lower and lower to the ground!

'When the car was first launched it wasn't finished. We got stuck at the border when heading for the Spanish Grand Prix as we had the wrong carnets – we were stuck in limbo at Customs. We unloaded the cars in the compound, where we went on building them.

'When we first started, the car had hardly done a race before it was changed. As with all things, we had to find our way along. The set-up of the rear suspension was totally different to what you might call a normal car, such as

RIGHT: Peter Warr, seen here in 1971, first worked for Lotus Engineering in 1958. In 1969 he returned to Lotus to be team manager, his tenure of office including the era of the Type 72. A period with Walter Wolf Racing followed, but by 1981 he was back with Chapman, holding the team together in the immediate years following the death of its founder. *(Ford)*

FAR RIGHT Eddie Dennis was Team Lotus chief mechanic for much of the Type 72's five-year career. *(Ford)*

the Type 49. We used ¼in bolts, which went through the wishbone, because "the Old Man" (Chapman) never wanted to see a ½in bolt on a racing car. They finished up ⅜in, sleeved down to go through the small rose joints.

'There were problems as to where the battery was to be fitted, whether it should be underneath the driver's legs or in the nose of the car. In the early days there were also problems with the oil tanks pumping oil out in the catch tank. These sort of things always reared themselves at the circuit. Another trouble-spot was the CV joints, which overheated. We had to grind the cage to relieve the load. However, it wasn't all doom and gloom by any means.

'I think the drivers found 72s quite comfortable. They were fairly roomy, compared to some of the other cars. I had the opportunity to drive a variety of Lotuses including the 72. We would be blasting the car up and down the main straight. On one run a reel of paper used for one of the test recording machines came adrift and flowed from the car as it sped along! We also used to drive the cars to the garage at Clermont-Ferrand and sit in them at the traffic lights.

RIGHT: Preparing the Lotus 72 of eventual winner Ronnie Peterson in the paddock at the Osterreichring in 1973. *(Sutton Images)*

EDDIE DENNIS NOTES PIT LANE AND PADDOCK CHANGES THAT COULD BE MADE TO A LOTUS 72 DURING A PRACTICE SESSION:

- 'There was always a need to find a flat surface for set-up changes. We had no travelling set-up pads like they have nowadays.
- 'The ride height was critical, proving that some things never change. The rising rate changed with ride height, but this could be adjusted by changing the length of the torsion bar link. Shortening the link increased the wheel rate, but would also change ride height, but then we'd correct for this by adjusting torsion bar stops ($9/16$in Allen bolts). If changing the length of the torsion bar link couldn't sufficiently change the wheel rate, then the torsion bars had to be changed for ones of a different rate (we colour-coded these). It was difficult to do so at the front due to their running through the fuel cell area. The torsion bars were more accessible at the rear. Care had to be taken over kerbs, as the rear torsion bar link could project below the plane of the undertray. The lowest part of car had to be the undertray according to the rules, but the torsion bar actuator arm was cranked so as to avoid the rear damper, and during suspension travel this could drop below the level of the undertray.
- 'The anti-roll bars were very easy to work on. As the front was, initially, non-adjustable, we'd have to change whole bar. There were various positions on the rear bar for the drop link in order to adjust the amount of anti-roll stiffness.
- 'We started with Girling dampers, but then switched to Konis later on. These were bigger, but no extra space was provided for them. The Konis were adjusted via top and bottom adjusters (bump and rebound). The Girlings just had six notches of bump adjustment on a knob at the bottom of the damper barrel.
- 'The toe-in was adjusted in virtually the same as with any modern-day car, with track rods front and rear, which were fairly accessible at both ends. At the rear you'd also get a touch of camber change as a result of a toe change.
- 'The camber was adjusted by winding the outer rod ends on the wishbones in or out. At the front a double-threaded collar on later versions made carrying this out very much easier.
- 'There wasn't a lot that you could do with the front caster, which was pre-set at around 1.5° to 2.5°. This did, though, make the car easier to drive. Inboard brakes also made for less of a handling problem.
- 'We'd sometimes change gear ratios during a session. The cam and pawl diff wasn't tunable at the track, though, and required careful rebuilds at the shop.
- 'We didn't lose much oil or water during a race. The water system was pressurised only by a 13psi rated filler cap; there was no header tank as such, just a long vertical filler pipe on the cross pipe linking the heads on the back of the engine. I notice that some of the 72s running now have a swirl pot and header tank to help reliability.'

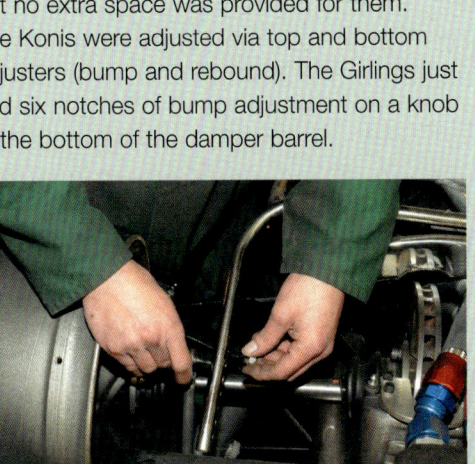

LEFT: A rigging bar sited across the front tyres of Ronnie Peterson's 72 at Interlagos in 1974. *(Sutton Images)*

BELOW LEFT: The rear anti-roll bar is easy to work on. *(Author)*

BELOW: Mechanic Stevie May (right) appears thoughtful, as does Dave Walker. *(Ford)*

ABOVE: **Eddie Dennis at Hethel in 2012. In the background is Bob Dance, another legendary Lotus mechanic, albeit one that didn't work on the Type 72.** *(Author)*

'I had a reasonably good rapport with Jochen Rindt. He'd do a bit of testing but then he'd get bored. He'd learnt his driving as he went along, while John Miles was more of a technical man. John was pushed to the back a bit because he was slower than Rindt, by a fair margin at times, but then John was a much more careful guy. You had to respect him when Jochen was killed and he said he couldn't go on.

'Emerson Fittipaldi was mature for his years. He wasn't a do-or-die driver, or someone who was going to fly off. He stepped into Jochen's shoes quite easily, although he was fortunate when he won the US Grand Prix. He didn't pass a single car – they all just fell by the wayside – but he brought his car home. I think he was using the engine from Jochen's car at Monza. It was a "special" engine with some of the best bits, and we managed to get it out before the car was impounded. Emerson reckoned that engine had a "big smile on its face".

'There were troubles when Ronnie Peterson arrived. Emerson's nose was put out of joint and he was concerned that information about his car was being given to Peterson. However, "the Old Man" wanted such information to be shared between the two. Towards the second half of the season Ronnie started to come to the fore, and Emerson's then wife, Maria Helena, accused me of giving the best engines to Ronnie. I don't think I was able to convince her otherwise. It had taken Ronnie about half a season to get used to the car. Such a lovely guy; he would come and talk to you at ten o'clock at night. He just liked to talk to mechanics; he enjoyed their company.

'When I became chief mechanic in 1971 I didn't get the chief mechanic's pay until I'd done about half of the season, and then I had to start on the last person's salary.'

Dennis' stint as chief mechanic should have ended with the 1973 season. However, Ken Leighton, his replacement for 1974, didn't last the season so he returned to the post to finish that year off. 'I'd done three years, and that was a life sentence when you worked for "the Old Man". However, I came back for a full season in 1975 and the following year was put in charge of research and development at Ketteringham Hall.'

Dennis recalls the state of exhaustion that would overcome him and the other Team Lotus mechanics. 'There was a time when Herbie Blash started to shake in Madrid. We just had to carry him, put him in the front of the truck and cover him with blankets. At the same race I went to get something to eat. The next thing I knew I was in the corner of the garage. I didn't know how I go there. I don't think you'd get anybody to do that sort of work nowadays.'

Derek Mower

Derek 'Joe 90' Mower and Dave 'Beaky' Sims (the Lotus mechanics were known for their sobriquets – Dennis was known as 'Jake') were the two mechanics for John Miles's Lotus 72 in 1970 and then Reine Wisell's car for the final two races of the year. They also worked together on the Swede's car during the start of the season, before Mower was persuaded by Mario Andretti – with whom he'd worked when the American had raced a factory Lotus 49 on three occasions in 1969 – to join Vel's Parnelli Jones Racing in the USA. Lotus 72 designer Maurice Phillippe had already left to work for VPJ. They weren't the only Lotus refugees to join the company: engineers John Baldwin, Dick Scammell and Sid Carr also added to the team's predominately English make-up at about this time.

'We all helped to build the cars as well,' recalled Mower. 'Because the factory-based fabrication section was small, the Formula One mechanics were also required to help build the chassis and a substantial amount of the suspension.'

Mower remembered some of the trials and tribulations. 'One big problem was the torsion bars. They didn't have the mathematical process to accurately work out which torsion bar they wanted to run. They were a sod to change. We also had a problem when the car was too wide. I remember working all night trying to narrow up the pods, as we'd run foul of the overall width measurement. It diluted the amount of engineering that we could do as we were too busy making it legal. There was another incident when the tie-wraps that held the oil pipes together on Jackie Stewart's car ended up in Emerson's radiator duct – they'd got hot, broken, and blown into our car. We changed the front bulkhead several times because of the anti-dive. The rivets got bigger and bigger every time because the holes got bigger. It was so much work, but it was a lovely car, though.

'At Monza we had a super engine that would pull a longer gear. With no wings the thing was a missile. After Rindt's crash, Denny Hulme reported that "he'd gone past me like I was painted on the road". That wasn't what caused the accident. That seems almost certainly to have been a broken brake shaft, although this wasn't proven. We loaded everything up except the car. We got into the truck and hightailed it to the border. We got stopped once and the chap looked in the back of the truck. I think he was looking for Jochen's car.

'At Spa we worked all day at the racetrack and then all night at a garage in Malmedy. We were staying in a lovely old house across the road. Beaky, Eddie and I were all in one room. One night Beaky woke me, saying: "90, 90, look at Jake." He was at the foot of his bed on his knees, working on it as if it was a car. We asked him what he was doing, and he said, "Adjusting the roll bar." And this was all in his sleep! We were that exhausted.'

'That weekend Beaky also collapsed. Chapman said, "Quick, put him in the truck. Don't let anyone see him." We did as ordered and he slept for the rest of the day.

'By the end of the season we were totally washed out. We'd been working full-on, 20 hours a day, seven days a week. Tiredness could result in some hair-raising moments returning from the circuits. The axle weights of the truck were likely to be in excess of the legal limit, and as a result they blew Firestones on a regular basis. One sunny afternoon, returning

LEFT: After his time with Team Lotus, Derek Mower left to join Maurice Phillippe in the United States. He enjoyed a long career there, returning to Europe to run a Formula 3000 team with his son Chris. *(Derek Mower collection)*

Ian Dawson

Ian Dawson joined John Player Team Lotus from the small racing car manufacturer Modus in the spring of 1975, the last year of the Type 72. Initially he ran Jacky Ickx's spare car. 'It was a bit of a shock. It was suffering front driveshaft failures and Ickx decided he didn't want to run any more. There was no doubt that the heyday of the 72 was over and that it had become a midfield-running car. Jacky went and I ended up running the second car for Jim Crawford, Brian Henton and John Watson.

'The problem, as I remember it, was that the Lotus 72 had basically lost its balance, and it didn't give the drivers any confidence. Technically the cars went during that year from coil springs, torsion bars, wide-track, long wheelbase; and did you move the engine from the tub, or did you move the gearbox from the engine? These things would appear on the job list. If it said "new front torsion bars" that meant taking the fuel tank out. You were probably faced with a 27-hour job list, and there weren't a lot of people at Team Lotus during this time. It was quite stressful. We worked massive hours, which is why some just went.

'Often the parts on the job list hadn't even been made, so they had to be made first. If you didn't have it you fabricated it in the truck.

ABOVE: There was nothing sophisticated in the way in which fuel was added to Grand Prix cars in the early 1970s. This shows Peterson's car at Zandvoort in 1973. *(Sutton Images)*

RIGHT: Ian Dawson moved on to endurance racing, entering a diesel car for the Le Mans 24-hours two years before Audi. *(Author)*

from a Grand Prix, I was driving while the rest of the crew were fast asleep. On the way up to Paris, we were crossing a long and extremely high viaduct when the front right tyre blew. The truck immediately veered to the right towards the very low barrier separating it from a long drop into the ravine below. I was now standing up, hanging on to the wheel and yelling at Eddie Dennis, who was sitting next to me. Eddie immediately arose from a deep sleep and also grabbed the steering wheel. We ground to a halt and made another wheel change.

'When we worked at Malmedy we used to drive the Formula One cars back from the pits – that's quite a long way. We used to come up to La Source hairpin and the brakes would be cold. There were several moments when there were almost shunts! It doesn't bear thinking about. It was a lot more work then, but a lot more fun.'

You'd be making a wide-track front suspension and heat-treating it in a bucket of oil.'

Dawson remembered that the car was in a state of constant change, both at the track and back at the factory. It was difficult to have a stable, two-car programme. Ronnie Peterson was becoming disillusioned and the drivers in the other car were constantly being changed.

'One thing that sticks in the mind is Jim Crawford in the pouring rain. He had some shoes with the right-foot toes cut out because he was so used to having them hooked behind the throttle pedal in case it stuck. Chapman asked him if it was the best clothes that he had and sent him off to the shops. He came back with new socks, new shoes, new underwear, observing, "That's the most anyone has ever spent on me!"'

Chapman also asked Crawford if he'd ever raced in the rain, only to be answered in the negative. 'So there he was at Monza in nearly monsoon weather in a Formula One car that he'd hardly driven before; definitely a baptism of fire.

'Crawford was just one of the boys. He was so easy to work with, but he was quick. He wasn't scared of anything. Then Brian Henton appeared; he was an interesting character to work with. He had a big shunt at the Osterreichring and then walked back into the paddock saying, "It's not too bad, you'll be able to fix that." It was like half the car was missing! Brian used to talk really loudly, leading Chapman to observe, "We don't need a radio with him."

'All Ronnie wanted to do was to have the car back where it was. After three days of testing, the car was put back and he went quicker than ever. On the last day he wanted to leave at lunchtime, proclaiming that the car was great. After he'd gone a photographer appeared with some shots that showed the Swede completely sideways round the back of the circuit. Chapman went mad, reckoning that the team had just wasted three days. That was Peterson – he'd drive anything. In the last race the Lotus 72 finished fifth, but that was a lot down to Ronnie's ability to drive it.

'The Lotus 72 was a hard car to work on. It was a battle, a lot of work with a mass of changes. You could lose track a bit. I had come out of Broadspeed [a leading tuner and saloon car entrant], where I'd been used to fabricating stuff, and Ralph Broad was a bit like Chapman, an extremely clever tyrant. It was an interesting period. It was a shame it was coming to an end.'

ABOVE: Spectators were able to watch as the Lotus 72s were fettled in the communal garages at the 1973 United States Grand Prix. *(Sutton Images)*

Typical between-race checks for a Lotus 72 in historic racing

In the 1970s a Lotus 72 would have been totally stripped between Grands Prix. Although a Type 72 may typically cover no more than 150 miles in an historic race meeting, it's still essential to carry out a thorough post-race check using a predetermined post-race check sheet. The example illustrated is that used by CGA Racing between the Nürburgring, Germany, and Portimao, Portugal, events in late 2011. A header gives the basic details, such as the fact that the car was Lotus 72/6, carrying the number 5, and the Cosworth engine was DFV0210LP. The tyres used were the standard Avons for this type of racing, and the driver was the car's owner, Katsu Kubota. The gear ratios in and out are also listed, as is the fuel situation. Fuel out in this case was four litres. Twenty litres were needed to run the car up, systems-check it and carry out the mechanical set-up. Filling 40 litres then set the team up for the Friday practice session, so there's no need to be concerned with that when it arrives in Portugal.

BELOW RIGHT: 72/6 has its own specific bay in CGA's Warrington workshops. *(Author)*

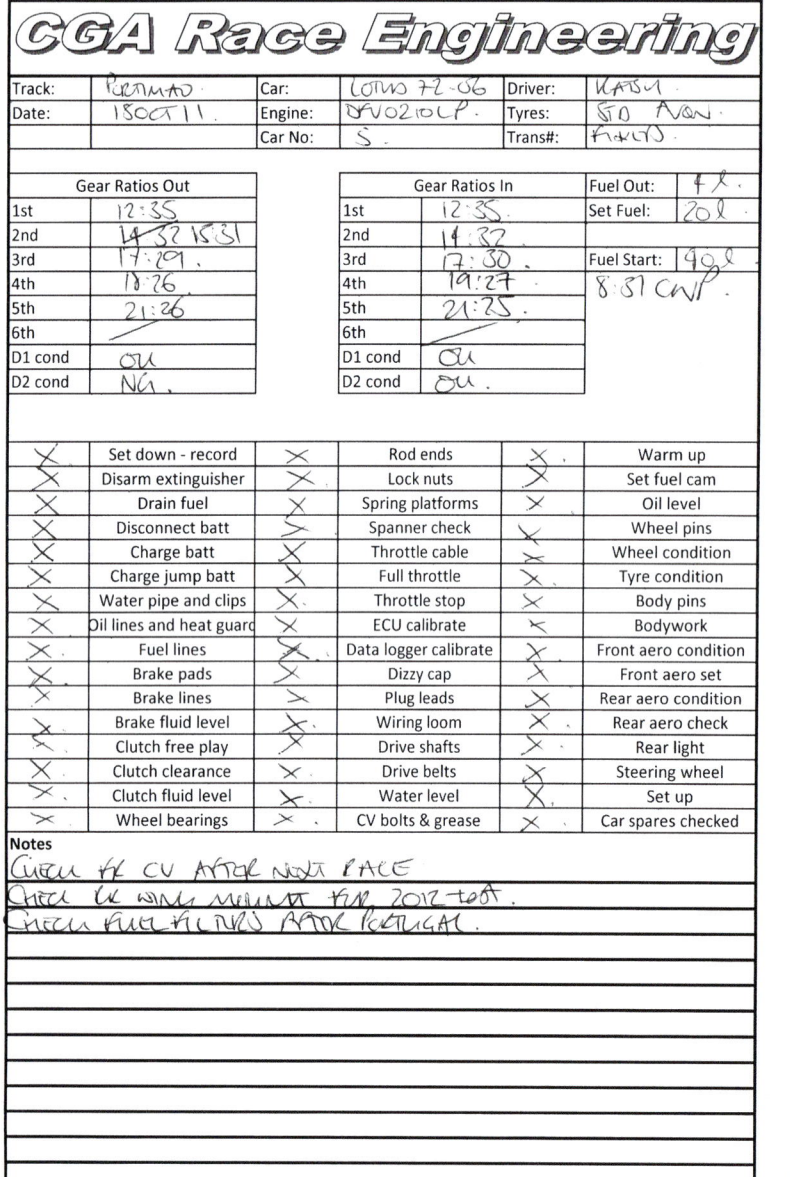

In terms of workshop practice, the 72/6 has its own specific bay within the Warrington workshop of the family concern, CGA Race Engineering, that prepared the car for Kubota. When it's stripped, it's stripped handed, left and right. Prior to its rebuild everything is directionally etched. 'It's definitely a labour intensive car, more than average,' said CGA's Alistair Bennett.

One of the critical elements of running the car will be its engine life and mileage, and close attention must be paid to this. This includes any special events that may have occurred in the previous race, such as being over-revved or overheated. The regulations permit the use of a simple data logger, which measures pressures and temperatures, to keep track of this. 'A good Cosworth will now cost between £80–85,000, so you have to be on top of them,' said Bennett.

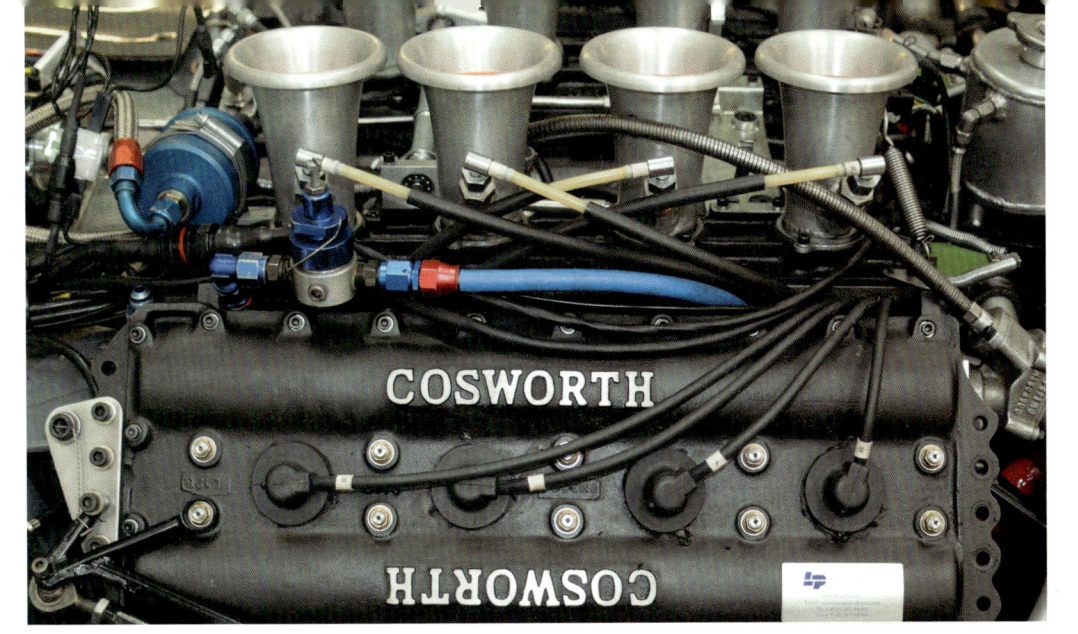

LEFT: Close attention must be paid to the engine between outings. *(Author)*

The team will carry out a 'set-down' when the car is rolled back off the truck. This enables it to monitor how the car might have changed during the previous race. Basically, this is the reverse of a set-up. The team will look at ride heights, corner weights, cambers, castors, toes, aero angles and trim. This then documents the changes that may have been made during the weekend and where the team may have deviated from any set plan.

This car requires a very high level of detail in terms of spanner checks whilst at the track. When it gets back to the workshop every nut and bolt that that can be accessed – over 95% of those on the car – has to be checked. Many of the bolts and fasteners are very highly stressed, and are consequently replaced as much as they possibly can be to maintain reliability. 'It does break stuff and shake stuff off. It rattles aircraft lock nuts loose. It transmits frequencies that will vibrate things off,' said Colin Bennett. 'Eddie Dennis said that for everything on the car you have to use lock nuts, lock wire and Loctite. There's a specific sub routine for the Lotus 72 that we don't do on any other car.'

Much of the work that should be carried out in the shop is relatively straightforward. However, MRO (maintenance, repair and overall) work has to be 'fantastically clean and organised. You need observational skills and ability to visually check what may have changed and try to understand why,' said Alistair. Typically, if you find a problem on the left-hand side you should

BELOW LEFT: The Type 72 required a particularly high level of spanner checks. *(Author)*

BELOW RIGHT: According to Eddie Dennis 'everything on the car' required lock nuts, lock wire and Loctite. *(Author)*

109

THE ENGINEER'S VIEW

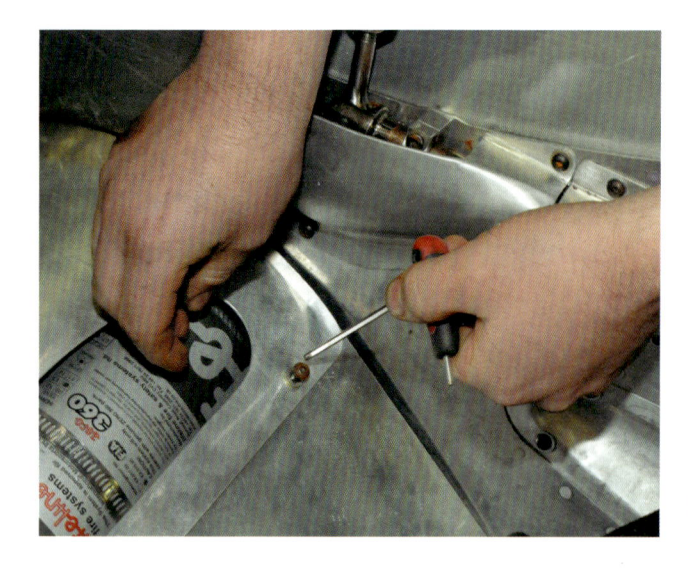

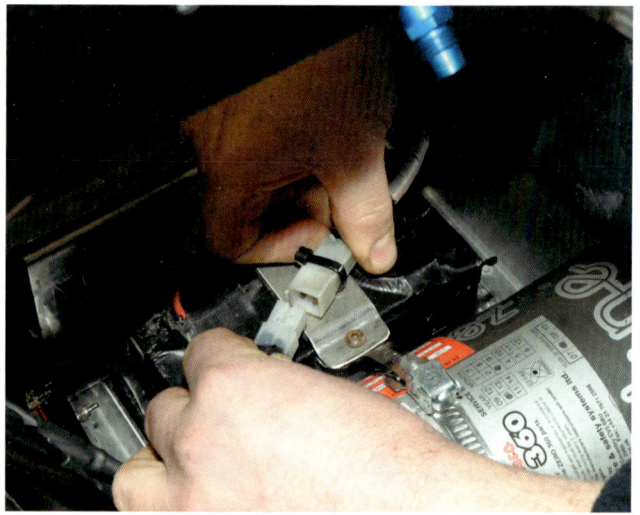

ABOVE LEFT: The fire extinguisher should be disarmed. Access is via a small panel under the driver's legs. *(Author)*

ABOVE RIGHT: Like the fire extinguisher, the battery – which should be disconnected – was moved to under the floor of the cockpit. *(Author)*

RIGHT: Close inspection should be made of the back of the radiator and the water system. *(Author)*

check its equivalent on the right. That's simply standard practice. Sixteen- or eighteen-inch stands are used to work on the car.

Initially, the fire extinguisher should be disarmed, the fuel drained out and the battery disconnected. The location of the fire extinguisher and battery on the Lotus 72 changed during its Grand Prix career but they were eventually both sited under the driver's legs. They live under a panel, with the battery the other side of a small bulkhead to the extinguisher. The battery should then be charged and left on a cycler. (With not many electrics to run, the battery is very small.) The jump battery should also be charged, a task that could easily be forgotten.

The mechanical checks should then be carried out. All the water pipes and clips are checked for condition. With the Type 72 there are aluminium water pipes, silicone hoses and clips that are located right in front of what will have been a large, hot, slick tyre, which may have been firing off stones and anything else that it may have run over. Therefore a close inspection should be made of the back of the radiator and all of the water system. You should look for any evidence of coolant weeping and check all the welds. A similar process should take place for oil lines and heat guards, except the oil system will typically feature fairly large diameter Aeroquip, in the case of 72/6, –12. This is heat-guarded from the tank, and tie-wrapped to keep it out of the way of the brake discs. If the heat guard goes missing the brake temperature can influence the oil temperature. Again, the condition of all the lines should be checked to see that none of them are frayed and there are no cracks. At the same time you should look to see that the lines haven't rubbed on anything else.

Checking the fuel lines is similar to the above. The fuel collector in the Lotus 72 is underneath the roll hoop, in between the driver and the engine. The much smaller type-6 hose should be examined – how it's picked up, whether it's touched anything or come loose.

The brake pads are easy to check. The pad level is determined by its thickness, as on a road car. The pistons should be examined for any contamination, cracks or heat marks. The cast iron brake disc check is also simple. Again look for any small surface cracks. Also look for cracks around drive pegs and mounting flanges. The brake and clutch fluid level are

against your clutch stop how much room you have. It's essential that the clutch doesn't go over centre, because it then won't return.

A standard turnaround won't require the wheel bearings to be stripped. 72/6 has sealed cartridge wheel bearings rather than roller tapers, and they're straightforward to service. With a wheel on and the car in the air you should try to rock the wheel bearings to see if there's any free play. Typically the wheel bearings will be replaced once a season, although spares should, naturally, be carried to the track because you can never predict when one may go wrong. Failure is usually caused by a special event, such as hitting a kerb hard.

Rose joints and rod ends are featured throughout the car. A simple lift and drop can check the condition of the rod ends. The lock nuts should be examined to see that they're all present, correct and tight.

It's difficult to adjust the front torsion bars once they've been installed, although the rears are relatively straightforward. There are access panels inside the chassis structure that can be removed to check that the circlips are still on the front torsion bars, as well as the muff couplings that couple the inner to the outer torsion bar.

The throttle cable, full throttle and throttle stop are all checked together. Make sure that

LEFT TOP: Checking the brake pads is a simple task. *(Author)*

LEFT MIDDLE: Brake and clutch cylinders are mounted on the front bulkhead. *(Author)*

BOTTOM LEFT: The rear torsion bars, by contrast, are relatively straightforward to adjust. *(Author)*

BELOW: A simple lift and drop can be used to check the condition of the rod ends. *(Author)*

BOTTOM RIGHT: Due to their location inside the chassis structure, the front torsion bars are difficult to adjust. This shows the rearward location inside the chassis. *(Author)*

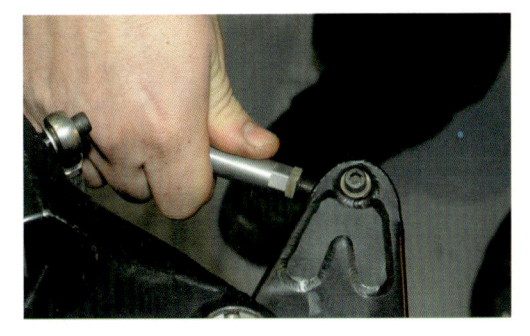

THE ENGINEER'S VIEW

ABOVE: ...and the water levels should be checked. Although a header tank wasn't installed during the 72's period racing career, CGA uses this safety-related modification to prevent water spilling out of the overflow in the event of the engine overheating. *(Author)*

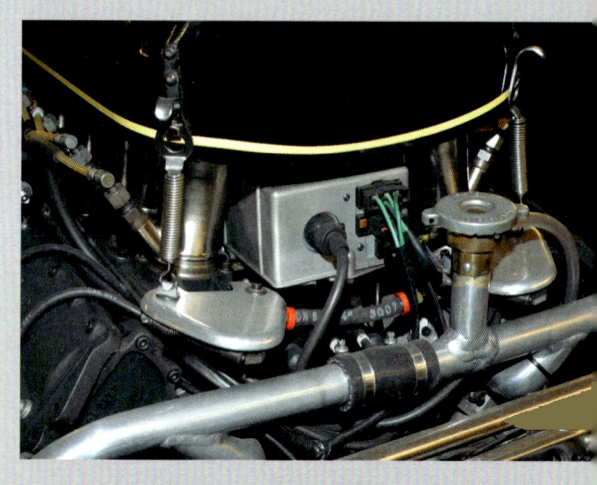

ABOVE: Prior to the engine being warmed up, the oil... *(Author)*

RIGHT: 72/8 is virtually as it was when it last raced, and therefore doesn't feature a header tank. *(Author)*

LEFT: The wheel pins should be checked. *(Author)*

RIGHT: The fuel cam is set with a small rod that has to be pushed in and turned to change the mixture setting. *(Author)*

the operation of the throttle cable is smooth and easy, and that its routeing hasn't changed. The cable is clipped in and routed underneath guttering on the right side of the cockpit. You should check that there's full throttle on the engine and against the stop, so that the tension isn't in the cable.

Although the engine will have come as a built item, the distributor cap, plug leads and wiring loom should still be checked – particularly if it's been wet, as the engine is open to the elements. The wiring loom is held under the opposite gutter to the wiring cable. Check that there's no chaffing, damage or movement, especially close to the contact points. As with any of these items, if there's anything wrong it should obviously be replaced.

The driveshafts should be visually checked to ensure that there are no cracks or marks. Every few races they should be removed and crack tested using magnetic particle inspection. This involves applying a magnetic field to the part. A fluid is then applied, the flux flows through the part and you can see if there's a crack. DPI (dye penetrant inspection) is also used, although this is usually for non-ferrous materials. Whenever there's a question mark about which method is better, CGA Racing will use both.

CVs and driveshafts tend to come as one package on a Grand Prix car like this. The cage, inner and outer will wear out at varying rates. These are manufactured by GKN Motorsports and have an excellent repeatable quality standard. The only drive belt likely to be checked behind the front cover is the main belt that drives the pump. You can take the aluminium cover off to check the belt, but this is more likely to be the task of the engine builder.

Assuming that the above checks have proved satisfactory, the water and oil levels should be checked. The engine is then warmed up and the data that this gives is recorded. This data should then be emailed to the engine builder for more detailed examination. The fuel cam is set for the next race using a small rod on the side of the engine, which has to be pushed in and turned. This changes the mixture setting.

The wheel pins should then be checked (there must be a safety pin within the wheel), and the wheel condition. The wheels should all be taken off the transporter, washed, and visually inspected for cracks. Twice a year they should be sent away for crack testing.

As far as tyres are concerned, liaise with the tyre supplier and generate a plan regarding what tyres you're going to need for the next race. The compounds are fixed for historic Formula One racing, but the weather forecast should provide an indication as to the percentage of what types are needed.

The condition of the bodywork and body pins needs to be examined. The Lotus 72 has a fairly large nose pinned on by two Dzeus

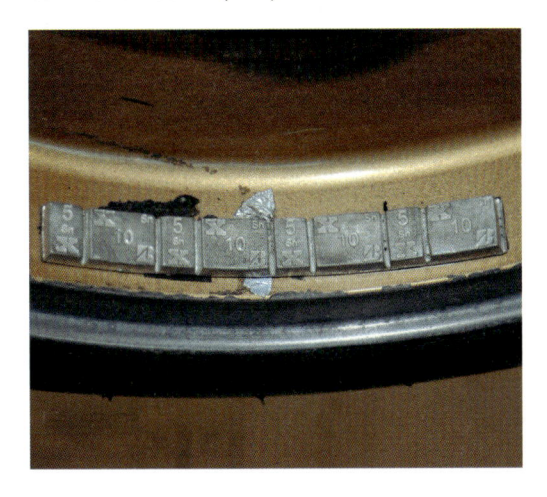

ABOVE: The nose is pinned on by two Dzus fastenings. *(Author)*

LEFT: The wheels should be checked and balanced, using self-adhesive wheel weights, every time a tyre is removed. *(Author)*

113

THE ENGINEER'S VIEW

RIGHT: Rain lights are particularly vulnerable to vibration and don't survive for long. 72/8 has a traditional, but less reliable, bulb light... *(Author)*

fastenings. Check that the bar in the nose hasn't moved and that there's no damage around the bodywork, airbox and rear wing. Ensure that neither of the front wings has been damaged. The aero devices at both ends hang off, so they're the easiest things to hit with.

Then, with the car in the air, the front aero can be set for the next race. If, for example, the car is going from Monza to Monaco, this will be vastly different. Likewise the rear aero should be checked and set.

Make sure that the rain light (which is attached to the back of the oil tank) works. Rain lights are subject to a considerable amount of vibration and tend not to survive for very long.

The final few items include spanner-checking the steering wheel, all the bolts in and around the clasp, and seeing that the quick-release is working.

About a day should then be spent setting the car up. CGA Racing has a nominated flat area in its workshop. If the torsion bars have to be changed, this should be done before the car goes on to the set-up pad. Log the set-up on a separate sheet. All the spares should be checked, making sure that they're present and correct, wrapped up and all loaded on to the truck.

RIGHT: ...while 72/6 is fitted with an LED light as is now preferred for historic racing. *(Author)*

FAR RIGHT: Spanner-check the steering wheel, all the bolts around it and the clasp, and ensure that the quick-release is working correctly. *(Author)*

114
LOTUS 72 MANUAL

Pre-race/demonstration preparations

In addition to the tasks that will have been carried out in the workshop between demonstrations or races, there will also be a list of pre-event tasks. In this case the example used is that for a demonstration by 72E/5, the example used by Classic Team Lotus for all events where the car is required to be driven. Given its historical value, 72E/5 is now only used for demonstration runs, its racing days being firmly over. Any requests to race it are now declined, although it has been used in historic competition in the past. Classic Team Lotus's other 72, 72/9, hasn't been started for many decades and is considered only suitable for static displays. It remains as it was in 1975.

Before Lotus 72E/5 leaves the Classic Team Lotus workshop, one of the mechanics will go over it with a job list. There may also be other jobs that became apparent at its last run. Any parts required will be listed on a booking-out sheet. Generally the car will be fuelled before it leaves the factory and the battery charged. When it arrives at the venue it will be rolled out of the transporter and put on display. A couple of hours before it's due to be run the tyre pressures will be checked, and the metering unit warmed up so that the quill shaft isn't damaged when the engine is started.

Classic Team Lotus Trackside Job List

- Mechanic: CHRIS
- Chassis: 72E5
- Driver: EMERSON
- Circuit: SAO PAULO STREET DEMO
- Event: PRE GRAND PRIX DEMO
- Date: 1st NOV 2010
- Issued by: CHRIS

Schedule:
- 5:30 — Preheat
- 6:00 — Engine Start
- 6:15 — Loading
- 6:30 — Depart Office
- 6:45 — Arrive Venue
- 7:00 — Unloaded
- 7:10 — Engine Start
- 7:30 — Ready to Run

1. ✓ Check tightness of wheel nuts
2. ✓ Check brake pad thickness and pad retention system is secure
3. ✓ Check condition of tyres (incl. Wets and Spares)
4. ✓ Spanner check as required (to include all necessary suspension and steering fixings)
5. ✓ Check suspension and steering joints for wear
6. ✓ Check wing assemblies and mountings for condition
7. ✓ Check feel of brake pedal
8. ✓ Check brake system for leaks
9. ✓ Ensure battery is fully charged
10. ✓ Arm Fire Extinguisher
11. ✓ Check tyre pressures (incl. Wets & spares)
12. ✓ Check / consider radiator blanking
13. ✓ Check / consider oil system blanking
14. ✓ Check brake temps, repaint as required and consider brake duct blanking
15. ✓ Check and record maximum engine revs from previous session
16. ✓ Set up timing beacon if required
17. ✓ Set up TV monitor as required
18. ✗ Check pit garage presentation, banners, tables, tool boxes etc.
19. ✗ Set up pit signals
20. ✓ Connect water heater
21. ✓ Drain fuel and measure — Add — litres — 50 litres in 1/11/10
22. ✓ Consider wet set up
23. ✓ Consider draining catch tank
24. ✗ Check Garage has suitable fire extinguishers
25. ✓ Check any new tyres are marked as necessary
26. ✓ Check inside of airbox for debris, damage and fixings security
27. ✓ Check operation of rear light
28. ✓
29. ✓ FIT CAMERA
30. ✓ LOCK WIRE STEERING COLUMN — DRILL BOLT
31.
32.
33.
34.
35.
36. FACTORY JOBS:
37.
38. Fuel pipe on aspr valve shows signs of cracking
39. Left front brake pipe close to FARB — Reposition
40. Check steering column lock wire

This sheet to be completed and kept with testing and practice log

The engine is then fired and warmed up.

Classic Team Lotus issues a set of running parameters for the car so that if somebody new is involved in running it they'll know, for example, what the tyre pressures are meant to be.

The first thing to be done before the engine is fired is to use a conventional hairdryer on the fuel metering unit. The machine tolerances are extremely fine, so if it's cold the quill shaft may twist, putting the timing out. The hairdryer should be set on the middle notch to avoid melting the injector pipes. It's imperative with a DFV that the metering unit is warmed up for about ten minutes to 'room temperature' before the engine is turned over. (CGA Racing has taken various steps to prolong engine systems and chassis life and has evolved a system of pre-heating and pre-checking the engine prior to running. This, it reckons, has given it the edge on reliability.)

The oil and water levels are then checked and the engine fired up. It should run at about 3,000rpm for the first two or three minutes to get the oil warmed up and circulating. Once the temperature is up to 50° to 60° the revs can be raised to 5–6,000rpm. The revs should be kept constant – there's no point in continuous blipping, just an occasional blip to clear the soot. The metering unit is mechanical, with five different positions. It should be set on full rich when the engine is cold, which is effectively like using a choke. Once it's warm the engine is then generally run one notch off full weak.

Following the first engine start, a series of trackside jobs need to be carried out, which will vary according to the type of event. Classic Team Lotus issues a generic job list for all its cars. The example on page 115 shows the filled-in job list for Emerson Fittipaldi's street demonstration run in 72E/5 at São Paulo in 2010. In this case such things as pit signals weren't needed, but it was necessary to add the fitting of a camera to record this particular event.

The outside temperature should be taken into consideration as it may be necessary to put blanking on the radiators if it's a cold day.

The engine should be warmed up on a rich setting. Once the temperature is up to 60°–70° the engine should be shut down and the metering unit reset to its run position, which is one off full lean. The driver can then get in, and with the isolator on, the ignition on and fuel pump on, start the engine up using the dash-mounted button. (Lotus 72s have electric starters.)

Even the older Cosworth DFV-engined cars with 450 to 460bhp are powerful beasts. 'You have to be very respectful of that horsepower,' said Classic Team Lotus team manager Chris Dinnage, Ayrton Senna's former mechanic. However, in terms of steering the car the Type 72 is one of the most responsive of all of Classic Team Lotus's cars. Obviously, on a demonstration you're not trying to extract the utmost from the car but rather to show it off in all its glory. But the fans don't just want to see it burbling around at 4,000rpm, so it's an idea to keep the revs up so that the car sounds as it would if it were being driven competitively. All this, naturally, depends upon where the demonstration is taking place. The Classic Team Lotus 72 had been driven on a track around

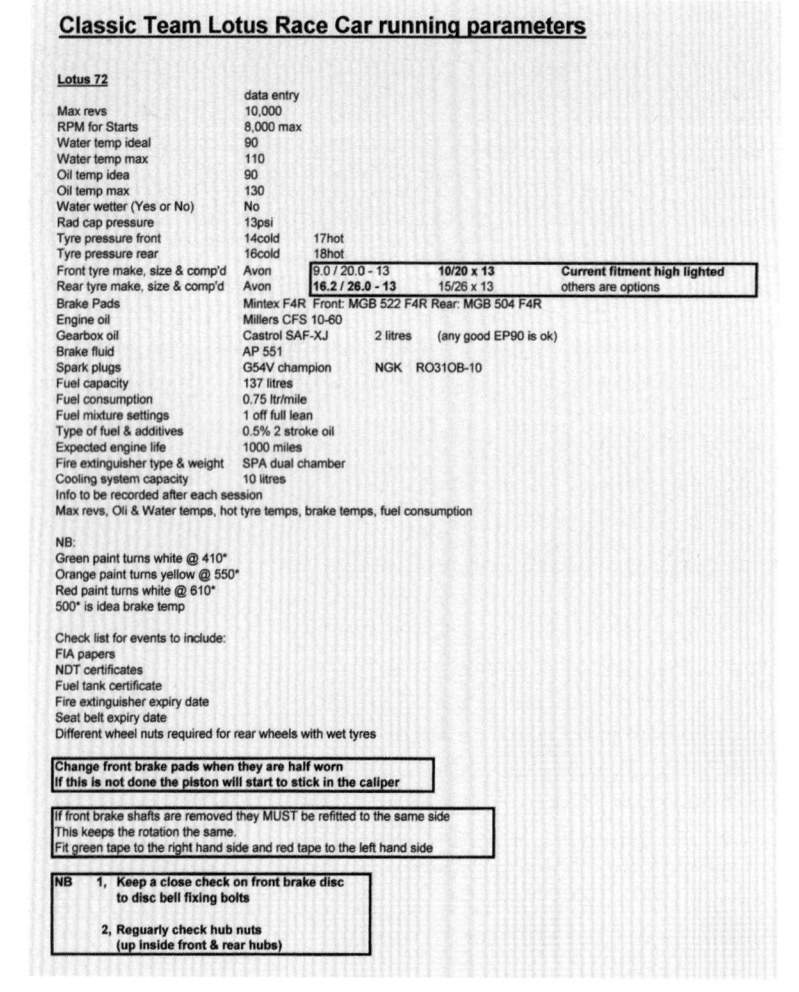

Classic Team Lotus Race Car running parameters

Lotus 72

	data entry			
Max revs	10,000			
RPM for Starts	8,000 max			
Water temp ideal	90			
Water temp max	110			
Oil temp idea	90			
Oil temp max	130			
Water wetter (Yes or No)	No			
Rad cap pressure	13psi			
Tyre pressure front	14cold	17hot		
Tyre pressure rear	16cold	18hot		
Front tyre make, size & comp'd	Avon	9.0 / 20.0 - 13	10/20 x 13	Current fitment high lighted others are options
Rear tyre make, size & comp'd	Avon	16.2 / 26.0 - 13	15/26 x 13	
Brake Pads	Mintex F4R Front: MGB 522 F4R Rear: MGB 504 F4R			
Engine oil	Millers CFS 10-60			
Gearbox oil	Castrol SAF-XJ	2 litres	(any good EP90 is ok)	
Brake fluid	AP 551			
Spark plugs	G54V champion	NGK RO31OB-10		
Fuel capacity	137 litres			
Fuel consumption	0.75 ltr/mile			
Fuel mixture settings	1 off full lean			
Type of fuel & additives	0.5% 2 stroke oil			
Expected engine life	1000 miles			
Fire extinguisher type & weight	SPA dual chamber			
Cooling system capacity	10 litres			
Info to be recorded after each session				
Max revs, Oil & Water temps, hot tyre temps, brake temps, fuel consumption				

NB:
Green paint turns white @ 410°
Orange paint turns yellow @ 550°
Red paint turns white @ 610°
500° is idea brake temp

Check list for events to include:
FIA papers
NDT certificates
Fuel tank certificate
Fire extinguisher expiry date
Seat belt expiry date
Different wheel nuts required for rear wheels with wet tyres

Change front brake pads when they are half worn
If this is not done the piston will start to stick in the caliper

If front brake shafts are removed they MUST be refitted to the same side
This keeps the rotation the same.
Fit green tape to the right hand side and red tape to the left hand side

NB 1, Keep a close check on front brake disc
        to disc bell fixing bolts

    2, Reguarly check hub nuts
        (up inside front & rear hubs)

(Classic Team Lotus)

the streets of Warsaw, which were narrower than Monte Carlo. This was just a matter of keeping it away from the walls. Conversely, speeds of 150–160mph aren't unknown during a demonstration at venues such as Silverstone or Snetterton. 'You're very conscious of what you're driving, as this is one of the crown jewels of our collection,' observed Dinnage.

(At the 2010 Classic Team Lotus Festival at Snetterton, all three of the drivers for the Formula One team known that year as Lotus (and subsequently Caterham) were used to demonstrate Classic Team Lotus cars, with Fairuz Fauzy, the reserve, in 72E/5. The drivers were asked to do a demonstration with no overtaking, but, racing drivers being what they are, the Malaysian and Heikki Kovalainen in a Lotus 77 set off and raced each other for three laps. Dinnage was driving a Lotus 79 that day and recalls the pair hurtling past him on the back straight … and he was doing over 140mph.)

If no more runs are to be made after the demonstration, 72E/5 will then be polished and put back on display. If it's to go out again, it will be checked over and go through the same procedure as earlier in the day before it goes out. When checking the tyres now, the pressures are less critical, and you're more likely to be examining them for signs of a puncture than making sure that they're set to exactly what they should be.

When a car comes back from a meeting it goes into the workshop. Each car has a technical bulletin book, which is added to whenever a new problem arises. This is a point of reference the mechanics can go to. A job list is written out. A general check-over means to go round each corner, take the wheels off, clean it, check such things as pad thicknesses, all the suspension joints for any wear or movement, make sure there's no free play in the steering system, have a look round all the suspension pickups and make sure there are no cracks. When you clean, you look. The cleaning is carried out with a small brush and cleaning fluid (generally brake cleaner), and a torch, inspecting everything as you proceed, from the front of the car to the safety light at the rear. With the Lotus 72, particular attention is paid to the front brake train, the CV joints, the brake shafts, inboard discs, the mountings of the calipers and the suspension. The gear linkage should be checked for any sloppy joints and around the fuel cells for any weeping or chaffed pipes. The same applies to the oil or water systems – anywhere that pipes might rub or touch the floor. If the team finds anything that it's not happy about then it will start taking the car apart, ahead of replace or repair. In the 1970s the cars would have been stripped completely between races.

(Classic Team Lotus)

ABOVE: Cosworth was responsible for some of the most successful racing engines of all time. (Ford)

Servicing the Cosworth DFV

Current owners of Lotus 72s will, typically, have their Cosworth DFV engines built and serviced by specialist operations such as Kimbolton-based Geoff Richardson Racing Engines, whose engine is used on such cars as 72/8, or Langford Performance Engineering in Wellingborough, which has, for example, built the engine for 72E/5. The power unit, though, can be the most expensive aspect of historic car racing, although Classic Team Lotus hopes to get 1,000 miles from a DFV between rebuilds. As far as historic racing is concerned, there's plenty of choice when it comes to what Cosworth DFV is used. Although the Lotus 72 never used a short-stroke version during its racing days, thanks to a slightly bizarre quirk of regulations it's possible to fit one today. However, this can result in difficulties in plumbing and throttle control.

During the time when the Lotus 72 was a current Grand Prix car, a Cosworth DFV would be rebuilt at approximately every 500 miles. These would be the result of the engine being fitted the night before a race, run in both warm-up and the race itself, and then left in for the following Grand Prix's practice session. In total the rebuild would take around 120 hours, including four hours of inspection.

Cosworth provided a structured rebuild programme to the top running teams, including Lotus, keeping card files of each DFV's exact specification. A full day would be spent on teardown of the engine. If it was in first-class condition the only parts that would be replaced would be the pistons and valve springs. It was possible to reuse all the nuts and bolts on the DFV, but Cosworth's experienced rebuild men could always spot a scrap thread. Once the parts had all been removed they'd be made ready for washing, visually inspected and crack detected.

New pistons would be first matched to the bores, then machined twice, first to set the squish height and then to determine the compression ratio. Each piston would have to weigh within a gram of its fellows; the same with the connecting rods. Each con rod would be tested to make sure that there was no imbalance between the big and small ends.

However, the first of the major sub-assemblies to be taken off the motor would be the metering unit and the electrical assembly, including the alternator and distributor. This would be cleaned and examined. Minor items like circlips would be routinely replaced. The process would also include pressure testing of the fuel system elements at 120psi and a thorough check of the electrics. This part of the rebuild would typically take about four hours to complete.

If the engine had been over-revved then the

big-end bolts would be replaced. Over-revving showed up on the pistons, valves and valve springs and as traces of white metal clinging to the scavenge filters. Parts to be reused, such as connecting rods and big end bearings, would be marked and matched up. Many of the parts – the block, heads, camshafts, crankshafts, connecting rods, valves and pistons – were manufactured in Cosworth's own foundry, forging and machine shop facilities. All the specialist engine work would be undertaken on Cosworth's premises. The delicate parts of the compound gear at the centre of the camshaft gear train would, for example, be crack tested and carefully inspected. Each gear would be examined for evidence of being over-travelled and its general condition would be noted.

The ignition black box would be tested, the rig simulating all the engine electrics, the circuitry being tested to over 11,000rpm and an oscilloscope displaying the amplifier signals. The coil would be routinely changed after every 12 months.

Seven to eight hours would be spent on the two oil pumps. The rotors and seals would be replaced, the castings crack tested and the numerous small parts reassembled. Rotors would have to be cleaned up and matched to their housings.

Assuming no damage has been sustained over its previous 500 miles, the engine would be reassembled and then dyno tested. Before final sign-off an industrial borescope would be used to peer deep into the combustion chamber. Valve clearances would be checked and an examination carried out for signs of dyno damage, such as a broken valve spring or signs that a piston or bearing has picked up. If anything was discovered, the engine would be taken down again and the error rectified. Otherwise it would then be on its way back to Hethel to be again installed in the back of a Type 72.

BELOW: Cosworth maintenance at the track – in this case John Robinson at work at Dijon-Prenois in 1974. *(Sutton Images)*

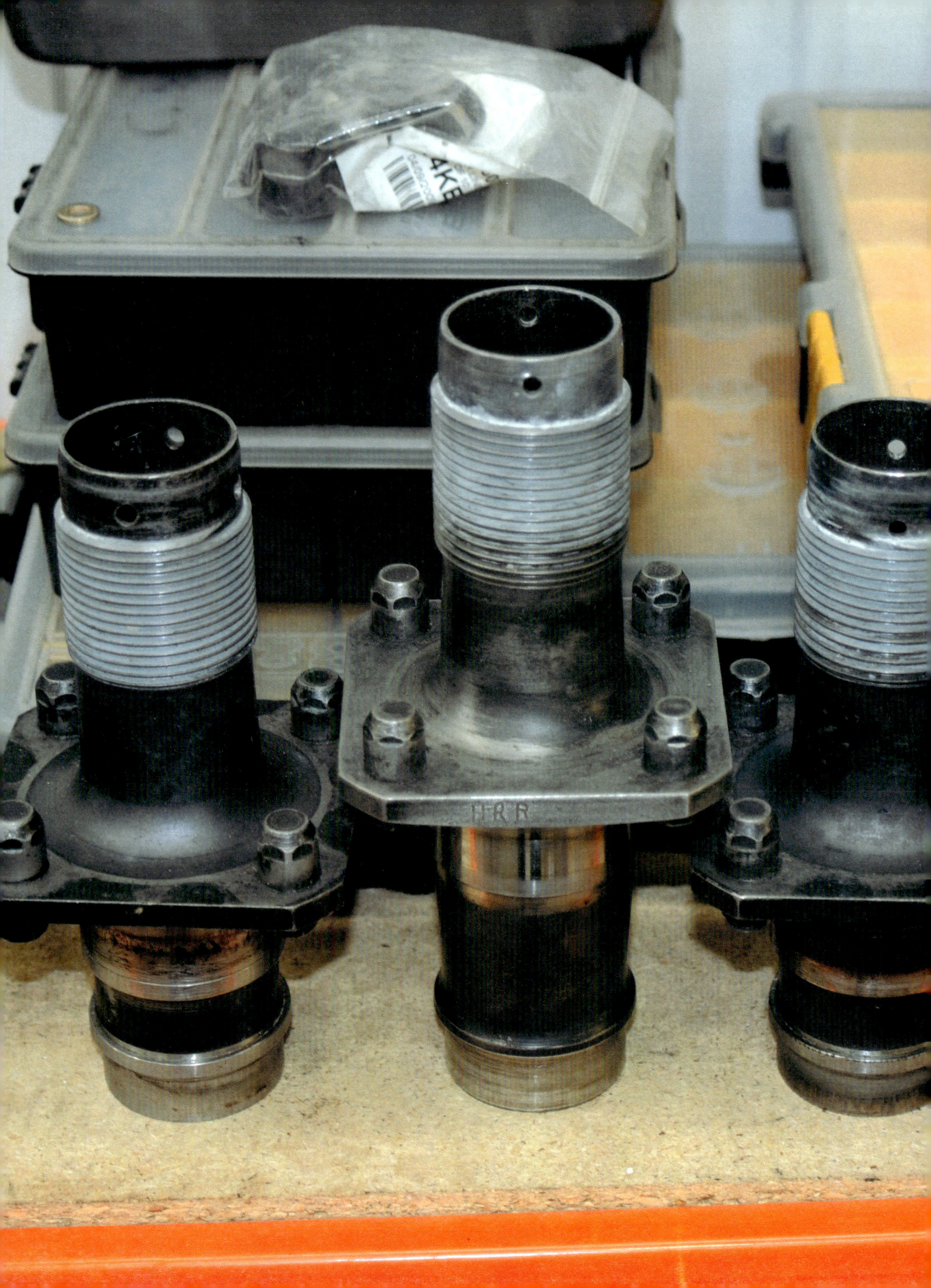

'We probably do more testing of materials than was ever done in period.'

Simon Hadfield
Owner of Simon Hadfield Motorsports and racing driver

(Author)

Chapter Five

Restoration and historic racing

Seven complete Lotus 72s exist today. Two remain with Colin Chapman's family. Of those in private hands, two are still in England, two in Japan and a third in the Netherlands. Despite their rarity, they occasionally change ownership. Levels of restoration have varied considerably depending upon how the owner wants to balance having a competitive racing car for historic events with one that retains as much as possible of its original detail.

As modern racing becomes increasingly expensive, ever more processional and often confined to 'spec' formulae, so the popularity of historic racing has risen. The 3-litre Formula One of 1966–85 was a long period, so it's logical that the newer and less significant cars now tend to be the ones that appear most often – this despite championships that use age-based class structures, awarding overall victory to whoever performs best in category. Because of their historic and monetary value, Lotus 72s are appearing less in racing and are more confined to demonstration runs, although one was completely rebuilt in 2011 to create a competitive racer. Those that have raced in historic meetings are 72/3, 72/4, 72E/5 and 72/6, with the first of these winning the Thoroughbred Grand Prix title in 1996.

Buying and maintaining a Lotus 72

With only nine Lotus 72s in existence, and two of those in a very badly damaged incomplete state, acquiring one is going to be difficult. However, a number of them have changed hands in recent years. As Classic Team Lotus owner Clive Chapman pointed out, a potential buyer's approach depends much on the condition of the car, the principle of any restoration required and the ultimate objective.

The question of provenance is unlikely to arise, as all the Type 72s are well documented. Some remain static in private collections, some go to shows and exhibitions as static displays or to events where they can make demonstration runs or race, but all are known and each chassis number accounted for. Rick Hall, of the historic racing car sales and restoration company Hall and Hall, points out that the first thing to do when buying any vintage racing car is to establish exactly which car it is and what its history is, to ensure that the car has proper provenance and a trail of owners. This is an important part of the car. However, unlike certain other racing cars there won't be an authenticity problem here; a replica has never been made of a Lotus 72.

The condition of the surviving Type 72s is varied. The two still owned by the Chapman family are preserved as they were when they finished racing with Team Lotus in the 1970s. The cars that have ended up in private hands, and in particular those that went to South Africa, can be very different. In general, said Chapman, 'you should treat everything with a high degree of caution'.

BELOW: At the Nürburgring in 2011, 72/6 owner Katsu Kubota donned a Ronnie Peterson-style helmet for early shooting of the film *Rush*, which mainly covers the James Hunt versus Niki Lauda battle of 1976. *(Jon Bunston)*

LEFT: One of the glories of Lotus 72 survival has been a number of opportunities to again see Emerson Fittipaldi at the wheel of 72E/5. Here he is on qualifying day for the 2010 Bahrain Grand Prix. *(Sutton Images)*

When it comes to establishing a price, it should be noted that even among the surviving Lotus 72s this will vary, and not just because of their state. The history is a major part of the value of the car. For example, 72/8 can be judged on the fact that it won three Grands Prix in the hands of Ronnie Peterson. Particularly pertinent, given the increasing importance of the Monaco Historic Grand Prix, one of these was the 1974 Monaco GP. There's a great demand for places on the grid at the event, held every two years, but a former Monaco GP winner is almost sure to be accepted.

Of course, there isn't just one price. Buying the car as it appears is one matter, but it may also need restoration work. There are no reference works to give a price, and vendors and buyers can only assess a figure based on the sums similar cars may have sold for. There seems little doubt, though, that a Lotus 72 is an appreciating asset. One of the cars is thought to have changed hands during the last few years of the 2000s, unrestored, for between £600,000 and £700,000. Restoration work is likely to have pushed this well above the million mark, and it's said that the owner of another recently restored version turned down an offer of £1.5 million in 2011. If the car is in need of restoration what you see is what you get. There are no guarantees.

Every bit of documentation and paperwork helps. They all add to the appeal of the car and its value. An HTP form (Historic Technical Passport) will say that the car is to the correct specification to go historic racing, but it won't mention chassis numbers.

Before buying, examine the monocoque in the first instance to ensure that it looks true and that the panels are straight and free from kinks. Make sure that the suspension is all in line. Look over the external condition of the engine and the gearbox – who rebuilt the DFV last, and what kind of mileage does it have on it? Has it

BELOW: Examine the external condition of the Hewland gearbox. *(Author)*

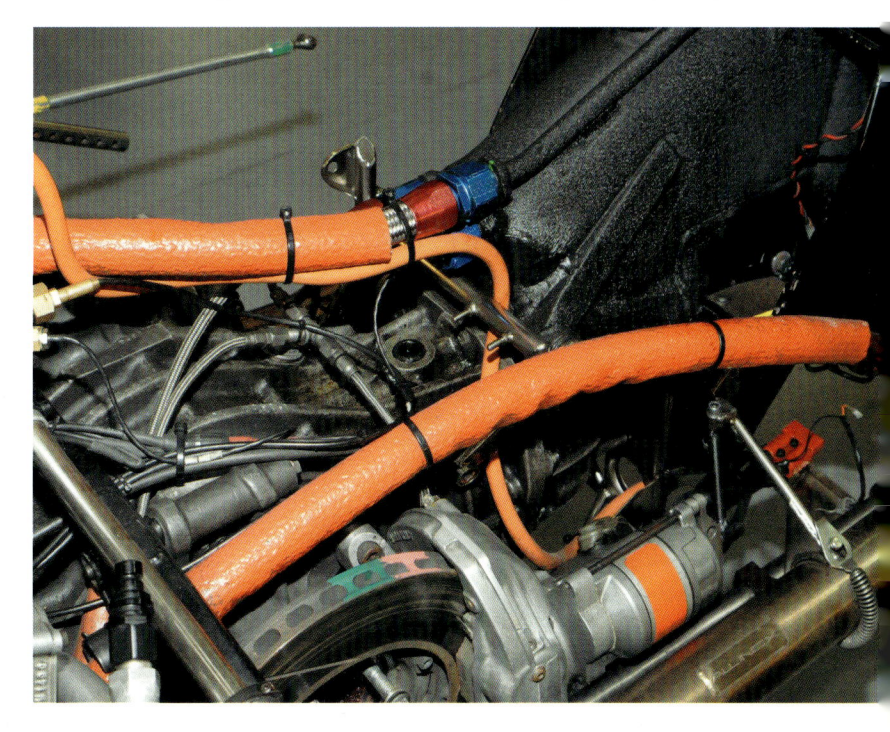

123

RESTORATION AND HISTORIC RACING

RIGHT: **Pedals should be subjected to non-destructive testing.** *(Author)*

been turned over regularly? These are really just the basics.

In terms of the restoration, much depends upon whether originality is paramount. The scale then runs through compromise to reliability and competitiveness. If your principle objective is to race the car to win, that won't necessarily be compatible with restoring the car and preserving as many of its original parts, as well as the original specification, as possible. As far as Classic Team Lotus is concerned, all the eggs are placed, as Chapman puts it, in the provenance basket. Thus, although CTL's 72E/5 has competed in historic races, no allowance has been made to make it competitive. By contrast, Katsu Kubota's 72/6 has been virtually remanufactured to allow it to be competitive in the second decade of the 21st Century.

The tub is the core of the car. On being acquired this should be stripped down to the bare tub and its condition examined. The suspension pickup parts will need to be subjected to NDT (non-destructive testing). 'We probably do more testing of metals now than was ever done in period,' observed classic racing car restorer Simon Hadfield. It may be that you'll wish to repaint parts of the tub or keep it as it was, possibly chipped and scratched, which is what Classic Team Lotus tends to do. When it comes to repainting the bodywork, CTL uses one of the original sign-writers, for this is very much an art. Something that isn't readily realised is that in 1973 there were three different golds used on the Type 72 – the John Player Special sign-writing, the vinyl sponsors' logos, and the gold paint of the roundels and the mirrors.

ABOVE: **A newly acquired 72 should be stripped down to the bare tub.** *(R&J Simpson Engineering)*

RIGHT: **A new cockpit surround will tend to be in clear Perspex rather than the original yellow.** *(Author)*

The cockpit surround was originally made from what has colloquially been called 'piss yellow' Perspex. If you're following the Classic Team Lotus philosophy of keeping the car as original as possible, it will be good to retain the original surround. A new one would have to be made from clear Perspex, which is hardly the same.

Pedals are another component where it's good to retain the originals, but these should certainly be subjected to NDT. Front suspension should also be NDT'd, and X-rayed. The front driveshafts are an important element that should also be condition tested, as should all the safety-critical components. The Type 72 is extremely complicated at the front – the tolerance, the types of bolts and the torques and CV joints used can be a nightmare.

A notable factor of the 72 was, as has been explained, its use of torsion bars. Classic Team Lotus has a plentiful supply of these, for as Clive Chapman says, he wouldn't like to make any more of them. Wherever possible CTL will use original parts. There are two principal sources of Lotus 72 parts, those that are on the Team Lotus drawings, and the proprietary parts such as the Hewland gearbox internals (available off-the-shelf), the Smiths instruments and the AP clutch – parts that the team didn't manufacture itself. If a part is damaged, an original spare may be used or, if this isn't possible, since the original drawings still exist a new part may be made. Wheels are an example of this, where CTL prefers to use the originals but will manufacture new ones from the original drawing if required.

This parts service isn't confined to CTL's own cars, and Chapman points out that it will often treat its customers' cars with more concern than its own. It has even been known for CTL to borrow parts from its own cars to keep customers' cars running. Amongst the private owners of Lotus 72s that it's known to have assisted with replacement parts are Alastair Morrison and Yoshio Fukuda.

In its efforts to maintain the authenticity of its Lotus 72s, Classic Team Lotus prefers to keep the original gauges and to have them serviced, although, in the words of Clive Chapman, 'living with the original gauges can be a nuisance'. If you're not going competitive racing it's also

TOP: The announcement of renewed John Player sponsorship at Brands Hatch in 1981 was a chance to bring out one of the Lotus 72s. *(Nick Collins)*

ABOVE: First page of the lengthy Lotus 72 parts list. Such invaluable documents are still held at Classic Team Lotus's Hethel base. *(Classic Team Lotus)*

125

RESTORATION AND HISTORIC RACING

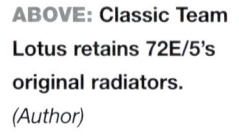

ABOVE: Classic Team Lotus retains 72E/5's original radiators.
(Author)

**ABOVE RIGHT:
The modern mirrors of Katsu Kubota's 72/6.**
(Author)

good to have an original specification steering wheel and, perhaps, the original seat. If these are the ones that were used in the 1970s they very much improve the history of the car. It would also be ideal to run with the original Walpres aluminium mirrors, but Chapman says that these are 'almost impossible to find, and a nightmare to live with'. Also tricky to source are the small fasteners for the cockpit surround.

Classic Team Lotus makes use of the original Serck Marston radiators, which are still sent back to now Unipart-owned Serck for servicing. It is, though, possible to fit aluminium radiators if you don't want to run with the original design. CLT also tend to run with the original ignition system for its earlier cars, including the Type 72.

Of course, if racing's a possibility there will be changes that have to be made whatever your desire to retain authenticity. The fuel cells will have to be replaced and modern seat belts fitted. A modern fire extinguisher will also have to be installed, although fitting one into the original slot can be difficult. Dampers are often played around with in historic motorsport, but this is another example of where Classic Team Lotus prefers to keep to the original specifications.

Insurance

When insuring such a car you'll be looking for a bespoke policy, and it's essential to go to a specialist insurance broker, one that's experienced in classic and historic cars. Only they will be comfortable with or knowledgeable about the heritage of the car and be able to relate to its value, which could be somewhere between £1 million and £1.5 million.

It's highly unlikely that a Lotus 72 would be stolen, although it is possible that component parts might. The biggest risk, outside racing, is likely to be if it's being transported to or from an event and is damaged in a road accident or perhaps a fire in the workshop.

The first type of insurance that should be looked at, advises Adrian Hardy of Ellis Clowes, is a storage and transit policy. This is a 12-month insurance that, as its name implies, covers the car when it's in the base workshop or garage, when it's trailered or transported to race meetings, and when it's in the paddock area or a pit garage. It won't extend beyond the line in front of the pit garage, or cover the car when it's under its own power. This is 'all risks' coverage, and with a car such as the Lotus 72 you'd probably have an excess of something like £1,000. The price, obviously, depends what you'll be doing with the car. If you just intend taking it to the Goodwood Festival of Speed or making a demonstration run such as those at the Classic Team Lotus Festival at Snetterton, then that will naturally be considerably cheaper than if you complete in ten race meetings throughout Europe. As a percentage rate to calculate the premium you're probably looking at something between 0.3% and 0.6% on the value of the car.

The owner of a Lotus 72 is likely to have a collection of cars. This will mean that the individual car cost will be lower than that suggested above.

You now have to decide whether you want to cover the car while it's in action. Some historic racers do, some don't. The coverage is certainly available, and costings again depend on the nature of the activities in which you'll be involved. The once-a-year appearance at Goodwood would be easy to cover. The car would only be doing a couple of runs up the hill per day, and providing the driver has plenty of experience and a reasonable record then the cost will not be astronomic.

A value of £1million to £1.5million is more of an intrinsic value than a rebuild. If you do damage the car then your rebuild costs will presumably be significantly lower. Hardy recommended that the owner goes for what's called a 'first loss' policy. This means that you don't insure the full value but select a figure. For argument's sake, if this is £100,000 you'll have a reasonably significant excess – you will probably have to bear the first £5,000 to £10,000 – and your premium for a race meeting would probably be around £2,000 to £2,500. At a race meeting this would include all official practice and the race or races themselves. The per meeting cost is likely to come down the more races you undertake. The insurance would cover the cost of repair or recreation of parts and for the labour. The cost can, of course, depend upon the circuit; Monaco is, after all, a very different place to Snetterton. As Hardy pointed out, though, there isn't a manual in which you can look up how much it would specifically cost to insure a Lotus 72 to race at, say, Portimao. The broker will come up with a figure based on past experience and knowledge of the sport. It will then negotiate with an underwriter – Ellis Clowes generally tends to use Lloyds – to hopefully agree a sensible package, and then inform the car's owner what's on offer.

The insurance business is particularly competitive when it comes to modern racing, but less companies seem to be interested in covering historic cars. Those that do tend to be staffed by people with an interest in the sector. Many of the underwriters with which Ellis Clowes deals also have an interest in the sport, and some of them race.

Racing opportunities

Period Formula One events

There are three series, ranging from a full FIA championship in Europe to a less formal series of races in North America in which the Lotus 72 is still eligible to race. In addition there's the prestigious Grand Prix de Monaco Historique, which takes place every two years and features races for 3-litre Formula One cars built from 1966 to 1978, with the type 72 eligible for a 1966–72 class. Several Lotus 72s have raced in this event, including appearances by Sean Walker and Keiichi Murakami in Classic Team Lotus's 72E/5, Alistair Morrison in 72/6, and former Minardi Grand Prix driver Alex Yoong in the same

ABOVE: One of the Chapman family's two Lotus 72s, 72/9, in storage prior to the formation of Classic Team Lotus in 1992. *(Author)*

ABOVE: Malaysian Grand Prix driver Alex Yoong was a competitor in the 2002 Grand Prix de Monaco Historique. He looked a likely winner until his car, 72/6, stuck in fifth gear and he was forced to finish second. *(Sutton Images)*

car when owned by David McLaughlin. Yoong finished second in 2002 after his car had stuck in fifth gear.

Historic Formula One

The Historic Formula One Championship is the most prestigious series open to the Lotus 72 as it is now sanctioned by the Fédération Internationale de l'Automobile (FIA), motorsport's governing body. It was originally known as the Thoroughbred Grand Prix Championship. The overall championship goes to the highest-scoring performer in one of four categories. The Lotus 72 is eligible for Class A, 1966–71 Formula One cars, or Class B, post-1971 non-ground effect Formula One cars. Michael Schryver took the trophy in 1996 competing in Class A. Others who have raced in the series with Type 72s have been Walker and Murakami in the Class B Classic Team Lotus car, and Morrison and McLaughlin, both in 72/6.

In all, cars from 1966 to 1985 are catered for, with grids averaging about 25. A typical season will have seven events in countries such as Germany, Belgium, Italy, England, Spain, France and Portugal. HFO became a support race for the British Grand Prix at Silverstone in 2012.

Masters Historic Racing

The Masters Historic Racing series, which first ran in 2004, includes a category for 3-litre Grand Prix cars built between 1966 and 1978. Grand Prix Masters, as it's known, became a championship in 2011. Events include the Silverstone Classic, Nürburgring Oldtimer Grand Prix, Zandvoort Historic Grand Prix and the Dijon Grand Prix de l'age d'Or. A typical season will include eight race meetings. The Lotus 72 is eligible for the Stewart class (named after thrice World Champion Jackie), which caters for cars from 1969 to 1971. The organisers say that Grand Prix Masters was created to give the owners of older cars the chance to be competitive, as the HFO tends to be the preserve of later machinery. (Against this it should be pointed out that the class structure means older cars can also take the overall HFO title and, indeed, a contemporary of the Lotus 72 won in 2011.) Lotus 72s have competed in the GPM driven by James King in Classic Team Lotus's 72E/5, Alistair Morrison in 72/6 and Patrick van Heurck.

All cars in both HFO and GPM must run in period livery. One significant difference is that HFO features standing grid starts while GPM races have rolling starts.

Historic Grand Prix

Historic Grand Prix is a North America-based series of races, rather than a championship, that caters for 3-litre Formula One cars built from 1966 to 1983. Around four events take place each year at tracks such as Road America, Lime Rock, Watkins Glen and the Circuit Gilles Villeneuve in Montreal. Although no Lotus 72s have yet run in any of these races there seem to have been plans in the past to do so. Lotus has, however, been represented by examples of Types 49B, 77, 79 and 81.

ABOVE: **72/3 took the Thoroughbred Grand Prix Championship in 1996.** *(Simon Hadfield Motorsports)*

BELOW: **Katsu Kubota during a particularly wet Historic Formula One race at the Nürburgring. Despite standing water covering much of the track, he brought the car home to third in class and fifth overall.** *(Jon Bunston)*

Restoration projects

Simon Hadfield Motorsports – 72/3

Although it never won a Grand Prix and was never the 'number one' driver's car at Team Lotus, 72/3 was probably worked harder than any other Type 72, thanks to its long South African career. Although now owned by Yoshio Fukuda, it was acquired for historic racing in the 1990s by Michael Schryver, and restored at Simon Hadfield Motorsports in Shepsted, Leicestershire.

BELOW: Simon Hadfield Motorsports ran 72/3 in virtually the same specification as it was raced by Dave Charlton. *(Simon Hadfield Motorsports)*

In historic racing 72/3 weighed around 575 to 580kg and was essentially in 1971 specification. It did, though, feature the deformable sides of the monocoque, as the tub had never been seriously damaged. These had been fitted late in the car's original racing life. After 72/7 had been badly damaged at Kyalami, Team Gunston borrowed 72/3 from Dave Charlton. The car was stripped down and rebuilt to 72E specification using salvageable parts from 72/7. Simon Hadfield remembered that you would occasionally pull off a part like the steering column or a disc bell and it would have 72/7 written on it. 'There wasn't the rigorousness in South Africa of lifeing.'

'In its original iteration the Type 72 was very light, but it became more robust and as it did so it finished more races,' said Hadfield. 'Before 72/3 was acquired, I went to see Classic Team Lotus's 72/9, which is essentially known as a lightweight version, but I couldn't see what was lighter. I presume everything was made just that bit thinner or smaller. There's this myth that the 72 wasn't that strong, but we have later cars in our workshop that were made in exactly the same way and yet people think of them as being robust.'

A couple of English club racers bought the

BUYER BEWARE

It could be said that, as with any car, the principle of *caveat emptor* (buyer beware) still holds good. In the early 1980s, David McLaughlin, who with his wife Lorina was to create the first historic Formula One series in Europe, was keen to buy chassis 72/6. At the time the car was in the Rembrandt Tobacco Company's Heidelberg museum along with 72/3, both cars in Team Gunston colours. Having been raced by Ronnie Peterson to four Grand Prix victories, 72/6 was considered to be far more significant than 72/3, which had been driven by John Miles and Reine Wisell before becoming the first of the South Africa-based cars, and had only won races in the South African Drivers' Championship. Both cars were preserved just as they had last raced.

After a couple of years of being constantly badgered by McLaughlin, the owner named what he recalls was an 'incredibly high figure for the time'. It was agreed that the car would be shipped to Heathrow, from where McLaughlin went to fetch it with a 'dodgy' two-wheeled trailer towed by a Ford Sierra. He found a 'very sorry-looking Team Gunston chassis sitting on a pallet, and was shocked to find that it was the less desirable 72/3. This was at the start of the Easter break, and McLaughlin was unable to contact anyone in South Africa. He spent the holiday period wondering whether a genuine mistake had been made or whether the seller was working a flanker.

The following week it transpired that somebody at the museum had been instructed to ship car number six to the UK, meaning chassis number six. However, 72/3 had carried race number six during its final season in the SADC, and for this reason it was this car that was sent. At first McLaughlin was asked if he'd like to simply swap chassis plates, but the real 72/6 was an ex-Peterson car, so it was something he wasn't prepared to do. The correct chassis was then sent and McLaughlin now recalls how, for some months, he had two Lotus 72s in his garage before the museum arranged for 72/3 to be returned.

72/3 back to the UK from South Africa and had it resprayed back to the original Gold Leaf Team Lotus colours. It went to auction but failed to sell. However, Hadfield suggested to Michael Schryver that this would be a fantastic car to buy. At first the asking price seemed too much for Schryver, but his brother Andrew chipped in and the pair purchased the car for Michael and Hadfield to race.

'We took it apart, photographing every bit as we did so. The engine was seized solid and was sent to J&F Engines. We put the monocoque on the jig and found that it was twisted. The floor, which curls round the side and picks up the deformable structures, had been changed. We undid the floor, came to the last three or four rivets and it went "bong" and sprang back dead square. What we think had happened was that the floor had been fitted by hand in South Africa.

'We took the tub apart and made jigs for it, cleaned everything and looked for cracks. There were quite a few in the front frame, which we welded up and put some wraps in. There were also some major cracks in the engine pickups. Everything was made good and properly surface-treated and the car put back together.

'We ran the car effectively as Dave Charlton

ABOVE: **72/3 in its time at Simon Hadfield Motorsports.** (Simon Hadfield Motorsports)

BELOW: **Simon Hadfield and his team took 72/3 apart, photographing everything as they did so.** (Simon Hadfield Motorsports)

RESTORATION AND HISTORIC RACING

had in 1972–73 – apart from using mag uprights, which we always use because you can crack-test them. You can't crack-test steel uprights. There'd been some updating when Team Gunston hired the car from Charlton after one of its own had been damaged. It still had rubbed bushes on the rear radius rod and evidence of where they'd been on the bottom link anchor plate. There had been an attempt to update the radiator mounts at the back. It was also fitted with a Lotus 76 oil tank. By sheer coincidence I had a customer at the time with a McLaren M10 that had the oil tank from 72/3 fitted at some time when both cars were in South Africa. In return for a new oil tank, the customer was happy to let me have the original.'

Hadfield acquired one of the original side scoop airboxes to try on the car, thinking that it would tidy up the air to the rear wing. In testing this proved to make the car nearly a second a lap slower. In Gold Team colours the 72 never ran with an anvil-shaped airbox, although 72/3 had used a horn-shaped box in its later time as a factory car. Hadfield was unable to locate one of these and so made one, but that 'killed' the 1971 spec single-piece rear wing, losing yet another second. When Hadfield asked Eddie Dennis about this he replied that the drivers in 1971 wanted an airbox because the other cars had airboxes, this being the only reason why the horn-shaped box had been fitted.

'Things bent and things moved on 72/3,' observed Hadfield. 'For example, there was on the rack a small cutaway where the disc protruded through the aluminium housing rack casing. This had small, riveted-on steel reliefs for the disc to actually pass into it. When we started running the car we didn't have the frame-to-bottom caliper stiffeners, which we then copied from 72/9. They were fantastic brakes but they'd move in the side of the rack. What counts against the car today is that it has very small brakes and is very soft. We know far more about racing cars now and they're very much stiffer.'

Like Sean Walker, who was able to race Classic Team Lotus's 72E/5, the 72 means a lot to Hadfield emotionally because of his father's involvement in Lotus, in this case as special

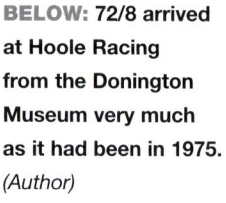

BELOW: 72/8 arrived at Hoole Racing from the Donington Museum very much as it had been in 1975. *(Author)*

LEFT: Although there's a small amount of delamination, the paintwork on 72/8 hasn't been touched. (Author)

events manager for John Player. (The black and gold colour scheme was designed by Barry Foley in the Hadfields' front room.) 'When I drove it, it was so accomplished.' Like Classic Team Lotus, Schryver and Hadfield used a long-stroke DFV, and as developments continued in historic racing so they fell down the grid. Schryver, though, won the Thoroughbred Grand Prix Championship in 1996 by winning his class.

'If you had told the ten-year-old me that I'd drive and race a Lotus 72, I'd have thought you were mad. This is the ultimate racing car.'

Sid Hoole Racing – 72/8

Lotus 72/8 led a sheltered life from the time that it was pensioned off at the end of 1975 and was loaned to the Donington Grand Prix Collection. It became the property of Lotus accountant and eventual chairman Fred Bushell before being sold to the museum's owner Tom Wheatcroft in 2001. Hall and Hall, which has an exclusive agreement with the Wheatcroft family, had been told that a number of the cars could be for sale if the price was right and said that it would find a buyer if possible.

In 2009 one was found in the person of leading Minneapolis-based film producer Bill Pohlad, and a price agreed. It has now been sympathetically restored at Hoole Racing in Kimbolton, Bedfordshire. It's in full racing condition and just as it came out of the museum. Although there's a small amount of delamination, the paintwork hasn't been touched. The original wheels have been crack-tested. All the suspension components are as were.

BELOW: Sid Hoole Racing's Peter Lawrence at work on a Hewland FG400 gearbox. (Author)

133
RESTORATION AND HISTORIC RACING

When the car arrived at Hoole Racing it was given a safety check. The brakes were all resealed and the front driveshaft hubs were crack-tested. Not much was done to the engine for its first outing. The injector pipes were changed, fresh oil was used, and it started first time out from the museum. It was later sent to locally based Geoff Richardson Racing Engines for a 'freshen up'. Both Hoole and Pohlad then tested the car before it was stripped down and a new bag tank made for it by ATL. 'Otherwise, apart from a bit of tidying up of the chassis, that was about it,' recalled Hoole Racing's Peter Lawrence, who was responsible for much of the work.

The original titanium rollover hoop has been replaced with a steel one. A larger extinguisher has to be fitted to meet current regulations, although this is still in the original location under the driver's legs. Lawrence reported that a number of different colour schemes were used for the 72's wheels in period: completely black, black centre and gold outer, or gold. Hoole Racing decided to use the gold finish.

72/8 – THE OWNER'S VIEW

Bill Pohlad* might be said to be of the Clive Chapman school of Lotus 72 owners. For him, the car must be as original as possible. His love of motor racing dates back to the mid-1960s – when he saw the film *Grand Prix* – following Graham Hill with BRM and then with Lotus. Many years later this is reflected in his collection that includes a 1.5-litre BRM P261 and Lotus 72/8. In the early 1970s, still a teenager, he got to know Jackie Stewart, following the Scot around to a number of Grands Prix.

'The Lotus 72 was a car I grew up with; it was a classic car from the very beginning.'

Not knowing that there was a market for old racing cars, Bill did become aware that there was one for such as drivers' helmets and race suits 'and became a little bit involved in that'. On discovering that people were restoring historic racers, he acquired one of the earliest P261s that was raced just the once, at Snetterton by Graham Hill. (He has since replaced this with an ex-Stewart P261.)

Pohlad was an understandable fan of Ronnie Peterson, so when 72/8 became available, 'it was a no brainer' to acquire it. 'I felt so passionately about it and just had to figure a way to do it.'

He had met restorer Sid Hoole through a friend, leading historic car and then endurance race entrant Duncan Dayton. At first they tried to buy Denny Hulme's 1967 Monaco Grand Prix winning Brabham when that came up for auction, 'but that wasn't right'.

'Sid's a real player in the industry,' said Pohlad. 'He knows a lot about the cars, and that comes from his own personal love of the era. He has been a great partner.'

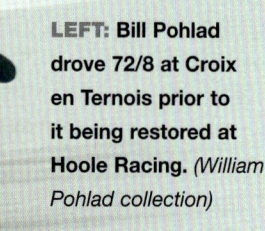

LEFT: Bill Pohlad drove 72/8 at Croix en Ternois prior to it being restored at Hoole Racing. (William Pohlad collection)

OPPOSITE: 72/8's Cosworth DFV has been 'freshened up' by Geoff Richardson Racing Engines. *(Author)*

RIGHT: The original titanium rollover hoop on 72/8 has been replaced by a steel version. *(Author)*

Hoole assisted with the buying of the BRMs and also the Cooper-Climax T60 with which Bruce McLaren won the 1962 Monaco Grand Prix. He also made Pohlad aware that 72/8 had come up for sale.

Pohlad recalls that the earlier 72/4 had come up for auction prior to this, 'but that was when I was not so savvy and not up to speed on how the whole thing worked.' The former Rob Walker 72 had probably been the first Formula One car that Bill had seen when he attended the US Grand Prix in 1970. Despite the fact that Fittipaldi won that day, securing the World Championship for Rindt, it was the blue 72 with Graham Hill at the wheel that left Pohlad with the biggest impression.

The 72/8, 'so fresh and original', became available. 'I know a lot of people like racing these cars and I like driving them but I am not that keen on racing them to the point where they lose their originality. I love the history of the cars and I like to keep them in an as-original state as possible. It's the smell and feel of it.' It is not just the fact that 72/8 won at Monaco, Dijon and Monza with Peterson at the wheel that makes this car special to Pohlad, it is the whole history of the car with 'that whole match up of car and driver.'

Shortly after acquiring the car, and before any restoration work was carried out, Pohlad had the opportunity to drive it at the little Croix en Ternois track. Engine tuner Geoff Richardson was amazed how the Cosworth engine fired up after years sitting in the Donington Collection. It was also his first time with the Cooper and, with the opportunity to drive all three of his cars, it was, as he recalled, 'an amazing occasion'.

'It was great to contrast the different cars. I started with the BRM as I had driven it before. Then I stepped into the Lotus 72 and it was amazing what a difference those few years had made between the cars. The BRM was more of a challenge to drive and then the Lotus was just so beautiful, so smooth, silky and driver friendly. It was like night and day.'

Although Pohlad had no particular plans for the future of 72/8, it is likely that it will take part in the feature film that his company River Road Entertainment is making about the Tyrrell team-mates, Stewart and Francois Cevert.

'The Lotus 72, particularly in the JPS colours, is a car that is so stunningly good to look at that, even if you are not an aficionado, you will appreciate it. It was such a major transition, changing from one style of car to another.'

* Bill Pohlad is the son of financier and Minnesota Twins baseball team owner, the late Carl Pohlad. The president of River Road Entertainment, he was executive producer of the Academy Award winning 2005 film *Brokeback Mountain* as well as the 2011 film *The Tree of Life,* which starred Sean Penn, Brad Pitt and Jessica Chastain, and for which he was nominated for an Oscar.

CGA Racing/R&J Simpson Engineering – 72/6

If Classic Team Lotus's 72E/5 is kept as original as possible, then Katsu Kubota's 72/6 could be said to be at the opposite end of the scale. Indeed, it could be argued that its restoration has resulted in an almost new but considerably stronger car. Faced with the question 'do you want it to be competitive or do you want it to be like the original car?', Kubota leaned towards the former. It should also be remembered that if an historic car is to be raced, it still has to pass a scrutineer.

Colin Bennett, a former Lotus mechanic who runs Warrington-based CGA Racing, which prepares the car, points to the fact that 72/6 retains its original appearance while making use of the materials now available. As he observes, you can only replace a certain amount before a car loses it identity. 'As far as is practical we use period techniques but with modern applications.

'Whilst this is a fragile car, there are parts from 1970 on it that you'd think wouldn't have lasted, but they have. It was also well engineered, and we didn't want to change that mark of Chapman's ability. We wanted to stick with it and improve it where we could, and that's what we think we've done with 72/6.

'We haven't touched the aerodynamics of

TOP: 72/6's chassis towards the end of its rebuild process. Note the new skins. *(R&J Simpson Engineering)*

ABOVE: 72/6's tub was completely rebuilt at R&J Simpson. *(R&J Simpson Engineering)*

RIGHT: Colin Bennett at work on the front end of 72/6. *(R&J Simpson Engineering)*

the car, which are the same as in 1974. We therefore know, pretty much, the downforce loadings that it will take. However, we have altered a few things like suspension settings, to work with the current tyres, these being the Avons that we've run for many years.'

Bennett compares the 72 to the ex-Ronnie Peterson March 761 that he also prepares for Kubota. 'The 72 is so fragile that you really have to examine the monocoque, and the appendages that come off it, carefully. You have to look at this car more than you would others of its time.'

When Kubota purchased the car, 'we were very aware that it had inboard front brakes. That was a difficult thing to achieve in 1970, and as a consequence a lot of parts broke.' Former Formula One designer Gary Anderson was therefore approached to look at the best way of addressing the problem of making a brake shaft that would last. The work was taken to R&J Simpson Engineering of Tamworth, for which Anderson worked as an external associate, where the tub was completely rebuilt and other components were made for the car. The structural integrity of these cars is all-important and modern-day methods of gluing and riveting are better than they were.

Bob Simpson said that he was unable to find conventional box section of sufficient quality for the front-end. This was therefore constructed using S514 welded down the seam and polished off, so that it effectively looks like the original but is much stronger. All the sheet work was made in L613. The sides of the chassis would originally have been made from NS3 aluminium using an English wheel, but Simpson used NS4, which is as stiff as possible. Although NS4 is harder to work, it gives more torsional rigidity. The fact that the chassis was stiffer allowed the rate of the torsion bars to be increased. An additional rollover bar was also installed.

Simpson reported that the chassis of the Type 72 is particularly complicated, made more so by the fact that the front torsion bars run inside the fuel tank. Thus jigging was critical. 'It was the most difficult car that we've ever built – there was very little clearance on anything.'

Because the cars now need considerably less fuel to take part in historic racing than they did in Grands Prix, Simpson was able to make the back end of the tub solid, rather than leaving the cut-out which meant that the bottom engine mounts flexed. Complete diaphragms with a couple of flanged holes were also used in the sides. The original ones were small and thin but it was possible to improve on this because of the smaller area being used for the fuel tanks.

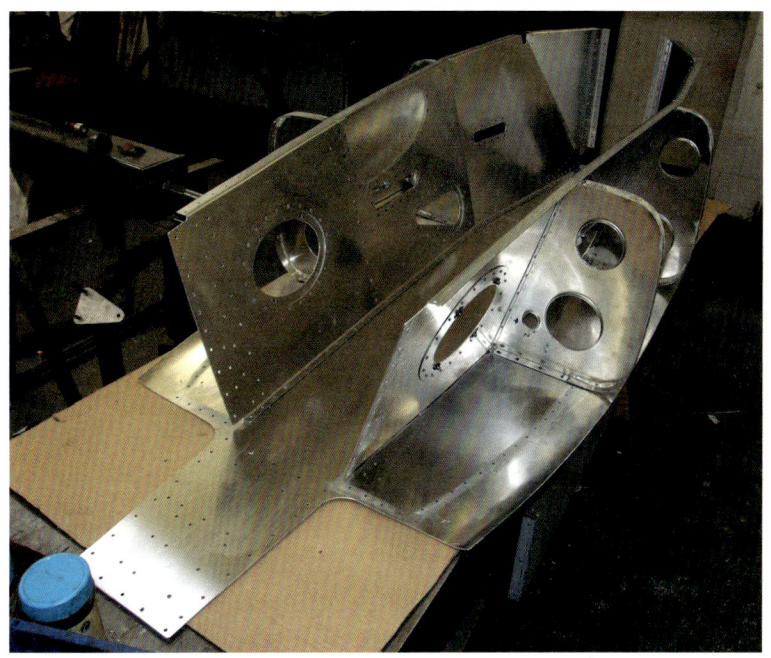

The suspension was remade, with uprights and wishbones being created from 4130 steel, heat-treated up to 28 to 32 Rockwell. New hubs and driveshafts were manufactured from heat-treated 300M, while the brake disc carriers were machined from one part, unlike the originals. New CV joints also had to be made.

TOP: Note the cut-out in the tub, into which a dish will be bolted that's been included to accommodate the driver's hips. *(R&J Simpson Engineering)*

ABOVE: Complete diaphragms with flanged holes were used in the sides of the tub. *(R&J Simpson Engineering)*

ABOVE: The suspension on 72/6 was remade and the brake disc carriers machined from one part, unlike the original. *(Author)*

ABOVE RIGHT: The CV joints had to be extensively modified from already existing GKN bespoke motorsport applications. *(Author)*

RIGHT: Former Grand Prix driver Mike Wilds carried out early testing of Katsu Kubota's rebuilt Type 72. *(R&J Simpson Engineering)*

GKN found one that had the same internal bearing tracks. Simpson & CGA reverse-engineered the old CVs to produce a brand new, spherical track CV joint with a copy of what was on the 72 welded round. In this way it looks identical to the original. 'We were very nervous about the brake shafts and the CV joints,' remembered Simpson.

Historically, the seat would have been made from two-part foam, 'Which,' said Bennett, 'would have been like a brick.' Thus CGA Racing now fits an energy-absorbing seat made out of a resin that's semi-deformable but has a memory, and is covered in a bacteria friendly, fire retardant covering.

At least seven months were taken up working on the project at R&J Simpson, but Bob says, 'I stopped counting the hours we worked on the car.'

At the conclusion of manufacturing its new parts, the car – in kit form – returned to CGA Racing for its build phase. 'The strip down, re-engineering and rebuild took at least 700 hours, without including the manufacturing phase completed by R&J Simpson. 72/6 was a challenging car to build, incredibly so for its year of manufacture,' said Colin Bennett's son Alistair.

CLASSIC TEAM LOTUS

Two Lotus 72s remain in the ownership of the Chapman family, and are thus maintained by Classic Team Lotus. This was established in 1992 to maintain and operate its own and customers' Lotus racing cars. A comprehensive service of restoration, maintenance and operation is provided from Team Lotus's original factory in Hethel, Norfolk. Colin Chapman's widow and son, Hazel and Clive, are the directors, while the staff includes stalwarts from the heyday of Team Lotus. The legendary Bob Dance, for example, has been with Lotus for over five decades, having started with the team as a mechanic in the 1960s. Team Manager Chris Dinnage joined in 1982 and became number one mechanic for Ayrton Senna; Nick Yallop joined in 1979 as a composites technician, while accountant Steve Allen has been with Team Lotus since the days of the Lotus 72. Martin Ogilvy, head of the Team Lotus drawing office for much of the 1980s, acts as a consultant on technical matters.

Classic Team Lotus operates a number of services useful to Type 72 owners. It restores, maintains and operates Team Lotus racing cars. The fact that many of its staff designed, built or operated the cars originally is a massive plus for customers. So, too, is the availability of a massive number of original drawings and components. New parts can also be sourced from the original suppliers, with the company's records ensuring that they're made to the correct specification. It is, understandably, claimed that Team Lotus is the only Formula One World Championship winning marque to have established a works team for historic motorsport.

The team has its own collection of cars, some of which are available for sale, although this doesn't include the 72s. These cars have been used at exhibitions, demonstrated on track and often raced. One of the 72s, 72E/5

LEFT: Clive Chapman at the 2010 Classic Team Lotus Festival, by his side a Lotus 72. *(Author)*

BELOW: Classic Team Lotus's chassis 72/9 hasn't run since its last Grand Prix. However, it's used as a static display, as seen here in company with a Type 25 at an *Autosport* International Show. *(Author)*

139

RESTORATION AND HISTORIC RACING

has been raced by such drivers as Sean Walker, but is now solely used for demonstrations.

The Classic Team Lotus Register exists to identify all the surviving single-seat, open-wheel Lotus racing cars and to make contact with their owners. Fifty-eight monoposto designs were built by Team Lotus, from the Type 12 to the Type 102. In total around 1,400 examples of these were built, of which nearly 550 – including eight Lotus 72s – have been identified as having survived.

It should be noted that Classic Team Lotus also protects, as well as promotes, the commercial interests of Team Lotus history. Its archive of original design drawings, photographs and actual cars can be made available to licensees.

In recent years Classic Team Lotus's 72E/5 has been out and about, although its days in historic race series would appear to be over.

The year 2007 saw it at the American Lotus Owners' Gathering in Colorado, the first time, it was reckoned, that a 72 had been back to the USA since 1975. Emerson Fittipaldi was guest of honour and demonstrated the car, which was also looked after by Bob Dance. It then made it back to the UK a few days later to run at the Goodwood Revival as part of a Tribute to Cosworth parade. The infamous 'The Stig' also drove the car in southern Spain for the BBC's *Top Gear* programme. That year finished in emotional fashion when 72E/5 was taken to the Montjuich Revival, the scene of its 1972 Spanish Grand Prix win. There could only be one driver that day – the original winner, Emerson Fittipaldi. In 2011 the car was back in Barcelona, this time demonstrated by Chris Dinnage.

The following season 72E/5 suffered a setback. A front outer CV joint failure in qualifying for the Jim Clark Revival resulted in

BELOW: Fairuz Fauzy, reserve driver for the Formula One team then known as Lotus, was an understandably enthusiastic pilot of 72E/5 at Snetterton.
(Author)

ABOVE: Work in progress on 72E/5 at Classic Team Lotus's evocative Hethel workshops. *(Author)*

BELOW: One of Classic Team Lotus's two Type 72s ready to be pushed out on to the unique grid at Snetterton on which one of every type of Lotus Formula One car was represented. *(Author)*

the car being withdrawn from the Monaco Historic Grand Prix. Just in case it appears that this particular 72 was getting all the limelight 72/9 was displayed on the Classic Team Lotus stand at the *Autosport* International Show at the start of 2009. The following year Fittipaldi was again reunited with 72E/5 when he demonstrated it at the Bahrain Grand Prix. It was the 40th anniversary of Emerson's first Grand Prix victory and, appropriately, the car was shipped to Brazil later in the season for him to drive it around the streets of São Paulo.

Examples of every type of Lotus Grand Prix car were assembled at Snetterton that year for the Classic Team Lotus Festival. All three of the team that was then know as Lotus Racing (now Caterham) were on hand to demonstrate a car each, with reserve driver Fairuz Fauzy pedalling 72E/5. Five-times Le Mans winner Derek Bell also got the chance to drive it in 2011 during the *Top Gear* live show at the Kyalami circuit in South Africa. Glen Waters, who had joined Team Lotus as a mechanic during the Type 72 years, was in charge of the car for the occasion, while Bell is said to have thoroughly enjoyed himself despite severe rain and thunderstorms. It's largely thanks to Classic Team Lotus that enthusiasts still have the opportunity to savour the sight and sound of a Lotus 72.

RESTORATION AND HISTORIC RACING

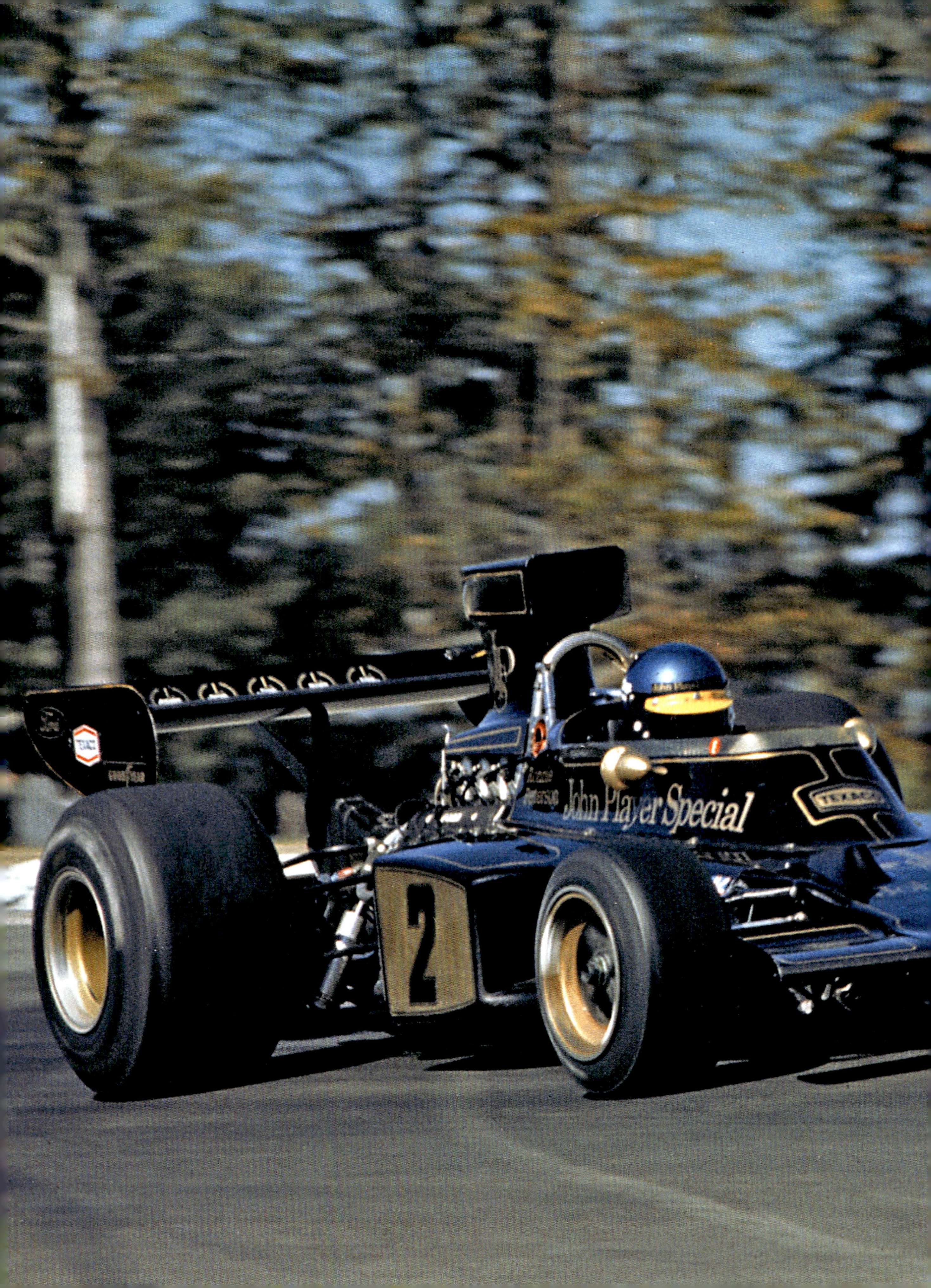
John Player Special
2

'Ronnie was such a lovely guy. He just liked to talk to mechanics; he enjoyed their company.'

Eddie Dennis
Chief Mechanic Team Lotus 1971–75

Chapter Six

Individual chassis histories

The lives of all the Lotus 72 chassis have been well documented. Some have changed little since their Grand Prix careers, while others have undergone major work, in particular the three that had a 'second life' in South Africa. Only one chassis number no longer exists, having been rebuilt into a later car. Some cars had illustrious careers, while others had little or no success.

(Ford)

RIGHT: **Rindt in 72/2 leads Brabham at Brands Hatch. He was only to win when the Australian ran out of fuel on the last lap.** *(Ford)*

BELOW: **Prior to the Type 72's 1 April 1970 press launch, Rindt managed a few wet laps with the prototype at the Hethel test track.** *(Ford)*

Team Lotus manufactured nine Type 72 monocoques. Monocoque number 1 was rebuilt into 72/4. The wreckage of 72/2 escaped from the Italian authorities into private hands. The fourth monocoque, in 72/5, was not repaired by Team Lotus after Emerson Fittipaldi's 1973 accident. The eighth monocoque was used in a new car for Ickx in 1974 and for which Team Lotus continued to use the identity number 5.

72/1

The prototype, which raced just seven times in 1970, always driven by John Miles. It finished only twice, in seventh and eighth places at Zandvoort and Clermont-Ferrand respectively. The majority of the anti-squat geometry was removed from the rear suspension after Spa, thus creating a one-off 72B. The other changes that created a 72C weren't made at this stage. After Brands Hatch the monocoque was dismantled and its parts used to create 72/4. Little of the original was left bar the seat back and the rear bulkhead.

72/2

Another car that only raced during 1970, this was Jochen Rindt's World Championship mount, the only other person to have used it being Alex Soler-Roig when he failed to qualify for the Belgian Grand Prix. After two races it was converted to 72C specification. The anti-squat and anti-dive were removed, the monocoque stiffened and a smaller and lighter FG400 gearbox installed. In this form it became competitive, winning three Grands Prix before Rindt's fatal crash at Monza. The monocoque was severely buckled, and the wheels, front subframe and suspension ripped off. The Italian authorities impounded 72/2 until in 1985 it was acquired by collector Guido Romani. Eight years later his friend Pier-Luigi Mapelli took over ownership, and it was eventually sent back to the UK to be restored. At the time of writing the restoration work had come to a halt and the chassis is currently in a workshop loft in England.

144
LOTUS 72 MANUAL

72/3

This chassis started a remarkable 59 races, and while it was never a Grand Prix winner it was a serial victor in the South African Drivers' Championship in the hands of Dave Charlton. It was the first chassis to be built to 72C specification and was driven in factory form by John Miles and then Reine Wisell before Charlton first tried it at the 1971 British Grand Prix. By this time it had been converted to 72D specification with twin parallel links at the rear. Using this car, now in Lucky Strike colours, Charlton won 22 races and took two SADC titles. Eddie Keizan then drove it for Alex Blignaut before it was returned to Charlton and mothballed.

When Team Gunston's 72/7 was badly damaged 72/3 was converted into a 72E with a deformable structure and brought back into action to replace it. It was retired to the Heidelberg Motor Museum before being mistakenly shipped to the UK instead of 72/6. It was returned to South Africa for a few years until John Brannigan and Rob Grant took it out of the country. Back in England it was resprayed in Gold Leaf colours and was eventually acquired by Michael Schryver, restored by Simon Hadfield and then, in 1999, sold to Yoshio Fukuda, a Japanese collector. Fukuda drove it, still resplendent in red, white and gold, at the 2006 10th Historic Automobile Festival in Japan, at which Team Lotus was honoured.

72/4

This was built up from 72/1 as a 72C, for Rob Walker. Driven by Graham Hill, it took part in just five races during 1970, retiring in all but one, in which it wasn't classified. It was sold to BRM factory driver Jo Siffert, remaining unused in his family's ownership following his death at Brands Hatch. The Fittipaldi brothers bought it in late 1972, repainting it and making it look externally like Emerson's championship-winning car, 72/5. Adrian Hamilton, son of 1953 Le Mans winner Duncan, bought most of the Fittipaldi's collection in 1985, selling 72/4 on to Brands Hatch owner John Foulston. The car was restored to race condition, and with Foulston's wife Mary at the wheel took part in a number of historic events. Foulston was killed testing another car in 1987 but for the next decade the car remained in the family's collection. The current owner is 'Joe' Willenpart from the Netherlands.

ABOVE: 72/3 started 59 races including (seen here) the 1971 Race of Champions at Brands Hatch. *(Ford)*

BELOW: Rob Walker's 72/4 was actually a rehash of 72/1. It raced just five times, driven on each occasion by Graham Hill. At Watkins Glen, Hill retired with a broken clutch. *(Sutton Images)*

72/5

This chassis appeared at the 1970 Italian Grand Prix, where Fittipaldi crashed it in practice, but was then used by him to win the US Grand Prix a month later. The car was modified during the early part of 1971 and by Monte Carlo had become a 72D. Fittipaldi was again its main driver, but a road crash saw him off the scene for a couple of races during which time Dave Walker took its wheel.

During 1972, 72/5 tended to be the spare chassis, although Fittipaldi used it to win three non-championship races – the Race of Champions and the Rothmans 50,000 both at Brands Hatch, and the Gran Premio d'ella Republica Italiana at Vallelunga – as well as the Austrian and Italian Grands Prix. At the latter race the Brazilian drove it to become the youngest ever World Champion after 72/7 had been damaged in an accident on the way to the track. Chassis 72/5 was then rebuilt as the first of the deformable-structure Lotuses, thus being re-designated a 72E. Again, it was often relegated to the role of a spare, but there was a last Grand Prix victory when Fittipaldi won the 1973 Spanish GP.

It was badly damaged in Fittipaldi's crash in the 1973 Dutch GP. The wreckage remains in the Classic Team Lotus stores.

72E/5

The eighth monocoque was built in 1974 and was allocated the number 5. It is referred to as 72E/5 throughout this book. In 1974 it became the regular mount of Jacky Ickx, winning the Race of Champions that year. Towards the end of its active life, 72E/5 was wheeled out for Jim Crawford and Brian Henton. For its last four races, it was given a 5-inch longer wheelbase by placing the oil tank between the rear bulkhead and the engine, thus becoming a 72F. 72E/5 remains in the hands of the Chapman family, and is now being used as part of the Classic Team Lotus collection of cars.

BELOW: **Fittipaldi in 72/5 chases Jo Siffert's BRM at the 1971 British Grand Prix.** *(Ford)*

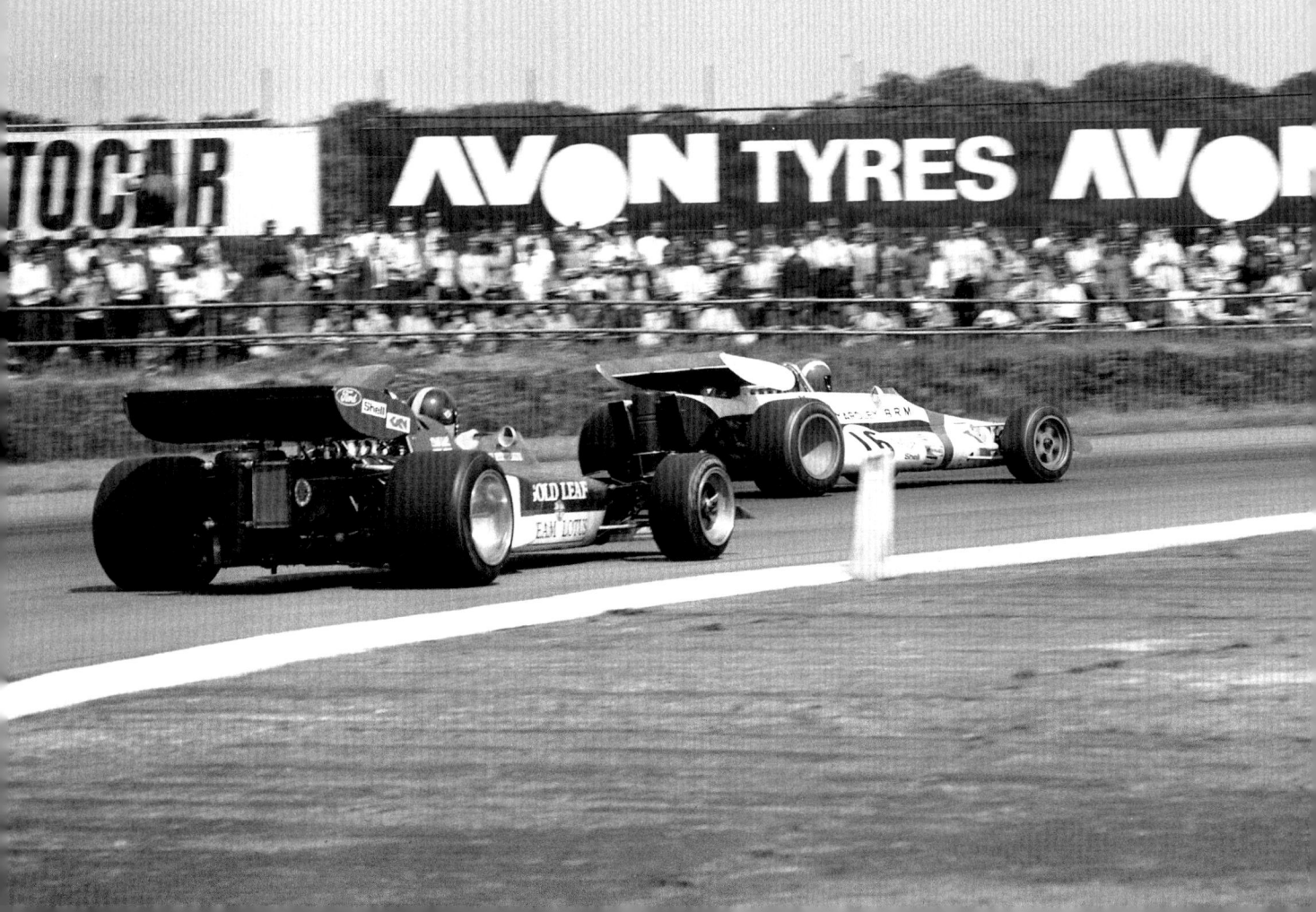

72/6

This was originally a 72D built for Reine Wisell for the latter part of 1971. Dave Walker used it for most of 1972, although the Swede was reunited with it for two races towards the end of the year. It was converted to the deformable structure 72E specification for 1973. It now became the regular mount for Wisell's ultra-rapid compatriot Ronnie Peterson. In his hands it became a winner, taking the French, Austrian, Italian and US Grands Prix. Thereafter it became one of the three 'South African' 72s. As part of Team Gunston, Ian Scheckter used it to challenge Dave Charlton for the SADC title in 1974, winning five races. Eddie Keizan took it over for its final season but the car had won its last race. Like 72/3 it was retired to the Rembrandt Tobacco Company's collection at Heidelberg.

Determined British collector Dave McLaughlin purchased it in the early 1980s. 72/3 was shipped to him by mistake, but he stuck to his guns and, refusing an offer just to swap chassis plates, made sure that 72/6 was his. 72/3 was returned to South Africa. McLaughlin restored the car in JPS colours and retained and raced it for about 24 years. Initially there was nowhere that he could compete with a 72, but he was instrumental in starting an HSCC series that included such cars. It was later owned and raced by Alistair Morrison. In 2011 72/6 was bought by Tokyo-based businessman Katsu Kubota, totally rebuilt by R&J Simpson, prepared by CGA Race Engineering of Warrington, and raced towards the end of the season. It was shipped to Japan in 2012.

72/7

This was built to 72D specification as Emerson Fittipaldi's main car for 1972 and 1973. He was the sole factory driver of the car with the exception of Dave Walker, who raced it just once, at the 1972 US Grand Prix. The Brazilian used it to win on six occasions, including the Silverstone International Trophy and three Grands Prix the first year and the two South American Grands Prix at the start of the following season. The deformable structure regulations meant that it was in 72E guise from the 1973 Spanish Grand Prix onwards.

For 1974 72/7 became the second of the Team Gunston cars, with Paddy Driver at the wheel. He was replaced by Guy Tunmer the following season, and at Killarney in July 1975 Tunmer scored the final contemporary victory for a 72 using this chassis. Later that month he crashed at Kyalami, damaging the car beyond immediate repair. The tub was sent back to the UK and by the time it returned Formula One cars had become obsolete in South Africa. There was some contention as to whether the crashed car was 72/6 and not 72/7, but this seems unlikely. 72/7 also went to the Heidelberg Museum before being acquired by a British collector, who wished to remain anonymous.

ABOVE: Ronnie Peterson used 72/6 to win the 1973 US Grand Prix. *(Ford)*

BELOW: 72/7 won six Grands Prix in the hands of Emerson Fittipaldi, including the 1972 race at Nivelles, Belgium. *(LAT Photographic)*

ABOVE: A practice crash with 72/8 in Austria meant that Brian Henton didn't start what would have been his second Grand Prix. *(Sutton Images)*

72/8

During 1973 Ronnie Peterson alternated between 72/8 and the older 72/6 once the latter had been converted to 72E specification. Likewise originally a 72D, 72/8 was also uprated after its first three races. Towards the end of the season it seemed that Peterson preferred 72/6, so 72/8 became his spare. However, when 72/6 was sold to Team Gunston for 1974 72/8 became his regular mount. With it he won in Monte Carlo, France and Italy and became again a serious contender for the World Championship. For Peterson's final race with the car, the 1975 French Grand Prix, its wheelbase was lengthened by 5in (127mm), making it a 72E.

For its final three races it was driven by Jim Crawford, John Watson and Brian Henton respectively. (There is some contention over whether it was also Crawford's car at Monza, although this is generally reckoned to have been 72/5.) The car then retired to the Donington Collection in Derbyshire, and was acquired by the museum's owner Tom Wheatcroft in 2001. In 2012 it was sold to American film producer Bill Pohlad and transferred via Hall and Hall to Hoole Racing for restoration.

72/9

Ronnie Peterson's contract with Lotus said that he was to have a new car for the 1975 season. With the Lotus 77 not yet ready, he was presented with a new 72 rather than a new design … and was not amused. After is first race the car had its rear suspension modified to accommodate cable-actuation of the torsion bar linkage. Another modification saw the front tack widened. In this guise it was unsuccessful, and prior to the British Grand Prix it was converted, as much as the regulations allowed, back to 1973 specification, although it was always referred to as a 72E. The changes were made to try and overcome handling problems that were now apparent, but it was found that these were down to the fact that the Type 72 – originally built to run on Firestones that had been designed for it – didn't suit the Goodyear tyre designs of the mid-1970s. Peterson was the only person to race 72/9, which never finished higher than fourth in Grands Prix. Still owned by the Chapman family, it is now part of Classic Team Lotus, but only used for static displays.

RIGHT: Jim Crawford raced 72E/5 in F specification at the 1975 Italian Grand Prix. *(Ford)*

OPPOSITE: Peterson in the so-called lightweight 72/9 at Monte Carlo in 1975. Having won the race the year before, he could only finish fourth this time. *(Ford)*

148
LOTUS 72 MANUAL

John Player Special
John Player
Special
John Player Special
DUCKHAMS
DUCKHAMS
GOODYEAR
5
MA
GENDARMERIE

The private entries

The early 1970s were still a time when private entries could start Grands Prix, while South Africa ran its own championship for Formula One cars. Thus a number of Lotus 72s fell into such hands, all but one of them South African. The exception was 72/4, a 72C that was rebuilt from 72/1 for Rob Walker. Walker had been the last privateer to win a Grand Prix when Jo Siffert drove his Lotus 49 to victory at Brands Hatch in 1968. His driver was now Graham Hill, who had left Gold Leaf Team Lotus following a major accident.

The car, sponsored by Brooke Bond Oxo and now in Walker's familiar blue livery, took part in only five contemporary races – the Oulton Park Gold Cup and four Grands Prix. It retired in four of these contests and, 23 laps down on the winner, wasn't classified in the other. In each case Hill was the driver while in Canada it was the sole Lotus, the factory having temporarily withdrawn following Rindt's fatal accident at Monza. At the end of the 1970 season Walker transferred his allegiance to Surtees, while Hill joined Brabham.

The South African Drivers' Championship ensured that three of the cars – 72/3, 72/6 and 72/7 – had long, active lives. The first of these was sold to United Tobacco Company to race in Lucky Strike colours and replace the Lotus 49C that driver Dave Charlton had been using. Yorkshire-born Charlton raced the car as a works entry at Silverstone in 1971 before shipping it to Africa, where he won eight races and the championship under the Scuderia Scribante banner. A foray to Europe for three World Championship events in 1972 yielded no results and the car returned to South Africa. During the next two seasons the dominant Charlton scored another 14 wins with the car and netted another two championships. 72/3 was then driven by Eddie Keizan and Guy Tunmer during two more seasons, but despite

BELOW: **The final appearance of the Brooke Bond Oxo sponsored Rob Walker car was in Mexico City, where it retired with overheating problems.** *(Sutton Images)*

a number of second places never won again. During the time that Charlton was driving the red and white car, Team Lotus ensured that it was kept up to date. For example, after its first two races with a periscope airbox Lotus supplied it with the latest anvil-shaped version.

At the end of the 1973 season rumours began to circulate that Team Gunston was planning to buy a couple of Lotus 72s for the South African series. These were to be for Ian Scheckter, the elder brother of 1979 World Champion Jody, and former motorcycle racer Paddy Driver. In early October it was announced that the two cars were 72/6 and 72/7, which had been driven by the likes of Peterson and Fittipaldi respectively. Scheckter and Driver were never able to pace themselves against Charlton in a similar car, as United Tobacco Company now purchased a newer McLaren M23 for the champion to stay ahead. 72/3 was acquired by Alex Blignaut Racing for Eddie Keizan to drive. It was updated to 72E specification, fitted with

ABOVE: Paddy Driver was a top motorcycle racer, finishing third in the 1965 500cc World Championship behind Mike Hailwood and Giacomo Agostini riding a Matchless. He also raced one of Team Gunston's 72s in South African championship events. He started the 1974 South African Grand Prix in the car, 11 years after he had crashed a Lotus-BRM 24 in practice for the same event. *(Sutton Images)*

LEFT: Dave Charlton was easily the most successful of the Lotus 72 privateers, winning the South African Drivers' Championship three times with such a car. *(Sutton Images)*

RIGHT: One way of keeping Jacques Villeneuve's interest at BAR was to let him drive a Lotus 72 at Valencia. The car was kitted out with Lucky Strike bodywork for a PR event to celebrate 30 years since Dave Charlton's start in the 1973 South African Grand Prix.
(Steve Slater)

BELOW: Local man Guy Tunmer raced in just one Grand Prix, driving one of Team Gunston's Lotus 72s to 11th place at Kyalami in 1975. *(Ford)*

an airbox that looked as if it had come from a Hesketh rather than a Lotus, and painted in blue and gold Embassy colours.

Scheckter won five of the final six rounds of the 1974 season with 72/6, proving that Charlton at last had a serious rival. However, the latter in the McLaren had won the first five races and took the championship again. A decision to swap from troublesome Firestone tyres to Goodyear rubber halfway through the season had proved too late. Keizan, now with Team Gunston, was unable to match Scheckter's performance the following season with the same orange and brown car, and it was left to Tunmer to score the 72's last contemporary victory in the 1975 False Bay 100. Subsequent damage to 72/7 meant that Charlton's old car was brought out of retirement and acquired by Team Gunston to see out the season. The regulations for the 1976 South African Drivers' Championship were changed to Formula Atlantic for 1976; the Formula One cars became obsolete, and the next time a Lotus 72 would race would be as an historic car.

The presence of Lotus 72s in South Africa did mean that their drivers had relatively competitive machinery to compete with the World Championship regulars when they annually travelled to Kyalami for the South African Grand Prix. Thus Keizan, Tunmer, Driver and Ian Scheckter all took part in one Grand Prix with the car. Thanks to his initial drive in the British Grand Prix and his subsequent three-race trip to Europe, Charlton was able to contest five GPs with his 72. Tunmer's 11th place in the 1975 South African Grand Prix was the best that any privately entered Lotus 72 could achieve.

THE PRIVATEER MECHANIC'S VIEW

Stan Collier, who had worked with BRP and Reg Parnell Racing, and long time Rob Walker mechanic Tony Cleverley went to Hethel to put together 72/4. Collier was unaware that some of the parts had come from 72/1 'We just used the bits they gave us,' he recalled.

'All Robbie wanted was a 72, so he would have accepted that,' added Cleverly, who had also worked on Walker's earlier type 49 at the factory. He reckoned that he and Collier were there for about a fortnight with the 72.

'It wasn't bad to work on, a bit complicated with that torsion bar system,' said Collier. 'The inboard brakes used to get a bit hot and we always had to put the coolers on them when they came in. Lotuses could be funny old cars to work on; they were a bit near the bone.'

Collier recalled how Walker 'parked the 72' and wound his team up at the end of the season to become a backer of Team Surtees. He believes that this was mainly due to concern for his friend Graham Hill, who had been involved in a serious accident the year before in a Lotus 49. 'Graham wanted to drive again but Rob Walker did not really want him to. Robbie realised that Graham was struggling a bit by then. He wanted Graham to retire. When Graham said no, instead of sacking him, he closed the team.' This did not stop Hill racing and he continued on with Brabham and then his own team until 1975.

Cleverley left Rob Walker at the end of the 1970 to set up a crash repair business in Capel. For about a month, the 72 went with him. 'Robbie just wanted to leave it somewhere,' he remembered. The garage also sold petrol and each morning Cleverley would wheel the car out on to the forecourt to attract sales, wheeling it back in when the working day was done. 'It was a bit of an attraction.'

When Walker took his Brook Bond Oxo sponsorship to Team Surtees, the car temporarily went with him, sitting unused in a corner of the works before being sold to Jo Siffert who, in 1969, had won the 1969 British Grand Prix with Walker's type 49.

BELOW: Despite the age of the design, four Lotus 72s started the 1975 South African Grand Prix. Eddie Keizan's Team Gunston car was one of them. *(Sutton Images)*

Epilogue

The Lotus 72 became one of the most instantly recognisable Grand Prix cars in history, an icon for many. It was driven by four of the greatest drivers of the era and took two of them to the World Championship, although only three of them won Grands Prix with it. During a five-year period it won 27% of the Grands Prix for which it was entered, a figure that perhaps sums up a sometimes dominant, sometimes troubled period.

The Type 72 wasn't quick out of the box, there was a perceived fragility, and in its final season it almost caused its high profile sponsor to withdraw, such was the trauma then surrounding it. However, its later record should be blamed on the failure of the Type 76, which caused the 72 to remain in service long after it should have been confined to happy retirement.

Although Colin Chapman and Maurice Phillippe introduced new standards with the 72, creating a car that was probably a couple of seasons ahead of its time, the other Formula One constructors didn't rush to copy its features. The Gordon Coppuck-designed McLaren M23 with which Emerson Fittipaldi won his second World Championship may have looked akin to the Type 72 – indeed, there are a number of comparisons, and the outwardly visual differences between the M23 and its M19 predecessor are similar to those between the Lotus 49 and 72; the shape of the M23 also had some of its origins in McLaren's M16 Indy car, as did the 72 with the Type 56.

However, there perhaps the similarities end. There were no torsion bars or inboard front brakes on the M23.

Against all this there were times when the Type 72 was undoubtedly the quickest car in the field and gloriously dominant. While conjecture in motorsport is a fraught pastime, who knows, its place in history may have been even more celebrated had Firestone continued to supply Lotus with bespoke tyres. One only has to listen to Emerson Fittipaldi to realise just how good the Lotus 72 could be when everything was going right for it. It was a package of technologies – such as torsion bars, inboard brakes and side radiators – that only someone with the imagination of Chapman could have put together in one winning car.

Given the fact that the prototype chassis, 72/1, was rebuilt into Rob Walker's 72/4, all of the cars are still in existence, and thankfully the tragic remains of 72/2 are in understanding hands. Brian Henton points to the caprices of chassis plates – the bane of a motorsport historian's life – which would indicate that there's myth in the story of the Lotus 72 as much as there is magic.

And magic there certainly is. The Lotus 72 has left us with some of the great images of the 3-litre era. Men with even the wealth of motor racing experience of Nigel Bennett still go misty-eyed about the thought of Ronnie Peterson in one of his spectacular four-wheel drifts through Silverstone's daunting Woodcote corner. 'You could hear the tyres squealing all the way through. Fabulous.'

Appendices

Lotus 72D specification (1973)

Chassis
Front suspension: Double wishbones, torsion bars.
Rear suspension: Parallel lower links, single top link, twin radius rods, torsion bars.
Suspension dampers: Koni.
Wheel diameter: 13in front, 13 or 15in rear.
Wheel rim width: 10 or 11in front, 15, 16 or 17in rear.
Tyres: Firestone.
Brakes: Girling.
Brake pads: Ferodo.

Steering: Cam gears rack and pinion.
Radiator: Twin Serck.
Fuel tanks: FPT fuel cells.
Battery: Varley.
Instruments: Smiths.

Engine
Type: Cosworth DFV.
Capacity: 2,993cc.
Bore and stroke: 85.6mm x 64.8mm.
Compression ratio: 11:1.
Maximum power and rpm: 450bhp at 10,000rpm.

Valves Inlet: 1.32in x 2.
Outlet: 1.14in x 2.
Valve lift: 0.4in.
Valve timings: 62, 86, 86, 62.
Pistons and rings: Cosworth/Hepolite.
Bearings: Vandervell.
Fuel system: Lucas petrol injection.
Fuel and oil: Texaco/Havoline.
Ignition system: Lucas OPUS.
Sparking plugs: Champion.

Transmission
Gearbox: Hewland FG400

Crown wheel and pinion: Hewland.
Drive shafts: GKN/Lotus.
Clutch: Borg and Beck.
Clutch lining: Ferodo.

Dimensions
Wheelbase: 99in.
Track: 58in front, 61in rear.
Engine weight: 365lb.
Gearbox weight: 98lb.
Chassis weight (tub): 68lb.
Formula weight: 1,213lb.
Fuel capacity: 42 gallons.
Fuel consumption: 6.5mpg (approx).

Lotus 72 World Championship Grand Prix history

1970		
19 April	Spanish GP – Jarama	4th Jochen Rindt 72/2 • DNQ John Miles 72/1.
7 June	Belgian GP – Spa-Francorchamps	Rtd Miles 72B/1 • DNQ Alex Soler-Roig 72C/2
21 June	Dutch GP – Zandvoort	1st Rindt 72C/2 • 7th Miles 72B/1
5 July	French GP – Clermont-Ferrand	1st Rindt 72C/2 • 8th Miles 72B/1
18 July	British GP – Brands Hatch	1st Rindt 72C/2 • Rtd Miles 72B/1
2 August	German GP – Hockenheim	1st Rindt 72C/2 • Rtd Miles 72C/3
16 August	Austrian GP – Osterreichring	Rtd Rindt 72C/2 • Rtd Miles 72B/3
6 September	Italian GP – Monza	DNS (fatal practice accident) Rindt 72C/2 • DNS Hill 72C/4 • DNS Miles 72C/3 • DNS Emerson Fittipaldi 72C/5.
20 September	Canadian GP – St Jovite	NC Hill 72C/4
4 October	US GP – Watkins Glen	1st Fittipaldi 72C/5 • 3rd Reine Wisell 72C/3 • Rtd Hill 72C/4
18 October	Mexican GP – Mexico City	NC Wisell 72C/3 • Rtd Hill 72C/4 • Rtd Fittipaldi 72C/5
1971		
6 March	South African GP – Kyalami	4th Wisell 72C/3 • Rtd Fittipaldi 72C/5
18 April	Spanish GP – Montjuich Park	12th Wisell 72C/3 • 13th Fittipaldi 72C/5
13 May	Monaco GP – Monte Carlo	5th Fittipaldi 72D/5 • Rtd Wisell 72C/3
20 June	Dutch GP – Zandvoort	DSQ Wisell 72C/3
4 July	French GP – Paul Ricard	3rd Fittipaldi 72D/5 • 6th Wisell 72D/3
17 July	British GP – Silverstone	3rd Fittipaldi 72D/5 • Rtd Dave Charlton 72D/3
1 August	German GP – Nürburgring	8th Wisell 72/6 • Rtd Fittipaldi 72D/5
18 August	Austrian GP – Osterreichring	2nd Fittipaldi 72D/5 • 4th Wisell 72/6
19 September	Canadian GP – Mosport Park	5th Wisell 72/6 • 7th Fittipaldi 72D/5
3 October	US GP – Watkins Glen	19th Fittipaldi 72D/5 • Rtd Wisell 72D/6
1972		
23 January	Argentine GP – Buenos Aires	DSQ Dave Walker 72D/6 • Rtd Fittipaldi 72D/5
4 March	South African GP	2nd Fittipaldi 72D/5 • 10th Walker 72D/6 • Rtd Charlton 72D/3

DNQ Did not qualify
DNS Did not start
DSQ Disqualified
NC Not classified
Rtd Retired
Wdn Withdrawn

1 May	*Spanish GP – Jarama*	1st Fittipaldi 72D/7 • 9th Walker 72D/4
14 May	*Monaco GP – Monte Carlo*	3rd Fittipaldi 72D/7 • 14th Walker 72D/5
4 June	*Belgian GP – Nivelles*	1st Fittipaldi 72D/7 • 14th Walker 72D/6
7 July	*French GP – Clermont-Ferrand*	2nd Fittipaldi 72D/7 • 18th Walker 72D/6
15 July	*British GP – Brands Hatch*	1st Fittipaldi 72D/7 • Rtd Walker 72D/6 • Rtd Charlton 72D/3
30 July	*German GP – Nürburgring*	Rtd Charlton 72D/3 • Rtd Walker 72D/6 • Rtd Fittipaldi 72D/7
13 August	*Austrian GP – Osterreichring*	1st Fittipaldi 72D/5 • Rtd Walker 72D/7
10 September	*Italian GP – Monza*	1st Fittipaldi 72D/5
24 September	*Canadian GP – Mosport Park*	11th Fittipaldi 72D/7 • Rtd Wisell 72D/6
8 October	*US GP – Watkins Glen*	10th Wisell 72D/6 • Rtd Fittipaldi 72D/5 • Rtd Walker 72D/7

1973

28 January	*Argentine GP – Buenos Aires*	1st Fittipaldi 72D/7 • Rtd Ronnie Peterson 72D/8
11 February	*Brazilian GP – Interlagos*	1st Fittipaldi 72D/7 • Rtd Peterson 72D/8
3 March	*South African GP – Kyalami*	3rd Fittipaldi 72D/7 • 11th Peterson 72D/8 • Rtd Charlton 72D/3
29 April	*Spanish GP – Montjuich Park*	1st Fittipaldi 72E/5 • Rtd Peterson 72E/8
20 May	*Belgian GP – Zolder*	3rd Fittipaldi 72E/7 • Rtd Peterson 72E/6
3 June	*Monaco GP – Monte Carlo*	2nd Fittipaldi 72E/7 • 3rd Peterson 72E/6
17 June	*Swedish GP – Anderstorp*	2nd Peterson 72E/6 • 12th Fittipaldi 72E/7
1 July	*French GP – Paul Ricard*	1st Peterson 72E/6 • Rtd Fittipaldi 72E/5
14 July	*British GP – Silverstone*	2nd Peterson 72E/6 • Rtd Fittipaldi 72E/5
29 July	*Dutch GP – Zandvoort*	11th Peterson 72E/6 • Rtd Fittipaldi 72E/7
5 August	*German GP – Nürburgring*	6th Fittipaldi 72E/7 • Rtd Peterson 72E/6
19 August	*Austrian GP – Osterreichring*	1st Peterson 72E/6 • Rtd Fittipaldi 72E/7
9 September	*Italian GP – Monza*	1st Peterson 72E/6 • 2nd Fittipaldi 72E/7.
23 September	*Canadian GP – Mosport Park*	2nd Fittipaldi 72E/7 • Rtd Peterson 72E/6
7 October	*US GP – Watkins Glen*	1st Peterson 72E/6 • 6th Fittipaldi 72E/7

1974

13 January	*Argentine GP – Buenos Aires*	13th Peterson 72E/8 • Rtd Jacky Ickx 72E/5
27 January	*Brazilian GP – Interlagos*	3rd Ickx 72E/5 • 6th Peterson 72E/8
30 March	*South African GP – Kyalami*	13th Ian Scheckter 72E/6 • Rtd Paddy Driver 72E/7 • Wdn John McNichol 72D/3
26 May	*Monaco GP – Monte Carlo*	1st Peterson 72E/8 • Rtd Ickx 72E/5
9 June	*Swedish GP – Anderstorp*	Rtd Peterson 72E/8 • Rtd Ickx 72E/5
23 June	*Dutch GP – Zandvoort*	8th Peterson 72E/8 • 11th Ickx 72E/5
7 July	*French GP – Dijon-Prenois*	1st Peterson 72E/8 • 5th Ickx 72E/5
20 July	*British GP – Brands Hatch*	3rd Ickx 72E/5 • 10th Peterson 72E/8
4 August	*German GP – Nürburgring*	5th Ickx 72E/5
18 August	*Austrian GP – Osterreichring*	Rtd Peterson 72E/8
8 September	*Italian GP – Monza*	1st Peterson 72E/8
9 September	*Canadian GP – Mosport Park*	3rd Peterson 72E/8 • 13th Ickx 72E/5
6 October	*US GP – Watkins Glen*	Rtd Ickx 72E/5 • Rtd Peterson 72E/8

1975

12 January	*Argentine GP – Buenos Aires*	8th Ickx 72E/5 • Rtd Peterson 72E/8
26 January	*Brazilian GP – Interlagos*	9th Ickx 72E/5 • 15th Peterson 72E/8
1 March	*South African GP – Kyalami*	10th Peterson 72E/9 • 11th Guy Tunmer 72E/7 • 12th Ickx 72E/5 • 13th Eddie Keizan 72E/6
27 April	*Spanish GP – Montjuich Park*	2nd Ickx 72E/5 • Rtd Peterson 72E/8
11 May	*Monaco GP – Monte Carlo*	4th Peterson 72E/9 • 8th Ickx 72E/5
25 May	*Belgian GP – Zolder*	Rtd Ickx 72E/5 • Rtd Peterson 72E/9
8 June	*Swedish GP – Anderstorp*	9th Peterson 72E/9 • 15th Ickx 72E/5
26 June	*Dutch GP – Zandvoort*	Rtd Peterson 72E/9 • Rtd Ickx 72E/5
7 July	*French GP – Paul Ricard*	10th Peterson 72E/9 • Rtd Ickx 72E/5
19 July	*British GP – Silverstone*	16th Brian Henton 72F/5 • Rtd Peterson 72E/9 • Rtd Jim Crawford 72F/8
3 August	*German GP – Nürburgring*	Rtd Peterson 7RE/9 • Rtd John Watson 72F/8
17 August	*Austrian GP – Osterreichring*	9th Peterson 72E/9 • DNS Henton 72F/5
9 September	*Italian GP – Monza*	13th Crawford 72E/8 • Rtd Peterson 72E/9
10 October	*US GP – Watkins Glen*	5th Peterson 72E/9 • 12th Henton 72F/5

Drivers' World Championship

1970 Jochen Rindt 1st 45 points (also Lotus 49)
Emerson Fittipaldi 10th 12 points (also Lotus 49)
Reine Wisell 16th 4 points

1971 Emerson Fittipaldi 6th 16 points (also Lotus 56B)
Reine Wisell 12th 9 points (also Lotus 56B)

1972 Emerson Fittipaldi 1st 61 points
Dave Walker and Reine Wisell – *did not score.*

1973 Emerson Fittipaldi 2nd 55 points
Ronnie Peterson 3rd 52 points

1974 Ronnie Peterson 5th 35 points
Jacky Ickx 10th 12 points

1975 Ronnie Peterson 12th 6 points
Jacky Ickx 15th 3 points
Jim Crawford, Brian Henton and John Watson – *did not score.*

Constructors' Championship

1970 1st 59 points (also type 49)
1971 5th 21 points (also type 56B)
1972 1st 61 points
1973 1st 92 points
1974 4th 42 points
1975 7th 9 points

BELOW: Final laps for the Lotus 72 – Ronnie Peterson in the 1975 United States Grand Prix. *(Ford)*

Lotus 72 non-World Championship race history

1970		
26 April	*BRDC International Trophy – Silverstone*	Rtd Jochen Rindt 72/2 • Rtd John Miles 72/1
22 August	*Gold Cup – Oulton Park*	2nd Rindt 72/2 • Rtd Graham Hill 72C/4
1971		
24 January	*Argentine GP – Buenos Aires*	7th Reine Wisell 72C/3 • NC Emerson Fittipaldi 72C/5
21 March	*Race of Champions – Brands Hatch*	Rtd Wisell 72C/3 • Rtd Tony Trimmer 72C/5
28 March	*Questor GP – Ontario Motor Speedway*	Rtd Fittipaldi 72C/5 • Rtd Wisell 72C/3
9 April	*Rothmans Trophy – Oulton Park*	7th Fittipaldi 72C/5
8 May	*BRDC International Trophy – Silverstone*	13th Wisell 72C/3
13 June	*Jochen Rindt Memorial Race – Hockenheim*	9th Dave Walker 72D/5 • 10th Wisell 72D/3 • DNS Tony Trimmer 72/5
7 August	*25th Anniversary Trophy – Kyalami*	1st Dave Charlton 72D/3
28 August	*False Bay 100 – Killarney*	Rtd Charlton 72D/3
19 September	*Rhodesian GP – Bulawayo*	4th Charlton 72D/3
10 October	*Rand Spring Trophy – Kyalami*	1st Charlton 72D/3
23 October	*Welkom 100 – Goldfields*	1st Charlton 72D/3
24 October	*Rothmans Victory Race – Brands Hatch*	2nd Fittipaldi 72D/5
1972		
8 January	*Cape South Easter Trophy – Killarney*	1st Charlton 72D/3
29 January	*Highveld 100 – Kyalami*	1st Charlton 72D/3
19 March	*Race of Champions – Brands Hatch*	1st Fittipaldi 72D/5 • 10th Walker 72D/6
30 March	*Brazilian GP – Interlagos*	5th Walker 72D/6 • Rtd Fittipaldi 72D/7
3 April	*Coronation 100 – Pietermaritzburg*	1st Charlton 72D/3
22 April	*Goldfields Autumn Trophy – Welkom*	Rtd Charlton 72D/3
23 April	*BRDC International Trophy – Silverstone*	1st Fittipaldi 72D/7 • DNS Walker 72D/6
14 May	*Bulawayo 100 – Bulawayo*	1st Charlton 72D/3
25 May	*Gold Cup – Oulton Park*	2nd Fittipaldi 72D/5 • Rtd Walker 72D/6
18 May	*Gran Premio Repubblica Italiana – Vallelunga*	1st Fittipaldi 72D/5
3 June	*South Africa Republic Festival Trophy – Kyalami*	1st Charlton 72D/3

5 August	Rand Winter Trophy – Kyalami	1st Charlton 72D/3
26 August	Van Riebeck Trophy – Killarney	1st Charlton 72D/3
28 August	Rothmans 50,000 – Brands Hatch	1st Fittipaldi 72D/5
10 September	Rhodesian GP – Bulawayo	Rtd Charlton 72D/3
30 September	Rand Spring Trophy	1st Charlton 72D/3
21 October	Welkom 100 – Welkom	1st Charlton 72D/3
22 October	John Player Challenge Trophy – Brands Hatch	Rtd Fittipaldi 72D/7

1973

6 January	Cape South Easter Trophy – Killarney	1st Charlton 72D/3
27 January	Highveld 100 – Kyalami	1st Charlton 72D/3
18 March	Race of Champions Brands Hatch	Rtd Fittipaldi 72E/5 • Rtd Ronnie Peterson 72E/6
30 March	Goldfields Autumn Trophy – Welkom	1st Charlton 72D/3
8 April	BRDC International Trophy – Silverstone	2nd Peterson 72E/8 • Rtd Fittipaldi 72E/5
23 April	Mercury 100 Pietermartizburg	1st Charlton 72D/3
26 May	South African Republic Festival Trophy – Kyalami	1st Charlton 72D/3
10 June	Bulawayo 100 – Bulawayo	4th Charlton 72D/3
1 July	Natal Winter Trophy – Pietermaritzburg	1st Charlton 72D/3
4 August	Rand Winter Trophy – Kyalami	1st Charlton 72D/3
25 August	False Bay 100 – Killarney	1st Charlton 72D/3
23 September	Rhodesian GP – Bulawayo	1st Charlton 72D/3
6 October	Rand Spring Trophy – Kyalami	1st Charlton 72D/3
20 October	Goldfield 100 – Welkom	Rtd Charlton 72D/3

1974

17 March	Race of Champions – Brand Hatch	1st Jacky Ickx 72E/5
13 April	Mercury 100 – Pietermaritzburg	2nd Ian Schekter 72E/6 • 3rd Paddy Driver 72E/7
4 May	Cape South Easte Trophy – Killarney	3rd Driver 72E/7 • 5th Scheckter 72E/6 • DNS Eddie Keizan 72E/3
25 May	South African Republic Trophy – Kyalami	2nd Keizan 72E/3 • 3rd Scheckter 72E/6 • 4th Driver 72E/7
15 June	Brandkop Winter Trophy – Brandkop	2nd Keizan 72E/3 • 3rd Scheckter 72E/6 • 4th Driver 72E/7
30 June	Bulawayo 100 – Bulawayo	2nd Keizan 72E/3 • 3rd Scheckter 72E/6 • Rtd Driver 72E/7
13 July	Natal Winter Trophy – Pietermaritzburg	1st Scheckter 72E/6 • 3rd Keizan 72E/3 • DNS Driver 72E/7
10 August	Rand Winter Trophy – Kyalami	1st Scheckter 72E/6 • 3rd Driver 72E/7 • Rtd Keizan 72E/3
15 September	Rhodesian GP – Donnybrook	1st Scheckter 72E/6 • 3rd Driver 72E/7 • 7th Keizan 72E/3
19 October	Goldfields 100 – Welkom	1st Scheckter 72E/6 • 2nd Driver 72E/7 • DNS Keizan 72E/3

1975

8 February	Cape South Easter Trophy – Killarney	2nd Guy Tunmer 72E/7 • Rtd Keizan 72E/6
16 March	Race of Champions – Brands Hatch	3rd Peterson 72E/9 • 4th Ickx 72E/5.
22 March	Goldfields 100 – Welkom	2nd Tunmer 72E/7 • Rtd Keizan 72E/6
29 March	Mercury 100 – Pietermaritzburg	3rd Keizan 72E/6 • Rtd Tunmer 72E/7
13 April	BRDC International Trophy – Silverstone	DNS Peterson 72E/9 • DNS Jim Crawford 72E/5
3 May	Brandkop Winter Trophy – Brandkop	Rtd Keizan 72E/6
31 May	South African Republic Trophy – Kyalami	3rd Tunmer 72E/7 • Rtd Keizan 72E/6
5 July	False Bay 100 – Killarney	1st Tunmer 72E/7 • 4th Keizan 72E/6
26 July	Rand Winter Trophy – Kyalami	3rd Keizan 72E/6 • Rtd Tunmer 72E/3
24 August	Swiss GP – Dijon-Prenois	4th Peterson 72E/9
1 September	Natal Spring Trophy – Pietermaritzburg	2nd Keizan 72E/6 • Rtd Tunmer 72E/3
4 October	Rand Spring Trophy – Kyalami	3rd Tunmer 72E/3 • DNS Keizan 72E/6
26 October	Donnybrook 100 – Donnybrook	2nd Tunmer 72E/3 • Rtd Keizan 72E/6

South African Drivers' Championship

1971 Dave Charlton (also Lotus 49)
1972 Dave Charlton
1973 Dave Charlton

Extracts from FIA Year Book of Automobile Sport, 1972

Single-Seater Racing Cars – International Formulae (Group 8)

Art. 293. – Formula No.1.
Validity: from the 1st January 1966 to 31st December 1875.
Engines with reciprocating pistons:
a) engine cylinder-capacity without supercharging: inferior or equal to 3,000cc;
b) engine cylinder-capacity with supercharging: inferior or equal to 1,500cc.
Number of cylinders: max 12.
Turbine engine
Utilization authorized on the basis of the Equivalence Formula given under Art. 252 j).
Minimum weight, without ballast: 550kg.

Art. 296. – Prescriptions and definitions applicable to racing cars of the 3 international formulae.

a) **Minimum weight:** the minimum weight is that of the car in running order i.e. with all lubrication and cooling liquids but without fuel.
   The ballast which is prohibited is that of a removable type. It is therefore permissible to complete the weight of the car through one or several ballasts incorporated to the materials of the car provided that solid and unitary blocks are used, and that they are fixed by means of a tool and offer the opportunity of being sealed on should the officials entrusted with the scrutineering of the car deem it necessary.
b) **The construction of the vehicle** must be symmetrical i.e. when the car is lifted laterally and weighed, the half weight on either side must be equal to half the overall weight, a margin of + or − 5% being allowed for the said half weight. To verify the above, the weighing must be done with all tanks full (fuel, water, oil) and a driver, weighing at least 75 kilos normally sitting at the steering-wheel (or a ballast of the same weight occupying the same place).
c) **Reverse gear:** all vehicles must have a gearbox including a reverse gear, which must be in working order when the car starts the events and able to be operated by the driver when normally in his seat.
d) **Compulsory automatic starter** with electrical or other source of energy carried aboard the car and able to be controlled by the driver when normally in his seat.
e) **Driver's seat** liable to be occupied or left without it being necessary to open a door or remove a panel. Sitting at his steering-wheel the driver must be facing the road.
   Moreover, the cockpit must be so conceived that the maximum time necessary for the driver to get in or out does not exceed 5 seconds.
f) **Safety harness:** Cars must be equipped with a 'six-point' safety harness, i.e. a harness made of two shoulder straps, one abdominal strap and two crutch straps. The wearing of this harness is compulsory.
g) **Coachwork:** No part of the coachwork, with the exception of the safety roll bar, shall exceed in height a horizontal plane, 80cm above the lowest point of the entirely sprung structure of the car.
   In other words, a car with its wheels and the mobile suspension elements removed, but without regard to the roll-over bar, must pass between two parallel planes separated by 80cm.
   Behind the front wheels, the coachwork shall not exceed a maximum width of 110cm.
   The coachwork ahead of the front wheels may be extended to an overall maximum width of 150cm.
   Nevertheless, any part of the coachwork ahead of the front wheels, exceeding overall width of 110cm, shall not extend above the height of the front wheel rims.
   Wheels shall be external to the coachwork.
   The coachwork opening giving access to the cockpit must have the following minimal dimensions:
   Length: 60cm;
   Width: 45cm, maintained over 30cm from the most rearward point of the seat-backrest towards the front.
h) **Braking safety system** which must include a double circuit operated by the same pedal and complying with the following:
   – the pedal shall normally control the four wheels;
   – in case of a leakage at any point of the brake system pipes or of any kind of failure in the brake transmission system, the pedal shall still control at least two wheels.
i) **Filling port complying** with the following requirements:
   – the filling port(s) and their caps shall not protrude beyond the coachwork material;
   – the opening shall have a sufficient diameter for allowing the air exhaust at the time of quick refuelling (in particular those done under pressure) and if necessary the breather-pipe connecting the tank with the atmosphere shall be such as to avoid any liquid leakage during the running.
j) **Oil catch tank:** the mounting of a tank(s) or device meant for collecting any oil spilling out of the engine and/or transmission is compulsory. This device must be conceived in conformity with the prescriptions of Art. 253 q).
k) **Exhaust pipes:** the outlet orifices of the exhaust pipes, when directed horizontally to the rear, must be placed at a height of more than 30cm and less than 60cm above the ground. If they are not entirely covered by an element of the coachwork, they may not protrude by more than 25cm beyond the overall length of the car.
1) **No refuelling of lubricant** is allowed for the whole duration of the event.
   The filling ports of the oil tanks and radiators shall provide the possibility of affixing seals.
   The leads sealing the filling port(s) of the lubricant tank(s) may not be removed at any time during the race.
   The leads sealing the filling port(s) of the radiator(s) shall be in place at the start of the race, but may be removed at any pit-stop.

Art. 297. – Safety devices: the safety devices and measures given hereafter must be complied with for racing cars of the international formulae.

a) Roll-bars:
Dimensions: the dimensions of the roll-bars must be as follows: the minimum height must be at least 36in (92cm) measured along the line of the driver's spine, from the metal seat to the top of the roll-bar. The top of the roll-bar must also be at least 5cm above the driver's helmet, when the driver is sitting In normal driving position.

The width must be at least 38cm measured inside the roll-bar between the two vertical pillars of the sides. It must be measured at 60cm above the metal seat on the perpendicular to the line of the driver's spine.

Strength: in order to obtain a sufficient strength for the roll-bar, two possibilities are left to the manufacturers:

a) The roll-over bar, of entirely free structural conception, must be capable to withstand the stress minima indicated under Art. 253 o) – III.

b) The tubes and brace(s) must have a diameter of at least 1$\tfrac{3}{8}$inch (3.5cm) and at least 0.090 inch (2mm) wall thickness. The material should be molybdenum chromium SAE 4130 or SAE 4125 (or equivalent in DIN, NF, etc.).

There must be at least one brace from the top of the bar rearwards at an angle not exceeding 60° with the horizontal. The diameter and material of the brace must be the same as those of the roll-bar itself.

In the case of two braces, the diameter of each of them may be reduced to 20/26mm.

Removable connections between the main hoop and the brace must comply with drawings nos. 10 and 11 of Art. 253 or with any other type approved by the FIA.

b) Cables, lines and electrical equipment: except if the cables, lines and electrical equipment such as battery, fuel pump, etc., are in compliance with the requirements of the aircraft industry as regards their location, material and connections, they must be placed or fitted in such a way that any leakage cannot result in:
– accumulation of liquid.
– entry of liquid into the cockpit,
– contact between liquid and any electrical line or equipment.

Should the cables, lines or electrical equipment pass through or be fitted in the cockpit, they must be fully enclosed in a cover of a liquid-tight and fire-proof material.

c) Safety fuel tanks
Formula 1 cars must be equipped with safety fuel tanks in conformity with the specifications FIA/Spec/FT3 (see Art. 253 j).

d) Red warning light
All Formula cars must be equipped with a rearward facing red warning light of at east 15 watts. This light must be mounted as high as possible on the centre-line of the car and be clearly visible from the rear. The warning light must be switched on by order of the clerk of the course.

e) Tank fillers and caps: it is recalled that on Formula cars, the tank fillers and their caps must not protrude beyond the coachwork.

The caps must be designed in such a way as to ensure an efficient locking action which reduces the risks of an accidental opening following a crash impact or incomplete locking after refuelling.

The fillers must be placed away from points which are vulnerable in case of a crash. The air vents must be located at least 25cm to the rear of the cockpit.

f) Electric circuit-breakers: it is recalled that since 1st January 1969, the fitting of a general electric circuit-breaker, clearly indicated, is mandatory for all cars taking part in speed races.

For Formula cars, this circuit-breaker must be indicated by a blue triangle with a spark and be easy to reach from inside as well as from outside the car.

g) Extinguishing system: All cars of the International racing formulae must be fitted with an extinguishing system conforming to Art. 269.

Art. 298. – Additional safety measures applicable to Formula 1.

The following safety measures will be valid exclusively for Formula 1 as from the dates indicated. If appropriate, these measures replace those mentioned above.

a) At least half of the extinguishing capacity must be placed forward of the engine but rearward of the foremost pick-up points of the front suspension. Waivers to this rule may be given by the CSI for an installation which can be considered to be within the main structure of the car. Applicable as from 1st January 1972.

b) Provision for a clearly indicated external emergency handle which can be actuated easily by the circuit rescue personnel even at a distance with a hook. This emergency handle shall simultaneously initiate the fire-extinguisher, cut off the engine and isolate the battery. Applicable as from 1st July 1972.

c) Compulsory fitting of a headrest capable of restraining 17kg under a rear-ward acceleration of 5G. Its dimensions shall be such that in no case can the driver's head be trapped between the roll-over bar and the headrest itself. Applicable as from 1st January 1972.

d) The use of magnesium sheet will be authorized only if its thickness exceeds 3mm. Applicable as from 1st January 1972.

e) The battery must be capable of starting the engine at least twice. However, it will be possible to start the engine in the pits or on the dummy grid with an external power source. In that case, the starter socket must be installed at the rear of the car and must face rearwards. If male sockets are used, they must be recessed and be provided with a cover. Applicable as from 1st January 1972.

f) Chromium plating of steel suspension members of over 45 tons per sq in tensile strength is forbidden. Applicable as from 1st January 1972.

g) Manufacturers may replace, inside the rubber safety tanks, safety foam by a supplementary internal bag, made of a supple synthetic material, which shall contain the fuel. The space between this inner bag and the elastomere outer bag to be pressurized with an inert gas. This type of safety tank eliminates the necessity of air vents and avoids any mixtures of air and fuel inside the tank.

h) It will be allowed to increase the overall width of the car to 130cm on condition that the supplementary 10cm on each side form a deformable structure, containing no fuel, fuel lines, electrical power sources or lines.

However, any aerodynamic device situated behind the front wheels must remain within 55cm on either side of the car's centre-line. Applicable as from 1st January 1972.

i) The part of the structure surrounding the fuel tank which is in direct contact with the external air stream, must include an aluminium sheet of at least 1.5mm thickness. The alloy used must be an aluminium-magnesium alloy with a minimum tensile strength of 14 tons per sq in and a minimum elongation of 5%. The use of other materials for the surrounding structure may be authorized by the CSI on condition that they ensure an impact resistance equivalent to the prescribed aluminium. Applicable as from 1st January 1972.

Useful contacts

Avon Tyres Motorsport
Bath Road
Melksham
Wiltshire SN12 8AA
Tel 01225 703101
Fax 01225 707 880
Website www.avontyres.com
■ *Supplier of tyres for historic Formula One racing.*

CGA Race Engineering
Forward Works
Woolston
Warrington
Cheshire WA1 4BA
Tel 01925 819980
Website http://cgaracing.com
■ *Historic racing car preparation and racing team.*

Classic Team Lotus
Potash Lane
Hethel
Norfolk NR14 8EY
Tel 01953 601621
Website
www.classicteamlotus.co.uk
■ *Maintains and races own and customers' Team Lotus racing cars.*

Ellis Clowes
27 Horse Fair
Banbury
Oxfordshire OX16 0AE
Tel 01295 221190
Website www.ellisclowes.com.
■ *Insurance broker.*

Geoff Richardson Racing Engines
7 Brook Road
Bicton Industrial Park
Kimbolton
Cambridgeshire PE28 0LR
Tel 01480 861599
Fax 01480 861561
Website www.geoffrichardsonengines.com
■ *Historic race engines supplier and rebuilder.*

Hall and Hall
Graham Hill Way
Cherry Holt Road
Bourne
Lincolnshire PE10 9PJ
Tel 01778 392562
Fax 01778 392561
Website www.hallandhall.net
■ *Historic racing car sales, restoration and race preparation.*

Hewland Engineering
Waltham Road
White Waltham
Maidenhead
Berkshire SL6 3LR
Tel 01628 827600
Website www.hewland.com
■ *Gearbox manufacturer*

Historic Grand Prix
4 Finch Road, North Salem
NY 10560, USA
Website
www.historicgrandprix.com
■ *Historic Formula One race organiser.*

Hoole Racing
Nene Road
Bicton Industrial Park
Kimbolton
Huntingdon
Cambridgeshire PE28 0LF
Tel 01480 861233
Website
www.hooleracing.co.uk
■ *Historic racing car preparation and racing team.*

Langford Performance Engineering
17 Bradfield Close
Finedon Road Industrial Estate
Wellingborough NN8 4RQ
Tel 01933 441661
Fax 01933 441549
Website www.lpengines.com
■ *New build and rebuild engines.*

Masters Historic Racing
The Bunker
Lower End Road
Wavendon
Milton Keynes MK17 8DA
Tel 01908 587545
Fax 01908 587009
Website
www.themastersseries.com
■ *Organiser of the Grand Prix Masters series.*

R&J Simpson Engineering
Unit 3–4 Mariner
Lichfield Road Industrial Estate
Tamworth
Staffordshire B79 7UL
Tel 01827 67898
Fax 01827 63783
Website
www.randjsimpson.com
■ *Restoration and reproduction of historic racing cars.*

Simon Hadfield Motorsports
Blackbrook Hill House
Tickow Lane
Shepshed
Loughborough
Leicestershire LE12 9EY
Tel 01509 506054
Fax 01509 600136
■ *Historic racing car preparation and racing team.*

Stuart McCrudden Associates
West Hall
Lea Lane
Great Braxted
Witham
Essex CM8 3EP
Tel 01621 892814
Fax 01621 892815
■ *Organises the Historic Formula One series.*

Index

Page numbers in **bold** include photographs or illustrations. Entries for cars are listed under the manufacturer's name, followed by the model name eg. Cooper-Climax, T60.

active suspension 23
aerodynamics 43–55, 93
Agostini, Giacomo 151
air ducts (drawing) **52**
airboxes 36, **51**, **52**
aircraft industry, influence of 31, 33, 37
Alex Blignaut Racing 145, 151–2
Alfa Romeo 33
Allen, Steve 139
Alunox **82**
American Lotus Owners' Gathering, 2007 140
Amon, Chris 16
ancillary systems 81
Anderson, Gary 137
Andretti, Mario 22, **23**, 27, 35, 94, 104
Angelis, Elio de see de Angelis, Elio
anti-dive 6, 15, 40, 41, 67, 90
anti-roll bars 57, 58, **66**, **103**
anti-squat 6, 15, 67, 90–1
removal of 40, 41, 58, 144
AP 84, 125
ARC Racing **85**
Argentine Grand Prix, 1973 19
Armstrong 67–8
Austin 7 30
Austrian Grands Prix
1964 24
1970 16, 58, 70
1973 19, **20**, 102
1974 21
1982 23
Autocourse 18
Autolite 18, 77
Autosport 35
International Show 2009 141
Avon Tyres Motorsport **73**, 161

Bahrain Grand Prix, 2010 123
Baldwin Dave 33
Baldwin, John 33, 104
BAR **152**
Bartels, Graham 101
batteries **56**, **57**, 59, **110**, 115
Belgian Grands Prix 15, 18, 19, 41
Bell, Derek 141
Bellamy, Ralph 19, 20, 30, 34, **35**, 37
Beltoise, Jean-Pierre 16, 26
Bennett, Alistair 108, 138
Bennett, Colin 109, 136–7, 138
Bennett, Nigel 31, 34, **37**, 154
between-race checks 108–14
Birchall, Arthur 101
Blash, Michael, 'Herbie' 100, 101
Blignaut, Alex see Alex Blignaut Racing

body pins 113
bodywork 113, 114, 124
Boeing, A160T Hummingbird 33
Brabham
  Brabham-BRM 24
  Brabham-Cosworth Formula Two 24
  BT33 **60**
  Jochen Rindt 25
  V8 Repco 620 engine 12, 134
Brabham, Jack 16, 24, 25
brakes 69–71, 72, 110–11, 117
Brannigan, John 145
Brazilian Grands Prix 19, 70, 73
BRDC International Trophy see International Trophy
Bridge, Dougie **101**
British Aluminium 30
British Formula One Championship, 1982 29
British Grands Prix
  1968 150, 153
  1969 153
  1970 16, 60
  1971 28, **100**
  1972 18
  1974 70
  1975 22, 64, 94
BRM
  British Grand Prix 1971 **146**
  engines 11, 12, 32
  International Trophy 1972 26
  P261 134
  suspension 30
Broad, Ralph 107
Brokeback Mountain (film) 135
Brooke Bond Oxo sponsorship 150, 153
BRP 18, 153
bungee wings 55
Bushell, Fred 133
buying vintage cars 122, 123–4

caliper mountings 117
Camel **23**
Campbell, Ian 101
cams
camshafts 78, 81
carriers 77, 81
covers 81
Canadian Grand Prix 17, **20**
Carr, Sid 104
CART races 26, 27
Cevert, Francois 135
CGA Race Engineering 108–14, 116, 136–7, 138, 147, 161
Champion 18, 77
Chaparral, Can-Am 43
Chapman, Clive 96, 122, 125, **139**
Chapman, Colin
  and Brian Henton 94
  career 10, **30**–1
  Cosworth DFV 3-litre engine 12, 13
  death of 23, 31
  and Emerson Fittipaldi **31**, 88
  and Ian Walker 95

and Jim Crawford 107
and Lotus 25 11
and Lotus 63 14
and Lotus 72 14–15, **19**, 21, 40, 55, 154
and Reine Wisell 92
rising rate suspension 63
Chapman, Hazel 139
Charlton, Dave
  British Grand Prix 1971 28, 145
  Dutch Grand Prix 1971 28
  Lotus 72/3 **130**, 131–2, 150
  South African Drivers' Championship 145, **151**
chassis
  construction 56–9, **58**, 137
  histories 144–9
  numbers 20
Chastain, Jessica 135
chief mechanics 100
Clark, Bobby 101
Clark, Jim 11, 13, 43, 100
  Classic Team Lotus
  72/5 146
  72/9 **127**, **139**, 141, 148
  72E/5 123, 124, **126**, 139–40, **141**, 146
  contact details 161
  parts lists 125
  pre-event preparations 115
  Register 140
  role of 96, 125, 139, 139–41
Classic Team Lotus Festival, 2010 **10**, 117, 141
Clermont-Ferrand, 1970 15–16
Cleverley, Tony 153
clutches 84, 110–11, 125
cockpits 59–61, **62**, **124**, 125
Collier, Stan 153
competitiveness of historic Lotus 72s 124, 136
composite Formula One cars 23
connecting rods **77**, 81
Constructors' Championships 10, 19, 20, 157
contacts 161
  Cooper
  Cooper-Climax 14
  Cooper-Climax T60 135
  Jochen Rindt 24
  Maserati V12 engine 12
Cooper Tire & Rubber 73
Coppuck, Gordon 154
Costin, Mike 12
Cosworth engines
  DFV V8 3-litre **12**, 19, 74–82, **109**, 116, 118–19
  DFY 23
Coughtree, Mike 100, **101**
Courage, Piers 15
Coventry-Climax engines 10, 11, 12, 30
crankshafts **76**, **77**, 81
Crawford, Jim 22, **29**, 106, 107, 146, **148**
CSI, changes in Formula One specification 12
CV joints 113, 117, 125, **138**
cylinders 76, **77**, 80, 81

dampers 67–8, 103
Dance, Bob **104**, 139, 140
dashboards **59**, **60**, **61**
Dawson, Ian 38, 101, 106–7
Dayton, Duncan 134
de Angelis, Elio **22**, 23
De Havilland 37
De Tomaso 15
Delta Formula Junior 31
demonstrations, venues 117
  Dennis, Eddie, 'Jake'
  career 100, 104, **104**
  and Emerson Fittipaldi 104
  and Jochen Rindt 17, 104
  and John Miles 104
  journeys to circuits 105
  and Lotus 72 55, 101–4, 109, 132
  and Ronnie Peterson 104, 143
  and Sean Walker 96
  on work exhaustion 105
designers, Lotus 72
  Colin Chapman 14–15, **30**–1, 154
  Martin Waide 33
  Maurice Phillippe 14–15, 32
  Nigel Bennett 37
Dijon Grand Prix de l'age d'Or 128
Dinnage, Chris 97, 116, 117, 139, 140
disc brake layout 69–71
distributor caps 113
documentation **125**
Donington Grand Prix Collection 133, 148
Donington Museum 132
Donnelly, Martin 97
Donohue, Mark 94
DPI (dye penetrant inspection) 113
drive shafts (drawing) **58**
Driver, Paddy 147, **151**, 152
drivers, Lotus 72 24–8
Drivers' World Championships history 10, 157
driveshafts 69, 113
Duckworth, Keith **12**, 13, 31, 74
Dutch Grand Prix 13, 15, 25, 41

electrical cut-off master switches **58**
electronic ignition system **85**
Ellis Clowes 126, 127, 161
engine temperature 49
engines
  Alfa Romeo 33
  BRM 11, 32
  Cosworth DFV V8 3-litre **12**, 19, 74–82, **109**, 116, 118–19
  Cosworth DFY 23
  Coventry-Climax 10, 11, 12, 30
  Ferrari 12
  Ford 12, 23
  Gurney 12
  Harley Davidson 33
  Lamborghini 23
  Maserati 12
  Mugen Honda 23

162
LOTUS 72 MANUAL

Pratt & Whitney 14
Repco 12
Serenissima 12
Weslake 12
Ensign 34, 37
European Formula Two Championship, 1971 27
exhaust systems **75**, **82**

FAI Automotive 96
  fatalities
    Jim Clark 13
    Jochen Rindt 16–17
    John Foulston 145
    Piers Courage 15
    Ronnie Peterson 22
Fauzy, Fairuz 117, **140**, 141
Fernandes, Tony 23
Ferrari
  275 LM 25
  F2002 10
  Grands Prix 16, 18
FIA (Fédération Internationale de l'Automobile) 12, 128
  Year Book of Automobile Sport, 1972 159–61
fire extinguishers **56**, **57**, **59**, **110**
Firestone, tyres 15, 17, 37, 72, 148
first loss insurance policies 127
Fittipaldi, Emerson
  accidents **17**, 35
  American Lotus Owners' Gathering 2007 140
  Argentine Grand Prix 1973 19
  Austrian Grand Prix 1973 **20**
  Bahrain Grand Prix 2010 **123**, 141
  Belgian Grands Prix 18, 19, 147
  Brands Hatch 1973 **19**
  Brazilian Grand Prix 1973 19
  British Grands Prix **16**, 18, **146**
  Canadian Grand Prix 1973 20
  career **25**, 27
  CART championships 1989 26
  drivers' championships 1973 20
  and Eddie Dennis 104
  German Grand Prix 1970 89
  Indianapolis 500 races 1989 27
  International Trophy 1972 18, 26
  Italian Grands Prix 16, 19, 21, **42**, 88, 89
  on Lotus 49 88, 89
  on Lotus 72 8, 88–9, 154
  and Lotus 72/4 145
  and Lotus 72/7 **147**
  and Martin Waide 36
  and McLaren 20, 26
  and mechanics 100
  Monaco Grand Prix 1972 **25**
  non-championship Formula One 1970 17
  Race of Champions 18, **19**, **89**
  Rothmans 50,000 Formule Libre 1972 18
  Rothmans World Championship Victory Race 1971 88
  São Paulo 2010 116
  Spanish Grands Prix 18, 19
  United States Grands Prix 17, 20, 25, **26**, **31**, 88
  World Championships 17, 19, 20, 25, 26, 28
Fittipaldi, Maria Helena 104
Fittipaldi, Wilson 26, 145
500cc World Championship, 1965 151

Foley, Barry 133
Ford
  105E engine 12
  Anglia 31
  DFV V8 engine 13
  HB V8 engine 23
  V8 IndyCar engine 12
Formula 5000 cars 14
Formula Atlantic 152
Formula Ford 14, 25, 97
Formula Junior 10, 12
Formula One
  change in specification 12
  regulations 19, 43, 55, 56, 58, 59, **61**
Formula Three 25
Formula Three Tecno 27
Formula Two 10, 13, 25
Foulston, John 145
Foulston, Mary 145
four-wheel drive cars 14, 17, 28, 30, 32, 47
Frank Williams 15
French Grands Prix 19, 27, 64, 68, 148
front-engined Formula One cars 10
fuel
  cams **112**, 113
  filler caps **58**
  injection systems 80
  lines 110
  pressure relief valves **80**
  pumps **78**, **81**, **82**
  systems 79
fuelling **106**, 115
Fukuda, Yoshio 125, 130, 145

Garner, Dougie 101
gauges 125
gears
  change assembly (drawing) **62**
gearboxes 19, 41, 82, **83**, **84**
gearshifts 60, **61**
  linkage 117
General Atomic, Predator 33
Geoff Richardson Racing Engines 118, 134, 161
German Grands Prix 10, 16, 20, **21**, 89, 94
Girling, dampers 103
GKN Motorsports 113
Gold Leaf cigarettes 145
Gooda, Steve 100, **101**
Goodwood Revival, 2007 140
Goodyear
  Lotus 72 tyres 19, 37, 68, 72, 73, 148
  product liability concerns 94
Gooze, Nick, on Nigel Bennett 37
Grand Prix de Monaco Historique 127
Grand Prix (film) 134
Grand Prix Masters 128–9
Grand Prix personnel, Team Lotus 100
Grand Prix results 10, 155–7
Grant, John 145
Gregory, Ken 18
Gregory, Masten 25
Group Lotus 23
Gurney 12

Hadfield, Simon 92, 120, 124, 130, 131
  on Lotus 72/3 132–3, 145
Hailwood, Mike 6, 16, 26, 151

Hall and Hall 122, 133, 148, 161
Hall, Rick 122
Hamilton, Adrian 145
Hardy, Adrian 126–7
Hardy-Spicer 69
Harley Davidson 33
Hart, Rex 100, **101**
Hayes, Walter 12
header tanks **112**
Heidelberg Motor Museum 145, 147
Henry, Alan 88
  Henton, Brian
    British Grand Prix 1975 94
    career 29
    and Colin Chapman 94, **95**
    and Ian Dawson 107
    on Lotus 72 **86–7**, 94–5, 154
    and Lotus 72/8 **148**
    and Lotus 72E/5 146
    United States Grand Prix 1975 22, **42**, 94–5
Herd, Robin, McLaren M2A 43, 47
Hethel, testing sessions 30
Heurck, Patrick van 129
Hewland Engineering
  contact details 161
  DG300 gearbox 41, 82, 84
  FG400 gearbox 41, 82, **83**, **84**, **133**
  FT200 gearbox 82
  gearbox maintenance **123**, 125
Hill, Damon 97
Hill, Graham 134
  Italian Grand Prix 1970 17
  and Lotus 25, 28
  and Lotus 72/4 37, 145
  Rob Walking Racing Team 24, 150, 153
  Spanish Grand Prix 1969 47
  World Championships 1968 13
Historic Automobile Festival, 2006 145
Historic Formula One Championship 128, 129 *see also* Thoroughbred Grands Prix
Historic Grand Prix 129, 161
historic racing 95–7, 108–14, 113, 122, 127–9
Hockenheim Rindt Memorial Race, 1971 28
Honda 23
Hoole Racing *see* Sid Hoole Racing
HSCC series 147
hubs **72**
Huckle, Gordon 100, 101
Hughes-Rayfield Special 15, **40**
Hulme, Denny 16, 55, 105
Hunt, James 94, 122

Ian Walker Racing 95
Ickx, Jacky
  Brands Hatch Race of Champions 1974 29
  British Grands Prix 16, 18
  German Grands Prix 16, **21**
  Le Mans 24 hour race 29
  and Lotus 72 20, 29, 106
  and Lotus 72E/5 146
  and Lotus 76 **28**
  Monaco Grands Prix 21, **29**
  South African Grand Prix 1975 22

Spanish Grand Prix 1975 22
World Championships 1970 25
ignition systems 81
inboard brakes 117, 153, 154
Indianapolis 500 14, 27, **40**
injection systems 81
inlets
  manifolds 81
  trumpets **78**
insurance 126–7
International Trophy
  1970 6, 15
  1971 92
  1972 18, 26, 147
  1973 **16**
Ireland, Innes 11
Italian Grands Prix
  1970 16, 48, **49**, 88
  1973 19–20, **42**
  1974 21, **22**, 68
  1975 148
  1976 27
Itoh, Yoshuatsu 100, 101

J W Automotive 74
J&F Engines 131
Japanese Grand Prix, 1976 22, 96
Jenkinson, Denis 18
Jim Clark Revival, 2008 141
John Player and Sons 21, 23, 95
  livery **8–9**, 10, 18, **19**, 20, 54, **125**, 133
Judd 23

Keizan, Eddie 145, 147, 150, 151–2, **153**
Kettlewell, Mike 18
King, James 129
Koni 68, **69**, 103
Kovalainen, Heikki 117
Kubota, Katsu
  Historic Formula One Championships **129**
  and Lotus 72/6 108, 124, 126, 136–8, 147
Rush (film) **122**

Lamborghini 23
lamp mountings, rear (drawing) **53**
Langford Performance Engines 82, 118, 161
Lauda, Nicky 122
Lawrence, Peter **133**, 134
Le Mans 24 hour race 24, 29
Leighton, Keith 100, 101
Lifeline, Zero 360 fire extinguisher **57**
lifespan, Lotus 72 40
link rods **68**
liveries
  Camel **23**
  Embassy 152
  Gold Leaf cigarettes 13, 95, 131, 145, **154**
  John Player Special (JPS) livery **8–9**, 10, 18, **19**, 20, **54**, **125**, 133
  Lucky Strike 145, 150, **152**
  national colours 13
  Rob Walking Racing Team 150
  sponsorship 10
Lobro 69
Lola 34, 37
Lola-Chevrolets 33
London Motor Show, 1956 10

Lotus
    7 30, 31
    11 30
    12 **10**, 30
    15 30
    16 **10**, 30
    18 **10**, 30
    21 **10**, 11
    23 30
    24 11
    25 **11**, 31
    26R 33
    30 33, 95
    33 11, 31
    38 31
    43 11, 32
    49 **13**, 15, 18, 25, 32, 47, **48**, 56, 59, 67, 95, 96, 97, 100, 104, 153, 154
    49B 129
    49B/C **49**
    49C 25, 71–2, 150
    49T **43**
    56 **14**, 15, 28, 30, 32, 47, 48, 67, 154
    56B 14, 17, 28, 47, 94
    57/58 F1/F2 project 14, 47
    58 33
    61 47
    62 33, 100
    63 **14**, 28, 30, 32, 47–8, 92
    64 35
    70 14, 33, 35, 48
    72 see Lotus 72
    72/76 hybrid 20–1
    73 93
    74 34
    76 21, 22, 27, **34**, **35**, 37, 84
    76/2 JPS/10 20–1
    76 JPS/9 20
    77 22, 37, 96, 117, 129, 148
    78 22, 34, 37
    79 22–**3**, 97, 117, 129
    80 23
    81 23, 129
    86 23, 31
    87 **22**, 23
    87B 96
    88 **22**, 23, 31
    91 22, 23
    92 23
    93T 23
    94T 23
    99T **23**
    102 23
    107 23
    750 Formula Mark 3 30
    administration order 1994 23
    Classic Team Lotus Register 140
    drawings 140
    Elan 33
    Elite coupé 30
    Europa 33
    Formula One models **10**
    Lotus-BRM 24 151
    Lotus-Climax 25 56
    post-Lotus 72 era 23
Lotus 72
    72/1 41, 67, **91**, 144, 145, 150, 153 see also Lotus 72 72/4
    72/2 41, 67, 82, 84, **144**, 154
    72/3 41, 42, **50**, 59, 67, **73**, **79**, 92, 95, 122, **129**, 130–3, **131**, 132, **145**, 147, 150, 151
    72/4 37, 41, 122, 135, 144, **145**, **150**, 153, 154

    72/5 19, 41, 42, **50**, **60**, 68, 144, 145, **146**, 148
    72/6 **20**, 42, **42**, **50**, **51**, **54**, **56**, 57, 59, **61**, **77**, **82**, 85, 108, 110, 111, **114**, **122**, 124, **126**, 127, **128**, 129, 136–8, 145, **147**, 150, 151, 152
    72/7 19, **42**, 130, **147**, 150, 151, 152
    72/8 20, 42, **50**, 59, **61**, **73**, **112**, **114**, 118, 123, **132**, 133–5, **148**
    72/9 20, 40, 42, 73, 115, **127**, 130, **139**, 141, 148, **149**
    72/76 hybrid 20–1
    72B 41, 144
    72C **40**, 41, 144, 145, 150
    72D **42**, **44–5**, 145, 146, 147, 148, 155
    72E **20**, 42, 130, 145, 147, 148, 151–2
    72E/5 42, **51**, **54**, 59, **61**, **82**, 84, 95, 96, **97**, **115**, 116, 117, 118, 122, **123**, 124, **126**, 127, 129, 139–40, **140**, **141**, 146, **148**
    72F 42, 146, **148**
    handling issues 15, 67, 72, 88
    mechanics 100, **101**, 104
    monocoque histories 144
    press launch of 144
    prototype **56**, **144**, 154
    race results 25, 27, 154
Lucas 80

Magnesium Electron 73
magnetic particle inspection 113
maintenance checks 108–14, 117
Mansell, Nigel 23, 27
Mapelli, Pier-Luigi 144
March
    89CE Indy 33
    701 27
    711 27
    721 27
    761 137
    drivers 27, 28
    German Grand Prix 1970 16
    tyres 94
Maserati, V12 engine 12
Masters Historic Racing 128–9, 161
Matchless 151
May, Stevie 100, **101**, 103
McCarthy, Vic 101
McLaren
    3-litre 12
    M2A 43, 47
    M10 132
    M16 154
    M19 34, 154
    M23 **28**, 88–9, 93, 151, 154
    McLaren-Oldsmobile 33
    tyres 37
McLaren, Bruce 135
McLaughlin, David 88, 127, 128, 147
mechanical checks 110
mechanics 100, **101**, 104, 105–6
MelMag disc wheels 35, 73
Mercedes-Benz, W163 15
metering units 78–9, 80, 115, 116
    failure of 19
Miles, John
    Belgian Grand Prix 1970 15
    career 28, 92
    and Colin Chapman 90, 92

    and death of Jochen Rindt 91
    Dutch Grand Prix 1970 **40**
    and Eddie Dennis 104
    Italian Grand Prix 1970 16, 17
    and Lotus 62 100
    and Lotus 63 4WD 92
    and Lotus 72 14, 28, 48, 90–2
    and Lotus 72/1 **91**, 145
    and Lotus 72/3 145
    and mechanics 104
    Monaco Grand Prix 1970 15
mirrors **126**
Modus 106
Momo **61**
Monaco Formula Three 27, 29
Monaco Grands Prix
    1960 10
    1961 11
    1970 15, 25
    1971 42
    1972 **25**
    1974 **21**
    1975 29, 149
Monaco Historic Grand Prix 96, 123, 141
monocoque
    chassis **56**
    Formula One cars 11, 13, 23, 31
    histories 144
Montjuich Revival, 2007 140
Morrison, Alistair 125, 127, 128, 129, 147
Moss, Stirling 10, 11, 30
Motor Sport Magazine 10, 18
moveable aerodynamic devices 55
Mower, Chris 105
Mower, Derek, 'Joe 90' 100, 101, 104–6
MPS 750 Formula car 31
MRO (maintenance, repair and overall) work 109–10
Mugen Honda 23
Murakami, Keiichi 127, 128

NACA ducts 58, 69, 70
NDT (non-destructive testing) 124
NGK **77**
Nilsson, Gunnar 22
non-World Championship race events 10–11, 17, 19, 157–8
Norman, Nick 101
North American Racing Team 25
nose 53, **54**, **113**–14
Nürburgring Oldtimer Grand Prix 128
Nürburgring pit garages **101**

Ogilvy, Martin 139
oil
    filler caps **51**
    levels **112**, 113, 116
    pressure pumps **79**
    radiators **51**
    scavenge pumps **80**
    sytems 79, 117
    tanks **49**, **50**, 53, 132
Oliver, Jackie **48**
owners 125, 130, 144–8

paddocks **100**, **102**, 103
Page, Theo 74
painting bodywork 124
parallel links **68**
parts lists **125**
Patrick Racing 26

pedals **124**, 125
Penn, Sean 135
Penske 27, 37, 94
Pescarolo, Henri 16
Peterson, Ronnie
    Argentine Grand Prix 1973 **35**
    Austrian Grand Prix 1973 19, **20**
    Belgian Grand Prix 1973 19
    Brands Hatch 1973 **19**
    and Brian Henton 94
    career **27**
    death of 22, 27
    and Eddie Dennis 104, 143
    European Formula Two Championship 1971 27
    Formula Three Tecno **29**
    French Grands Prix 19, **20**, **27**
    German Grand Prix 1974 20, **21**
    and Ian Dawson 107
    Italian Grands Prix 19–20, 21, **22**, 27, **42**
    and Lotus 72 27, 28, 33
    and Lotus 72/6 **147**, 148
    and Lotus 72/8 134, 148
    and Lotus 72/9 148, **149**
    and March 27
    Monaco Formula Three 27, 29
    Monaco Grand Prix 1974 **21**
    and Nigel Bennett 154
    Race of Champions **19**, **93**
    and Tyrrell 27
    United States Grand Prix 1975 22
    World Championships 1971 27
Phillippe, Maurice
    career 18, **31**, **32**, 33
    and Emerson Fittipaldi 88
    and Lotus 72 10, 14–15, 30, 63, 154
    Vel's Parnelli Jones Racing 104
Pickles, Jim 100, 101
pistons **77**, 81
pit garages **101**, **107**
pit lane changes 103
Pitt, Brad 135
plugs **77**
    leads 113
Pohlad, Bill 133, **134**, 148
Pohlad, Carl 135
post-race checks **108**
practice sessions, mechanics' work 103
Pratt & Whitney 14
pre-event preparations **115**, **116**
privateers 150–3
Prüller, Heinz 16, 88

quill hub arrangement 74
quill shafts 115, 116

R&J Simpson Engineering 137, 138, 147, 161
race meeting insurance 127
Race of Champions
    1971 28, 93, 94, 145
    1972 18, 146
    1973 18, 19, 89
    1974 29, 146
    1975 64
race results 155–8
Race Tech **60**
radiators **110**, 116, **126**
radius rods **69**
rain lights 1**1**
Ralt 34
rear camber adjusters **63**
rear-engine Formula One cars 10